everyday TRANSFORMATION™

The Human First Approach to Digital Change

WARREN CASS & WARREN KNIGHT

ABOUT THE AUTHORS

WARREN CASS

Warren Cass is a leadership, culture and communication consultant, keynote speaker and best-selling author of 'Influence' and co-author of 'Everyday Transformation'.

He is an expert in driving agile culture change within organizations. With years of experience as a transformational leader, Warren has honed his skills in inspiring teams to embrace agility and adaptability in an ever-changing business landscape.

WARREN KNIGHT

Warren Knight, a renowned Global Advisor and Expert in Digital Transformation, keynote speaker and author of 'Think Digital First' and co-author of 'Everyday Transformation'.

He is a catalyst for organizations, empowering them to forge a formidable competitive edge. With unwavering dedication spanning 15+ years, he equips leaders with the confidence, skills, and tools to embed digital into their core of their transformation.

Together their mission? To enable businesses to achieve ambitious objectives by keeping ahead of change, fostering resilience and creating a more agile culture, deeply connected to engaged communities.

DEDICATED TO OUR WHY

We would like to dedicate this book to the two people who support us the most in all our endeavours. They are our wise council, our cheerleaders, and take care of everything important to us, especially while we are away from home working with clients. Thank you, Janet, and Zoe, we love you and appreciate all you do.

Like most fathers, we work, we build, and we create for our children. They are the only legacy that really matters. Elliott, Jodie, Dixie, and Blossom... This book is for you too.

everyday TRANSFORMATION™

The Human First Approach to Digital Change

WARREN CASS & WARREN KNIGHT

"When digital transformation is done
right, it's like a caterpillar turning into
a butterfly, but when done wrong,
all you have is a really fast caterpillar."

George Westerman

Published by
HiveMind Publishing
Middle Farm High Street
Kempsford
Gloucestershire
GL7 4EY
United Kingdom
www.Hivemind-Group.com
www.Everyday-Transformation.com

ISBN 978-1-7395100-0-8

CONTENTS

Gonna change my way of thinking, make myself a different set of rules. Gonna put my best foot forward, and stop being influenced by fools

Bob Dylan

INTRODUCTION

What's It All About?

The lyrics opposite from the song 'Gonna change my way of thinking' say it all really. The rules of business success have in the last 20 years been screwed up and tossed out, but not replaced by anything that promises longevity.

Change isn't a choice, it's a constant which we ignore at our peril.

Here is another quote for you…

"It is not the most intellectual of the species that survives;
it is not the strongest that survives; but the species that survives
is the one that is able best to adapt and adjust
to the changing environment in which it finds itself."

In 1963 Leon C. Megginson, a Louisiana State University business professor, uttered these words in a speech referring to the work of Charles Darwin's 'On the Origin of Species' and his interpretation of the central idea.

This quote would go on to be refined and streamlined, and then falsely attributed to Darwin himself. It is rather amusing that the quote itself has 'evolved'.

But let's examine the words and adapt them for the current business landscape. As these words are written we wonder if this has always been the case? Once upon a time being the established player presented privileges and opportunities that the competition simply didn't get. Markets (and consumers) were more risk averse therefore financial stability and brand recognition inspired more confidence.

Today we live in a world where people are more resilient and less afraid of change. Why? Because it's constant. This rollercoaster of the last 40 years with sweeping changes in technology, demographics, culture, consumerism, and environment (to name but a few areas) have re-programmed us to be less resistant... and more adoptive of new solutions.

It is because people have been conditioned to be less concerned with the status quo and wanting to be seen as the cool early adopters of 'new stuff', that the established brands have had to seriously up their game when it comes to innovation. They simply have less control than they used to.

In this book we aim to explore in more detail the waves of change, and more importantly the widely accepted yet misunderstood strategy of digital transformation to ride this wave.

We are going to share what it is, why it often fails and what you can do to combat that. We will explore the key strategies to influence organizational change and the key ingredients to ensure adoption. Plus, we are going to give you a framework from our digital literacy and innovation programme which fast tracks your best talent to become your 'Everyday Transformation™' change makers.

So Who Are We and Why Do We Care?

We 'The Warren's' (Warren Cass and Warren Knight) are individually international keynote speakers, best-selling authors and subject matter experts.

Together we founded Hivemind Group, a specialised training and consultancy firm helping organizations navigate digital change, and equip their talent with the essential knowledge, skills and tools to thrive in today's rapidly changing environment.

We work with organizations all over the world (and in multiple sectors), to help them gain clarity on their vision and roadmap for digital change, then reinforce that by helping them identify and develop the skills required.

We have delivered in telecoms, government, food manufacturing, banking and finance, tourism, construction, aviation, retail, technology, and law enforcement to name just some of the sectors.

We believe this exposure to diverse cultures, operating models, and industries, provides us with a broader perspective and drastically increases the continued value we offer.

But It Is Not About Us... It's About You!

If you are interested, our individual profiles are at the end of the book. But actually, this book is about you. Written in a way that will hopefully make you think about your current situation and examine what best practice might look like for the organization and human beings you serve.

Now unless you are a serial digital transformation specialist, roaming from company to company leading change then moving on (unlikely we know), then you are probably slightly overwhelmed by the enormity of the subject and the responsibility of leading the charge. This is the correct human response.

Our objective in writing this book for you is that it provides the big picture and then breaks down the component parts so at any time you can revisit if you are stuck or looking for inspiration at a particular part of the journey.

Because it has been designed to be picked up and referred to often, we may repeat several key points throughout... unapologetically.

You are likely to get value from this book if at least one of the following statements is true;

- You are a leader.

- You are a stakeholder of change.

- You are convinced change is inevitable and want to understand how to navigate it for the best chance of success.

- You are unconvinced significant change is necessary for your organization and want to validate your position (spoiler alert... we will hopefully convince you to change your mind).

- You have customers and would like to keep them.

- You would like to understand digital transformation and be able to confidently talk about it with colleagues.
- You would like to position yourself as an invaluable champion of change in your organization.

OK, assuming you are still reading and one of them was true, let us share how we are going to help you reflect on your current situation and path forward throughout this book.

At the end of each chapter there is a section called 'Reflection Section' where we will ask you a few questions or suggest some actions to get you moving forwards in your digital transformation journey.

It is designed to help you take some time to pause and think about what we discuss and how it relates to you and your organization. You may not know the answer! And that's ok. But hopefully it will provoke you to have the conversation with your colleagues and ask the questions.

We agree with Tom Peters that in the current high-velocity environment, *"If you're not confused, you're not paying attention."* There is an abundance of confusion, as there are possible solutions. So, our intention with this book is to simplify and hopefully be more helpful. Everyday Transformation™ provides several frameworks, methodologies, and tools to help you make sense and adapt to the demands of your current situation.

We will focus less on asserting TRUTH, than we will on the methods and mechanisms to help you change the most fundamental elements of your organization. We intend to provide a clear path for leaders almost anywhere in the organizational hierarchy, to guide the transformation process at the most foundational level.

Ultimately though, it is about applying the knowledge… ***"To know and not to do, is not yet to know"*** Quote attributed to many great thinkers including Confucius, Laozi, and Stephen Covey to name a few.

Additional to this, we believe context is probably the most important part of sharing knowledge. To that end, in the last chapter of this book we will be sharing with you a number of sections specifically contextualising the content for different organizational roles such as HR, ICT, Finance, Operations etc. so you can either understand your role in the process better or better still empathize with the challenges of your colleagues.

The Challenge With Books of This Nature

In times of rapid change, especially in the realm of technology, a book on digital transformation is essentially out of date within weeks of release. We recognise this to be a challenge and would like to keep you up to date with our latest thinking.

Every year we will be updating the content and distributing the latest digital edition of the book to anyone who has a copy. You can visit www.

everyday-transformation.com to register for updates and find up to date content on emerging technology, new useful frameworks and latest interviews from experts on the topic.

You will also be able to find templates for some of the exercises we share for download.

There is also an extensive alphabetically ordered, glossary of terms you can download which explains every acronym, label, abbreviation, and phrase in connection to digital transformation.

Digitization Vs Digitalization Vs Digital Transformation

Since the beginning of the digital age, digitization and digitalization have been well used buzzwords. More recently, digital transformation has also become a popular phrase in strategy and technology conversations. They're often mistakenly thought to be different words with the same meaning, but actually they are three different technology concepts that have unique implications for your organization.

Digitization refers to the process of converting analog information, such as paper documents or physical media, into a digital format that can be stored, accessed, and manipulated electronically. This process involves scanning, capturing, and converting information into digital files or data.

Digitalization refers to the broader transformation of business processes, products, and services through the use of digital technologies. This can involve using digital tools to automate tasks, streamline workflows, and create new business models and revenue streams.

While digitization and digitalization are related, they refer to different aspects of the digital transformation journey. Digitization is a necessary first step in the process of digitalization, as it involves converting analog information into a format that can be digitized and used within digital systems. Digitalization, on the other hand, involves using digital technologies to drive business transformation and create new value for customers and stakeholders.

What Is Digital Transformation?

Digital transformation refers to the process of using digital technologies to fundamentally change how businesses operate and deliver value to their customers. It involves a shift from traditional, manual processes to automated, technology-enabled processes that are more efficient, agile, and customer-centric. A re-imagining if you like, of the way things are done.

Digital transformation encompasses a wide range of technologies, including artificial intelligence, cloud computing, big data analytics, and the Internet of Things (IoT). By leveraging these technologies, businesses can streamline their operations, improve their products and services, and gain a competitive edge in the marketplace.

However, digital transformation is not just about technology. It also involves a cultural shift within an organization, as employees must be upskilled and empowered to work in new, digital ways. It requires a willingness to experiment, innovate and iterate, to embrace change, and to put the customer at the centre of everything the business does.

Digital transformation is a complex and ongoing process that requires a strategic approach with careful planning, investment, and execution. But for those businesses that are able to successfully transform themselves, the rewards can be significant, including increased revenue, greater efficiency, and improved customer satisfaction, to name just a few benefits.

It transcends beyond the more traditional roles within organizations like operations, sales, customer service etc. and instead asserts that every department has a responsibility to think customer centric evolution. Asking them to take a step back and take a fresh look at the big picture. Not just at the possibilities today, but to anticipate the potential and challenges of the future.

This requires an understanding of current trends and predictive insights to future trends. It requires more customer empathy than ever before. Most importantly it requires an organizational culture that enables this very necessary re-prioritisation.

A Short History of Digital Transformation – The World's Longest Revolution

So now that we have defined digital transformation let's look at its origins and how it has evolved over the years.

It would be a near impossible task to find a business today which hasn't already incorporated some form of digital technology into their operations. Technological innovation has been slowly but surely revolutionising the way we work and generally live our lives. More than this, Digital Transformation will likely continue to play a pivotal role in shaping and evolving the global business environment for many decades to come.

But where did it all begin? Well, the term 'digital transformation' itself was coined relatively recently to describe the adaptations companies all over the world are undertaking. But the process which the term describes originates much earlier than the 21st century, at a time when technology was steering organizations towards digitization.

As discussed previously, digitization and digitalization whilst intrinsically related, are not the exact same thing. Digitization came first and describes the shift from analogue to digital technology. This was kickstarted in the late 40s by American mathematician, electrical engineer and computer scientist, Claude Shannon and his famous paper, A Mathematical Theory of Communication.

Soon afterwards, the invention of the microchip and the semiconductor transistor changed the technological landscape forever by making digital computing possible.

Next came the ARPANET which in 1969 made its debut (eventually leading to the modern internet), slightly preceded by Moore's law (1965), an observation made by Gordon Moore, founder of Intel and CEO at the time, that the number of transistors in an integrated circuit appeared to double every two years.

Riding the digitization wave, the 70s brought us home computers, arcade video games, and a growing demand for data entry, as organizations doubled their efforts to transfer their records into a digital format. In the 80s Workforce automation came into play, along with another pivotal invention – the World Wide Web (1989).

Digital Business Transformation in the 21st Century

Following the invention of the Web, we witnessed a global surge in technological innovation, with internet users reaching 1 billion in December 2009 and mobile phones becoming commercially available. Before the decade was over, stage one of the digital revolution had swept across the globe.

But the technological evolution didn't end there, instead of reaching a plateau, it evolved into digital transformation as we know it today. From 2010, organizations started reimagining the way they interacted with their customers, using digital channels to engage.

The next shift for companies expanded across all departments, redefining how companies used data and consumer insights to generate new business models.

The huge wealth of data organizations continued to gather prompted yet another shift – this time towards big data, a unified digital network which connected various business systems and processes. Enlightened with this new potential for connectivity, companies started shifting away from intermediaries and focused on establishing direct relationships with their customers.

Today, digital transformation is a strategic approach rather than just a technological upgrade. The term was first used in 2015 by Deloitte following research on the most successful technology adoptions at the time. Since then, organizations have been reinforcing their digital ambitions by upskilling their talent and redesigning company culture to see it as an ongoing process rather than simply a one-off project.

From its early conception in the 50s, through the leap in the 90s caused by the invention of the Web, and all the way into the 21st century, digital transformation has been gradually shaping all aspects of our lives and will continue to do so for decades to come.

Resistance To Change Is Futile

To quote the 'Borg' for all Star Trek fans… "resistance is futile". Actually, today resistance has very real consequences. We have all heard the countless accounts of market dominant companies that have fallen by the wayside in the last few decades.

Established brands that have resisted change, or lacked the agility to adapt, simply covering their eyes and ears in the hope that the disruption goes away and doesn't affect them.

Brands like Kodak, Blockbusters, Blackberry, Sears, Pan Am, Yellow Pages, My Space to name but a few. But let's be very clear, many of these casualties were avoidable had they just invested in the future rather than rest on their laurels.

For example, it was as recent as 2008 when Jim Keyes, Chief Executive of Blockbuster said in an interview, "Neither RedBox or Netflix are even on the radar screen in terms of competition." Fast forward just two years to 2010 and Blockbuster were filing for bankruptcy.

But it is not the lack of foresight of brands gone by that your business needs to be concerned about, it is the resistance you will meet from some of your people, staff, stakeholders, leadership, and even from some of your more traditional clientele.

We will be exploring this in much more detail further on in this book as well as providing strategies to mitigate the influence of resistors.

We assert that no organization today would brag about its constancy, sameness, or status quo compared to ten years ago. Consistency is seen today more often as stagnation than stability, and organizations that are not in the business of change and transformation are generally viewed as bloody minded. The scary uncertainty that traditionally accompanied major organizational change has been replaced by the scary uncertainty now associated with remaining the same.

Peter Drucker (the godfather of modern management) concluded that *"We are in one of those great historical periods that occur every 200 or 300 years when people don't understand the world anymore, and the past is not sufficient to explain the future".*

Relentless, unpredictable, and often surprising change makes it extremely difficult for any organization or leader to keep up to date, to predict the future with any degree of accuracy, or to maintain steadiness of direction. The failure rate of most planned digital transformation initiatives is dramatic.

70%

OF DIGITAL TRANSFORMATION

FAIL

Why Digital Transformations Often Fail

Digital transformations are complex and challenging undertakings that require significant time, resources, and effort to execute successfully. Despite the best of intentions, many digital transformations fail to deliver the desired results, and this can be due to a variety of reasons. From the conversations we have regularly with CIO's, CTO's, CDTO's and HR/HC leaders, here are the most common.

- **Lack of a clear strategy:** A well-defined and comprehensive digital transformation strategy is the foundation of any successful transformation. Without a clear direction, digital transformations can become chaotic, unfocused, and ineffective. Organizations need to establish a clear set of goals, objectives, and action plans, and ensure that everyone involved in the transformation understands their role in achieving these goals.

- **Inadequate leadership:** Effective leadership is essential to the success of digital transformations. Leaders need to be visionary, inspiring, and knowledgeable about the latest digital technologies and trends. They also need to be able to communicate the vision and goals of the transformation clearly and engage employees in the process.

- **Resistance to change:** Digital transformations often involve significant changes to the way organizations operate, and this can be unsettling for employees. Organizations need to manage the change process carefully, provide training and support for employees, and communicate the benefits of the transformation clearly and consistently.

- **Lack of buy-in from employees:** Digital transformations are not just about technology; they are about people and culture. Organizations need to engage employees in the transformation process and provide them with the resources, training, and support they need to succeed.

- **Insufficient investment:** Digital transformations can be expensive, and organizations need to be prepared to invest in the technology, resources, and personnel required to execute the transformation effectively. Organizations need to have a realistic budget and funding plan in place, and they need to be willing to allocate the necessary resources to ensure the success of the transformation.

- **Underestimating the complexity of the transformation:** Digital transformations can be complex, involving many different technologies, processes, and people. Organizations need to understand the scope of the transformation, the interdependencies between different components, and the impact that the transformation will have on different areas of the business.

- **Failing to manage the risks:** Digital transformations can be risky, and organizations need to be prepared to manage these risks effectively. They need to identify potential risks, assess the impact, and put contingency plans in place to mitigate the impact.

- **Ignoring the cultural impact:** Digital transformations are not just about technology; they are about people and culture. Organizations need to be aware of the cultural impact of the transformation, and they need to make sure that the culture supports and enables the transformation.

- **Not focusing on the customer:** Digital transformations should be customer-focused, and organizations need to understand the needs and wants of customers. They need to make sure that the transformation is aligned with the customer experience and that it delivers the desired outcomes for customers.

- **Failing to measure the success of the transformation:** Organizations need to measure the success of the transformation and track progress against their goals and objectives. They need to be able to assess the impact of the transformation and make any necessary adjustments to ensure that they are on track to deliver the desired outcomes.

- **Failing to measure what matters:** Failing to measure what matters is a significant contributing factor to digital transformation failure for several reasons. Firstly, without clear and relevant metrics, organizations lack the means to assess the success and impact of their digital initiatives. Measuring the wrong indicators or not measuring at all can lead to misguided decision-making, wasted resources, and missed opportunities for improvement. Secondly, digital transformation involves complex changes across various aspects of an organization, and without proper measurement, it becomes challenging to identify bottlenecks or areas that require optimization. Thirdly, data-driven insights are crucial for refining digital strategies and aligning them with business goals. Without meaningful measurements, organizations lack the visibility needed to make informed adjustments and ensure their transformation efforts are on the right track.

Even the biggest companies, known for their technology leadership and innovation, have a track record of making avoidable mistakes, particularly when attempting to leverage technology to enhance their operations. Let's explore three of the most notorious digital transformation failures and consider how they could have been prevented:

Case Study – Hershey, the renowned American brand known for its world-famous chocolate cookies, cakes, milkshakes, and beverages, faced a significant challenge in 1996. They recognized the need for a more robust Enterprise Resource Planning (ERP) system to replace their fragmented legacy IT systems.

They selected their new CRM, and a new supply chain management solution with the intention to streamline their operations. The entire implementation was projected to cost $112 million.

Originally planned to span 48 months, Hershey's leadership decided to expedite the rollout to 30 months to finish before the looming Y2K issue. However, this decision led to rushing the implementation and sacrificing proper testing. The pressure to meet the shorter timeline and complete the system migration in the midst of peak operations caused significant problems.

Unfortunately, the new ERP system encountered issues, resulting in over $100 million worth of orders remaining unfulfilled, even though Hershey had the necessary inventory. As a result, the company's quarterly revenues plummeted by 19%, and its stock value dropped by 8%.

Key Lessons Learned:

The rushed implementation without adequate testing and the unfortunate timing of the rollout during peak business periods proved to be a costly mistake for Hershey, highlighting the importance of careful planning and consideration in digital transformation initiatives.

Case Study – Revlon the hair and beauty brand. In February 2018, Revlon underwent a rollout of a new ERP system. Unfortunately, the migration was not adequately planned, leading to significant disruptions in the company's production and order fulfilment processes. The issues were observed across their operations in 22 countries.

When the aftermath of the implementation settled, Revlon faced severe consequences. The company incurred losses of over $64 million due to unshipped orders. Additionally, their stock price dropped by 6.9%, causing financial distress. Furthermore, the investors took legal action, filing a lawsuit against Revlon to claim damages resulting from the financial underperformance caused by the ERP system rollout.

Key Lessons Learned:

- Thoroughly test CRMs, ERPs, and IT systems before deploying them to identify and address potential issues in advance.
- Develop robust backup solutions that can step in to mitigate challenges and ensure business continuity in case of any problems during the implementation.
- Implement a well-planned change management strategy to navigate the transition smoothly while switching to new tools and solutions, ensuring seamless adoption and minimizing disruption to operations.

Case Study – Ford. In 2014, the classic American car company, embarked on a digital transformation journey by creating a new segment called Ford Smart Mobility. The objective was to develop digitally enabled cars with improved mobility features. However, challenges arose when this new segment was not effectively integrated into the broader Ford organization. It operated separately from the rest of the company, both in terms of its location and its lack of cohesion with other business units.

Despite significant investments in the new venture, Ford faced quality issues in other areas of the company. This led to a dramatic drop in the company's stock price, and the CEO eventually stepped down a few years later.

Key Lessons Learned:

The lesson we learn from this is the importance of integrating digital transformation efforts with the overall company strategy. In Ford's case, the digital transformation was perceived more as a pivot into a new business area rather than a holistic transformation of the organization. For digital transformation to succeed, it must be fully integrated into the company, aligning with its goals and strategies.

Organizations need to approach digital transformations with a clear strategy, effective leadership, and a focus on the customer. They need to be prepared to invest in the technology, resources, and personnel required to execute the transformation effectively, and they need to be aware of the cultural impact of the transformation and the risks involved.

Let us not underestimate that last point regarding culture. Several studies cite the biggest reason given for failure was a neglect of the organization's culture. In other words, failure to change the organization's culture sealed the fate of the other kinds of changes that were initiated.

By avoiding the common pitfalls, organizations can increase their chances of success and deliver the desired outcomes for their customers and employees, and we will be going into detail on all of these issues in the pages that follow.

And lastly, a failed digital transformation doesn't necessarily mean the inevitable demise of a company, but it can be extremely costly in lost money, time, resources, credibility… and competitive advantage.

EVERYDAY TRANSFORMATION™

What Is Everyday Transformation™?

Everyday Transformation™ is our structured approach to digital change, which puts humans at the heart of innovation and where the evaluation of opportunities/possibilities is the responsibility of all and the daily modus operandi.

It refers to the process of generating and implementing new ideas or solutions to improve everyday life experiences. This type of innovation focuses on finding creative and practical solutions to common problems or challenges that people face in their daily lives.

We believe when you start from the top down, with a people and culture first approach, you maximise your potential for success because you have the capability to overcome adversity and the mindset to adapt.

The challenge for most with the traditional approach to a digital transformation is actually defining what 'done' looks like? Where is the finish line? Is it an updated proposition for the customer? Or replacing legacy systems? Is it a one-off event or a continuous process?

Success for us is leaving clients with an organization that is agile and equipped for whatever situation may arise. Whether it be disruption to their market, changing customer needs, new regulation, pioneering new tech that changes expectations, or a global pandemic.

When an organization has the confidence that whatever the challenge, their people are up to the task, their processes enable the appropriate action and their leadership empower decision-making and are strategically aligned.

This approach has no end destination! It is a continuous commitment to the potential and opportunity of change.

No destination I hear you think! How do we know if we were successful? Or how can we secure budget? Etc. Of course your journey starts with a discovery stage and a roadmap for the next 2 to 5 years, maybe longer. But what we are saying is it doesn't stop here, change is the new normal, and that is a much more appropriate thought to get your head around and guide your thinking.

The Word Digital Is Misleading

Another thing that confuses many and normally results in a debate early on with our clients and their stakeholders is the inclusion of the word 'digital' in digital transformation. It sets the expectation that this is all about technology, when in actual fact it is equally about change, customer centricity, organizational culture, streamlining processes and brand positioning... amongst other things.

We have never found a professional yet who is an expert in all of these disciplines, so if it is your responsibility to drive the digital aspirations in your organization then you will need to be inclusive with all levels of employee, persuasive when painting the picture of future possibilities, consultative with all areas of the business and key stakeholders and humble enough to ask for help/advice/guidance and feedback.

Examples of Everyday Transformation™ can include developing new products or services that address a specific customer need or problem, creating new approaches or methods to accomplish routine tasks more efficiently, or finding new ways to engage with colleagues and stakeholders to build stronger relationships.

Everyday Transformation™ can be fostered by creating an agile culture, where people are open-minded and creative, have a healthy willingness to experiment and take calculated risks, and possess a strong desire to improve and make a difference in their roles.

Most importantly, EVERYONE in the organization takes collective ownership of the new way things are done, and accountability for the part they play in their role. Where your people are highly communicative and transparency isn't just a value written on the wall, but one lived and breathed as individuals have the confidence to ask for help, share mistakes and self-identify areas for their own personal and professional development.

Lastly, before we move on... organizations often talk about customer centricity, but it is often rhetoric and not mirrored by their practices. A central premise of Everyday Transformation™ is about putting yourself in the shoes of the people you serve. This might be the external customer, an internal team or external partner, if you are a leader, it would include the team that follows you. By truly, empathetically, and sincerely considering their needs, and the reason behind those needs, we can take steps small and large to help them better and improve the relationship.

Later in this book in the 'People' section we will explore this topic in more detail.

Global Trends and New Opportunities

We are currently going through one of the most significant changes ever experienced in human history. Old businesses will change, and new businesses will emerge. We are already seeing a shift in services our clients are adopting in response.

The dramatic metamorphosis in businesses today is impossible to ignore. Across every industry, profession or sector, new emerging trends are constantly reshaping the landscape. Whilst some will be fleeting, others will endure and be around for some time to come. In many ways the world has never been so small, or its corporations so big. Global disruptions caused by the pandemic, the war in Ukraine and the subsequent soar in energy prices have introduced new challenges for organizations, but with them new opportunities.

For example, post-pandemic economic growth reduced unemployment in many of the leading economies. This coupled by an increasing demand for skilled applicants, meant the job market became more competitive. Businesses have been quick to adapt to these disruptions, embracing digitalization and the gig economy, turning to innovative online solutions, and putting contingent workforce strategies in place.

The issue for many though is resistance to these forces of change, after all there is comfort in knowing what to expect. How many times have you heard people embrace disruption with enthusiasm? "Rarely" is your likely response. Yet we can easily rationalise that any disruption produces winners and losers. So, the question is do you want to innovate, or stagnate? Be the disruptor, or the disrupted? Leverage the emerging opportunities or protect the legacy approach? It really is that binary, and whilst most will tell you they are progressive and future thinking, the budget they allocate to such initiatives contradicts their assertion.

Here are some of the global trends currently impacting the workplace... (side note - This is one of several areas we are going to keep up to date on www.Everyday-Transformation.com)

Remote/Hybrid Working

An obvious starting point is remote and work-from-home trends. The pandemic advanced the development of virtual collaboration tools and video conferencing significantly in a short period of time. Those advancements were inevitable eventually, but definitely accelerated due to demand and circumstance. Companies with the ability to digitalize their workload (or whose propositions are digital) have been able to reduce the overheads associated with physical offices, and invest in talent, regardless of their location.

Fewer hours spent commuting has improved employee wellbeing and can improve retention. When your people thrive, it has a positive impact on your customers and your business.

Digital Nomads and Global Talent

Because of the above, digitalization brought significant changes to many roles, creating the ongoing ability for talent to work remotely from anywhere. As long as the employee can manage their schedule and provide their expertise, there is no reason why a company should only look 'locally' for the perfect candidate.

How We Define 'Workplace' Will Change

New expectations will be established for these working conditions, redefining work life and personal life boundaries. The workplace will no longer simply be an office where people attend each day. We will need to reimagine the purpose of a workplace, likely becoming collaboration hubs to achieve common objectives, as opposed to just simply a place for people to work. Unnecessary overheads such as rent, travel, rates etc will be cut, leaving no option but to encourage virtual interactions and replace physical face-to-face meetings.

Change in Work Habits Will Lead to Urban Transformation

With the change in demand for commercial real estate will come a fall in price and open up new ways of utilisation. We are already seeing an increase in space sharing collaboration hubs, or offices repurposing as event spaces. This in itself is allowing whole industries to be reinvented and reimagine their evolving surroundings.

More Organizations Will Develop a Contingent Workforce

Companies and people are embracing on-demand workforce models and platforms which are improving workforce planning, financial management and access to diverse skills. A contingent workforce refers to a group of workers who are not regular, full-time employees of a company but are hired on a temporary, part-time, or contract basis. These workers may include freelancers, independent contractors, consultants, seasonal employees, or temporary workers.

The use of contingent workers has become increasingly popular in recent years as it allows companies to be more flexible and responsive to changes in demand for their products or services. It also enables them to access specialized skills and expertise for specific projects or tasks without having to hire full-time employees. Contingent workers are typically paid on a per-project or hourly basis and are not entitled to the same benefits or job security as regular employees. However, they may enjoy greater flexibility and control over their work schedules and have the potential to earn higher rates of pay.

The Increasing Popularity of the Gig Economy

Similar to a contingent workforce but typically less involved, is the gig economy. The gig economy refers to a growing trend in which individuals work independently, often through online platforms or mobile apps, to complete short-term, project-based tasks or jobs. This includes work in areas such as ridesharing, food delivery, freelance writing, web design, and many others. Workers in the gig economy are typically considered independent contractors rather than traditional employees, and as a result, are often responsible for their own taxes, insurance, and other benefits. While the gig economy offers greater flexibility and control over work schedules, it can also present challenges related to job security, income stability, and the lack of traditional employment benefits.

Some of the biggest beneficiaries of the gig economy are people who ordinarily have less access to conventional jobs or are less able to accept traditional work arrangements. This has helped build the gig economy, which has been especially embraced by Gen Z, who prefer flexible work arrangements and a work-life balance.

Upskilling and Re-skilling Become a Major Priority as Organizations Are Forced To Reinvent Themselves

All industries will require transformation to their business models in order to remain competitive. New operating models and value-chains will significantly increase a need for new skills which might not be readily available in a competitive job market. Last year, the World Economic Forum warned of disruption to the labour markets of 15 developed and emerging countries that would lead to a net loss of over 5 million jobs, and the creation of millions of new jobs particularly linked to emerging technology. The learning and development departments will need to go through their own transformations to help their workforce quickly reskill and upskill.

Business Immigration

Business immigration has never been more critical. Research continuously shows that immigrants are 'job makers', not 'job takers'. Especially in developed countries. Skilled immigrants in particular are plugging gaps in healthcare and technology (amongst other fields) and are also benefiting companies by providing fresh, outside expertise and insights.

Globalisation will be redefined with more emphasis on social capitalism

The world is increasingly interconnected, with businesses operating across borders and cultures. This presents both challenges and opportunities, as businesses navigate different legal and regulatory environments, cultural norms, and language barriers. The pandemic or the 2008 subprime mortgage market in the US are great examples of the potential domino effect that can arise from an issue in one country and the consequential serious impact on the entire world economy.

Many believe a new form of globalisation will emerge, that recognises interdependence and the impact the collective actions of countries can have on humanity. This will result in organizations changing policy and management models with an even greater focus on corporate social responsibility. Social capitalism will drive companies as their customers demand it. Business strategies focussed not only markets and market regulation, but also what is good for their local communities and the wider society.

Diversity, Equality, Inclusion (DEI)

Even though these have been important topics for some time, DEI is being emphasized by globalization and digitalization processes. When employees feel seen, appreciated and supported, you won't need a better employer branding strategy than your own employees. We will be covering this topic in more detail later in the book.

Sustainability Isn't New, But...

Over the next decade, sustainability will not be just a trend, it is an expectation for every business. Strategy should consider more than just sustainable development goals (SDGs) as environmental, social and governance (ESG) considerations are more important to customers and investors, leading to increased demand for sustainable products and services. This has prompted many businesses to adopt environmentally friendly practices and to invest in renewable energy, as well as focussing on human rights, improving supply chain management, and ethical sourcing and distribution.

Digital Acceleration and Everyday Transformation™

Digital transformation is a process that can take years to complete. Now smaller rapid innovation initiatives can be completed in just a few weeks. Digital acceleration refers to the rapid transformation and adoption of digital technologies and processes within an organization, industry, or society. It involves using digital tools to enhance and streamline business processes, improve communication, increase efficiency, and drive innovation. The COVID-19 pandemic has accelerated digital change, as businesses and organizations have had to quickly adapt to remote work and digital channels for communication and transactions. Digital acceleration can lead to increased productivity, improved customer experiences, and new business models, but it can also create challenges such as cybersecurity risks and the need for upskilling and reskilling of the workforce as discussed above.

Artificial Intelligence Will Impact All of Us

AI is increasingly being used to automate routine tasks, analyze data, and improve decision-making. This will transform many industries, from healthcare to manufacturing, and is likely to have a significant impact on the future of work over the next few years. More on this later!

Supply-chains Will Fragment and Reconfigure Themselves

Supply chains will fragment further with technology platforms integrating them. The future of supply chains is likely to be marked by increased use of technology (automation and robotics), data, and collaboration, as companies seek to build more efficient, sustainable, and resilient supply chains that can adapt to the challenges of an ever-changing business landscape.

New Mindsets Will Drive Culture and Future Success

If technology-enabled transformation is the vehicle, people with new mindsets will be in the driver seat in order to ensure successful implementation and continuous adaptation. Cultural change will become one of the most important priorities for every board room which is why we wrote this book. The ground rules, beliefs, and assumptions that drive culture will require rethinking with a new set of mindsets driving employee and business success.

In fact, one of our most in demand workshops right now, applicable to everyone in an organization is Agile Mindset... More on agile later.

Case Study – DBS: A great example of an organization that has managed to cultivate an agile mindset throughout the organization and reaped the rewards is DBS Bank in Singapore.

DBS CEO Piyush Gupta said *"Behaving like a start-up meant shifting the bank's mindset from that of a mature multinational to one that is more nimble, more agile; one which is constantly learning, experimenting, and innovating on the fly. To effect this change at scale, we had to teach our people how to use the tools of innovation and provide them with opportunities to apply these tools in an environment where it is safe to take risks. This effective culture shift created through a programme of 'culture by design' has been instrumental to our success so far and will be key as we navigate the disruptions in our industry going ahead."*

In all interviews with the bank leadership what consistently came across were the digital and purpose-focused elements of the transformation and how these permeated every level of the organization. The willingness from the leadership to resource the change enabled a building up of the workforce's innovation 'muscles' to create a start-up culture – quite a feat for an organization of 30,000+ people.

And the result... they have won the award for world's best bank not once, but twice since.

Frameworks – One Size Does Not Fit All

Throughout this book we will be giving you key insights and strategies for improving your internal process when embarking on Everyday Transformation™. But for this book to truly guide you we want to discuss the process, system, methodology, model or framework you might use to lead your organization's digital change.

Frameworks or methodologies can be highly valuable in various contexts as they offer a structured and organized way to approach complex problems, analyze situations, and make decisions. But whilst frameworks offer numerous benefits, it's important to recognize their limitations as well. Frameworks are simplifications of complex realities and may not capture all nuances or unique circumstances of every situation. They should be used as tools to guide analysis and decision-making, but not as rigid prescriptions. Flexibility and critical thinking are essential to effectively apply frameworks and adapt them to specific contexts...

...But in the context of a digital transformation, applying a methodology, or indeed creating your own nuanced approach can massively help structure your thinking and equally importantly provide the explanatory power required to persuade stakeholders to get on board.

But the benefits don't stop there... Here are some of the key benefits and explanatory powers of frameworks:

- **Structure and Organization:** Frameworks provide a structured approach to understanding and analyzing complex concepts or problems. They offer a systematic way to break down complex ideas into more manageable components, enabling clearer thinking and better organization of information.

I am not here to speak the Truth. I am here just to give you a method to perceive it.

Jaggi Vasudev

- **Conceptual Clarity:** Frameworks help in developing a shared understanding of a particular concept or domain. By defining key concepts, relationships, and principles, they establish a common language and mental model that can be easily communicated and shared among stakeholders.

- **Problem-Solving and Decision-Making:** Frameworks offer a structured methodology for problem-solving and decision-making. They provide a step-by-step process or set of guidelines to approach complex problems, helping to identify relevant factors, consider different perspectives, and evaluate potential solutions or options.

- **Analytical Tools:** Frameworks often include analytical tools or techniques that facilitate data gathering, analysis, and interpretation. These tools can help in organizing data, identifying patterns, conducting assessments, and deriving insights from complex information.

- **Contextual Understanding:** Frameworks provide a broader context and perspective for understanding a specific subject or problem. They help identify the interconnections, dependencies, and influencing factors within a system, enabling a more holistic understanding of the situation.

- **Communication and Collaboration:** Frameworks serve as a common reference point for communication and collaboration among stakeholders. They enable effective communication by providing a shared language and structure, facilitating better understanding and alignment of ideas.

- **Knowledge Transfer and Learning:** Frameworks serve as a means to transfer knowledge and learning from one context to another. They encapsulate key principles, concepts, and best practices, allowing others to leverage existing knowledge and experiences when tackling similar problems.

- **Efficiency and Consistency:** Frameworks promote efficiency and consistency in problem-solving and decision-making processes. By providing a predefined structure and guidelines, they help streamline processes, reduce redundancy, and ensure a consistent approach across different scenarios.

- **Scalability and Adaptability:** Frameworks can often be scalable and adaptable to different contexts or levels of complexity. They provide a foundation that can be customized or expanded upon to suit specific needs, allowing organizations to apply the methodology to different situations and scale it as required.

Examples of effective frameworks which help you structure your thinking and have great explanatory power include SMART Goals, SWOT analysis, Porter's Five Forces Model, Ansoff Matrix, Kotter's change process etc.

A digital transformation framework is simply a tool, often used by consultants and leaders, to analyze a business to assist it to reposition themselves in a digital economy as well as agreeing approach (part of the philosophical alignment). Modern digital transformation frameworks are powered by data driven insights and differ from older management consulting frameworks which tend to be more subjective in nature. They are used to create a repeatable method of diagnosis, strategic planning, and implementation.

A good framework keeps focus on the things that matter; customer value, market position and competitors, rather than getting distracted by the shiny objects of technology. Don't get us wrong, technology should act as an important inspiration, but in our experience, many opportunities can be missed when the technologists deliver. This is because more often than not they deliver exactly what has been asked for. It's what was asked for, that's often the problem. When it comes to the Everyday Transformation™ of a business, technology is simply the enabler, not the actual destination.

So, are you clear on what your business is transforming into? Can it be clearly articulated? If not, you most likely need frameworks and models that can help guide your thinking, planning, innovation, communication, and technology/platform selections.

The challenge is, when you take a closer look at most of the digital transformation frameworks touted by consulting firms today, you'll find they are exactly the same as the old management consulting tools they've used for the past 50 years. Tired and subjective. They worked well in an analogue context but were not designed for the digital age.

Today we have to show fresh insights, in context with the customer's business, before our senior stakeholders take them seriously. But how do we get fresh insights...? Data + Frameworks – that's the key!

In what Areas Should a Digital Transformation Framework + Data Help You Gain Clarity?

In its essence, the aim of a digital transformation framework is to create clarity amid the volatility, uncertainty, complexity and ambiguity. Here are five key areas tackled by most frameworks:

Analyze your customers. What do your customers' need? What problem do you solve? How high is the demand for your proposition (product or service)?

Analyze your core strategy. What problems are you trying to solve? Where do you want to see your business in 1/3/5 years? What differentiates you from your competition?

Evaluate your competitors. Who are your competitors? Size? Geography? What makes them unique? What's their online footprint? Understanding this data will help you identify a niche you can own.

Examine your resources. By resources we mean time, skills, infrastructure, and budget. What do you have available and how can you leverage them to get what you need for your digital transformation journey.

Data removes all subjectivity creating roadblocks. It moves the conversation away from opinions and towards facts. By overlaying a framework, you start to paint the bigger picture with context. Armed with your current state analysis and the future state positioned in your strategy you can build the compelling business case for change.

Finally overlay the 'as-is' state of the business or business unit and create an inspirational 'to-be' state using supporting data and the chances of getting the business case accepted grows significantly.

Introducing The Transformation Insight Framework™

This book is divided into six main categories which relate to the Transformation Insight Framework™... but before we tell you what they are, let us share where they originated from.

Today, virtually every leader in business has seen or used the popular 'holistic' People Process Technology framework, used to help understand and manage change in their organization.

TRANSFORMATION INSIGHT FRAMEWORK

HIVEMIND

PHILOSOPHICAL	PEOPLE		PROCESS		PLATFORM		PARTNER
Mission / Vision	Talent Readiness	Culture	Operations	Innovation	Automation	Connectivity	Distribution
Values	Learning & Development	Agile Practices	Comms	ESG	Cyber Security	Data & Analytics	Development
Strategy	Leadership	Structure	Information	Governance & Risk	Technology	Infrastructure	Support

PROPOSITION (PRODUCTS AND SERVICES)

Business Model	Brand	Sales & Marketing	Supply Chain	Product Lifecycle	Customer Experience	Community	Collaboration

The origins of this model date back to the early 1960s when Harold Leavitt (management expert) created his "Diamond Model" which was a framework representing the interdependencies among four components present in every organization: structure, people, technology and tasks.

His model asserted that changes to one area would likely affect the other three. So, to maximise the chances of successful change, we must evaluate, understand, and manage the impacts across all four areas.

In time, structure and tasks were combined to make process, transforming the diamond into a "golden triangle" with the components most commonly used today: people, process and technology. Still with the assertion that if one area shifts, the other two must also adapt to maintain a balance as the change process advances.

Later in the 1990s, Bruce Schneier (Harvard lecturer and internationally renowned security technologist) popularized this version of the framework, essentially creating a common language around it.

A huge amount has changed since then: Cloud has re-engineered our relationship with technology, replacing mainframes and in-house data centres. Agile project management methodologies like SCRUM, LEAN and Kanban have reduced waterfall to a less frequent, situationally specific approach. Mobilization has broken the shackle of the desk allowing humans to work anywhere (and wasn't that needed in 2020). Social media has democratized communication and amplified the voice of the customer. Digital technologies have evolved faster than any innovation in human history transforming how we work, learn, and collaborate.

On top of this we have seen societal changes, geopolitical changes, environmental changes, and a pandemic to name just a few. So effectively with all this change in the last three decades disrupting business and technology, the People Process Technology framework remains a go-to model.

When digital transformation started picking up pace, many believed the People Process Technology framework would become obsolete. Because of the major shifts in the way we work the framework is still considered by many to be more beneficial than ever. But we use a slight twist on this positioning for the **Transformation Insight Framework™** with the following six Ps.

- **Philosophical** Alignment
- **People** Alignment
- **Process** Alignment
- **Platform** Alignment
- **Partner** Alignment
- **Proposition** Alignment

At the highest level, the philosophy is the specific direction and guiding principles for your organization, the people are the individuals who build and deliver solutions. The process is about how they build and deliver them. The platform is what they've developed, deployed, and supported. And the partners are the agency experts, data suppliers, JV's, and other service providers.

When working with organizations we don't necessarily deep dive in all areas, but we do perform an overview assessing the company's transformation capabilities through these five different lenses.

Remember, this framework is designed to provoke questions and map the big picture in your organization. How you use it to collect data and analyze in context to provide insight, will inform, and guide your strategy.

In each section of the book, we will break down the framework and address the component parts. Also, to accompany the **Transformation Insight Framework™** we have created a downloadable Transformation Insight Assessment™ which you can find by visiting www.Everyday-Transformation.com.

First let's start with a high-level overview…

Aligning Philosophy

Philosophical alignment is essential for the success of digital transformation initiatives. It helps to create a shared vision and purpose, ensures consistent messaging, facilitates cultural transformation, enables faster decision-making, and promotes greater agility. When stakeholders are aligned philosophically, it creates a foundation for success and helps to ensure that everyone is working towards the same end goal. Most importantly it provides a common language and authority for cooperation.

Aligning People

When evaluating people, we look at how they perform both individually and as a team. What is the cultural experience and is it attracting the right talent? Are roles well-defined and staffed appropriately? Does the mix of skills and experience meet the project needs, or are there gaps? Do team members work well together, collaborating effectively and jumping in to help one another to ensure goals are met? Are all teams working in sync with the organizational vision? Are they empowered, engaged, and aligned with the business's goals? Having people in place with the right skills, experience and attitude are pivotal to success.

Aligning Processes

Are the processes, systems and structures enabling the right behaviours or slowing things down? Are you using modern methodologies, like Agile? Are you inspecting and adapting, and holding retrospectives to continuously improve? Do you have an Agile playbook? Is your development process documented and followed? Are your people aligned with the processes: Do they understand them and how they fit into it? How do you elicit requirements and then prioritize them? How do you communicate progress to all stakeholders? How do you onboard?

Aligning Platform

The core foundation of successful digital transformation is platform, a platform that can fit within the existing IT infrastructure or that can integrate with the IT ecosystem. While many people advocate for adding "data" or "information" to the golden triangle framework (turning it back into a diamond), we consider it to be part of the platform. Does the data architecture and structure adhere to best practice. Lastly, what is the support structure for both end users and the underlying platform infrastructure?

Aligning Partners

Partners can play a critical role in digital transformation by bringing in expertise, resources, and technologies that complement an organization's capabilities and help accelerate the process. This is not restricted to the process of transformation, but may also benefit training, customer reach, data acquisition, preferred technology and operating models. Successful partnerships require open communication, mutual trust, and a shared commitment to the goals of the transformation initiative.

Aligning Propositions

Our propositions are essentially the value we add to our market to generate revenue, i.e. our products and services. To succeed today and in the future, businesses must deliver innovative solutions at a quicker pace, whilst managing risk with more control and meet the increasing demands of the customers and stakeholders.

You will notice on the model that Proposition extends across all of the other Ps... this is because every one of the other five areas impacts what and how we deliver value to our customer, and we believe putting the customer front and centre is the only sensible way forward in digital change.

Effectively understanding and prioritizing the Six Ps during times of change can provide the visibility and confidence necessary to achieve that.

The **Transformation Insight Framework™** is simple yet powerful. It's also very flexible. Here are some scenarios where its construct can help guide effective change:

- When considering key strategic partners to help throughout the transformation process, considering values, knowledge, experience and process.

- When considering merger or acquisition as part of organizational evolution in regard to values, brand and audience.

- When evaluating if a technology-enabled service is compatible with the platform of an acquiring company.

- When deciding to invest in a company whose platform will serve as the foundation for a series of add-on acquisitions or product developments.

- When looking to take a technology used internally and make it a platform for use by end customers or users (think Uber, food delivery services etc.).

- When exploring JVs for co-development serving the same audience with a shared data strategy.

All of That Said…

Reading this book will answer many of the questions you have, but in reality, it will generate even more questions that need to be answered for you to make informed decisions about your way forward.

If you agree that **DATA + ANALYSIS = INSIGHT**… then the challenge is what data do we collect? What are the useful metrics to measure? And what process will we follow to assess?

DOWNLOAD: To guide you through the **Transformation Insight Framework™** we have designed a 24-step self-assessment which will ask you the key questions and map essential stakeholders. Visit www. Everyday-Transformation.com

PHILOSOPHICAL	TRANSFORMATION
Mission / Vision	**INSIGHT**
Values	**FRAMEWORK**
Strategy	
PROPOSITION	
Business Model	

PHILOSOPHICAL ALIGNMENT

What Do We Really Mean by Philosophical Alignment?

It is important that we are using language the same way when it comes to a guiding book like this, so let us explain what we mean.

In the context of digital transformation, philosophical alignment refers to the agreement between an organization's core values and the principles underlying the digital technologies and processes being implemented. It recognizes that digital transformation is not just a technical or operational change, but also a cultural and philosophical shift.

A digital transformation initiative that is philosophically aligned with an organization's core values and principles is more likely to be successful, because it will be easier to integrate with the organization's existing culture and business strategy. Conversely, a digital transformation initiative that conflicts with an organization's core values may face resistance or even outright rejection from employees or customers.

For example, if an organization values transparency and customer privacy, it may seek to implement digital technologies and processes that prioritize data security and user consent. On the other hand, an organization that values innovation and risk-taking may prioritize experimentation and rapid prototyping in its digital transformation efforts.

Philosophical alignment is particularly important in digital transformation because the technology is often complex and rapidly evolving, making it difficult to assess its impact on an organization's values and culture. By focusing on alignment, organizations can ensure that their digital transformation initiatives are aligned with their broader strategic goals and values, therefore are more likely to succeed over the long term.

Of course, the second part to this is the agreement on overall transformation approach and often this comes first whilst the organization is yet to determine precise direction, but knows evolution is necessary, so as not to become obsolete like many brands before.

Alone we can do so little, together we can do so much

Helen Keller

When we work with companies in the early stages, we often workshop with senior leadership and stakeholders to ensure this alignment is there from the start, and the transformation team have the mandate to continue.

One North Star

The phrase "North Star" is often used metaphorically when setting a vision or goal because the North Star, also known as Polaris, has been used for centuries as a navigational guide for travellers. The North Star appears to stay fixed in the sky while the other stars rotate around it, making it a reliable point of reference for determining direction.

The North Star's position has made it a useful guide for travellers, sailors, and adventurers since ancient times. It was particularly important for those traveling across long distances, such as across the ocean, where other navigational aids like landmarks or maps were not available. Thus, the North Star came to represent a constant and reliable point of reference in a changing and uncertain world.

By analogy, the North Star has become a symbol of the guiding principles or values that organizations use to navigate their own journeys. The idea is that, like the North Star, these guiding principles should remain constant and unwavering, even as the surrounding environment changes. Thus, the phrase "North Star" is often used when setting a long-term vision that reflects an organization's core values or mission.

Particularly Important for Digital Transformation

Having one North Star is incredibly important when it comes to digital transformation as it often involves a significant shift in the way a company operates, so can help ensure that everyone is moving in the same direction, working towards the same ultimate goal. Without it, different departments or teams may have conflicting priorities, leading to confusion and inefficiency. It will keep the focus on the most important aspects of your transformation. With so many potential areas to invest in or changes to make, it can be easy to get side-tracked or overwhelmed. A clear direction will help ensure that all efforts are focused on the most impactful changes.

It is also a source of motivation and inspiration for employees throughout the transformation process. By rallying around a common goal, employees can feel a sense of purpose and excitement about the changes taking place, which can be critical for maintaining momentum and driving success.

Your North Star helps you to prioritize your digital initiatives. By aligning all digital investments towards a common goal, you make data-driven decisions and ensure you are investing in the initiatives that are most likely to drive digital transformation, and are congruent with your brand values.

A North Star is typically a quantifiable metric that can be tracked and measured over time. This provides a tangible way to measure progress and create a sense of accountability within the organization. By setting a clear goal, everyone is responsible for achieving it, which can help to drive performance and ensure that everyone is doing their part to contribute to the organization's success.

A North Star is only effective if it is supported by leadership and has their buy-in.

Without leadership support, a North Star can become a meaningless goal that is not taken seriously by the rest of the organization.

Here are a few reasons why North Star without leadership buy-in does not work:

Lack of resources: Without leadership support, it can be challenging to secure the resources needed to achieve your North Star. This can result in a lack of investment in the digital transformation efforts and can hinder progress towards your goal.

Lack of alignment: If leadership is not aligned with the North Star, it can be challenging to get everyone on the same page. This can lead to confusion and conflicting priorities, making it difficult to achieve your digital transformation goals.

Lack of motivation: When leadership is not fully committed to the North Star, it can be challenging to motivate employees to invest in the digital transformation efforts. This can lead to a lack of enthusiasm and engagement, making it harder to achieve your goals.

Lack of accountability: Without leadership buy-in, it can be challenging to hold teams accountable for achieving the North Star. This can result in a lack of progress and make it difficult to track performance and make adjustments as needed.

Having leadership buy-in is critical for success. Leaders need to be fully committed to the vision and be willing to provide the necessary resources and support to achieve it. Without this support, your digital transformation efforts may struggle to gain traction and may not lead to the desired outcomes.

Here are some steps that can help you create a compelling North Star:

Define your purpose: Start by defining the purpose of your organization's digital transformation. What are the goals you hope to achieve through digital transformation? What are the key business outcomes you are looking to drive? By defining your purpose, you can establish the foundation for your North Star.

Identify your customer value proposition: Next, identify your organization's customer value proposition. What value do you provide to your customers, and how can digital transformation help enhance that value proposition? By understanding your customer value proposition, you can develop a North Star that is focused on delivering value to your customers.

Conduct a SWOT analysis: Conduct a SWOT (strengths, weaknesses, opportunities, threats) analysis to identify the key challenges and opportunities facing your organization in the digital landscape. This can help you identify the areas where you need to focus your digital transformation efforts.

Develop a long-term vision: Based on your purpose, customer value proposition, and SWOT analysis, develop a long-term vision for your digital transformation. What does success look like in five or ten years? What are the key milestones you need to achieve along the way? This vision should serve as the basis for your North Star.

Communicate your North Star: Finally, communicate your North Star clearly and consistently throughout your organization. Make sure everyone understands the vision and how their work contributes to achieving it. By aligning everyone towards a common goal, you can ensure that your digital transformation efforts are focused and effective.

Creating a North Star is not a one-time event. It requires ongoing review and refinement as your organization's needs and priorities evolve. However, by following these steps, you can create a North Star that provides a clear and compelling direction for your digital transformation efforts.

Framing the Conversation

Framing the conversation of change within an organization is an essential step towards ensuring that the change is well-received and effectively implemented. It requires clear communication, transparency, and collaboration and done well ensures you get the correct level of buy-in from stakeholders.

Pre-discovery your framing is aimed at senior leadership and key stakeholders to ensure buy-in and essentially only agree the approach and desired outcome. When you have certainty on these two things you can start to spread the message beyond.

Here are some steps that can help you frame the conversation of change within the wider organization:

Start with the why: Begin the conversation by explaining why the change is necessary. What is the problem that you are trying to solve, and how will the change help to address it? By starting with the why, you can help people understand the rationale behind the change, which can help to create buy-in and reduce resistance.

Communicate the benefits: Clearly communicate the benefits of the change, both for the organization and for the individuals involved. Explain how the change will make things better, faster, or more efficient, and how it will benefit the organization as a whole.

Use Data to back up your plan: Framing your plan with data will enable you to get buy-in and it is worth spending time collecting, evaluating, and using data to tell the stories that support the vision. Data should be used to reinforce your decision making and reduce uncertainty. To keep the conversation grounded, provide facts.

Keep it simple: Wherever possible keep it simple and try not to over complicate. Your colleagues need to understand it and see where they fit in the great scheme of things. Giving them clarity on what is expected of them and their role moving forward is essential for progress.

Address concerns: Acknowledge any concerns or fears that people may have about the change. Be open and transparent about the potential challenges and explain how you plan to address them. This can help to alleviate any concerns and build trust among the stakeholders.

Provide a roadmap: Provide a clear roadmap for the change, including timelines, milestones, and key deliverables. This can help people understand the process and what to expect, which can help to reduce anxiety and uncertainty.

Involve stakeholders: Involve stakeholders in the change process and seek their input and feedback. This can help to build ownership and create a sense of collaboration, which can improve the chances of successful implementation.

Follow-up: Follow up regularly to ensure that the change is progressing as planned and to address any issues that may arise. This can help to keep people engaged and committed to the change.

Developing One Common Language

Our ability as human beings to use language is the significant differentiator between us and other animals. Gestural theory states that human language developed from gestures that were used for simple communication, which many scientists believe was developed as a direct result of one person needing to teach another person a new skill, more specifically, toolmaking. Two types of evidence support this theory. Gestural language and vocal language depend on similar neural systems. The regions on the cortex that are responsible for mouth and hand movements border each other.

Thomas Morgan from the University of California at Berkeley presented research that stone toolmaking played a crucial role in the evolution of language and teaching among our prehistoric ancestors. The first verbal communications, which likely happened approximately 2.5 million years ago, were likely about toolmaking. The study suggests our human ancestors may have developed a primitive form of language so they could teach each other how to make stone age tools, an essential skill for survival.

When people share a common language, it will bring them together. When they don't, it can divide them. This is the premise of a study published by Deloitte who concluded that organizations who establish a common language to advance digital transformation, one that transcends technology, are likely to be more successful.

A common language is the most obvious binding element in any society

Michael Howard

Language and Digital Transformation

Digital transformation is all about promoting a different vision of life. The mistake many companies make is treating digital as if they are 'doing digital', this is digitization at its worst, as if it's some checklist of things to do without giving the context or the why behind the change. In contrast organizations who embrace 'being digital' shift the paradigm in relation to culture and operations. They recognise it isn't just about buying the latest digital tool, but more about creating a new process, system or mindset. Helping people to understand why digital transformation is necessary, requires explanation and persuasion.

For many organizations, digital transformation is simply a matter of survival. Leaders seek to determine how to maintain competitive advantage and enable a winning strategy that doesn't just withstand disruption but embraces it to generate new possibilities. Digital transformation efforts often raise questions, like why do so many transformations fail to deliver measurable impact? Why is it so hard to drive change, or create a strategy that can evolve with technology and shifting core assumptions? We believe the answer lies in the lack of a common language. Creating a common, strategically linked language for digital change, could be the answer to achieving digital advantage.

How Does Language Help?

Finding the right language to help employees and stakeholders alike to understand why digital transformation is necessary, and starts with a vision that can be supported by a coherent strategy.

Often this is where digital transformation efforts get derailed. The Deloitte research found that 85% of CEOs accelerated digital initiatives during the pandemic, yet most can't articulate their overall strategy, or the progress they made... just that they made a tech investment. This is 'digitization' at its worst. If CEOs can't say their digital transformation resulted in new business advantages, including leaner processes and improved adaptability, then they haven't really transformed. They go on to note that C-level executives have different agendas, focuses and needs. Often, they lack awareness in other areas of the organization and don't speak to each other when making tech decisions, or if they do, they struggle to communicate effectively.

Everyday Transformation™ is a team sport that requires a playbook to coordinate across divisions with a consistent approach. A common language will enable executives to have tech-adjacent and tech-agnostic conversations that transcend any individual technology and go to the heart of their processes and culture. Like our earliest ancestors, who needed to teach toolmaking, leaders need a common language to ensure things are done correctly.

Creating a common language in a digital transformation can have several benefits, including:

Transcending behavioural and structural barriers: Everything in an organization is interconnected. A common language ensures leaders across business functions can speak thematically about shared requirements, avoiding unnecessary spend and addressing new threats or risks.

Improved communication: A common language allows all stakeholders in a digital transformation project to speak the same language, reducing misunderstandings and confusion. This, in turn, can improve collaboration and efficiency.

Better decision-making: A common language allows stakeholders to better understand the data and analytics involved in a digital transformation project, making it easier to make informed decisions.

Creation of a plan beyond a single technology: Platforms, capabilities, and initiatives often involve multiple digital and physical technologies securely working together. As these technologies combine, they become greater than the sum of their parts to bring new capabilities and greater value.

A playbook for future evolution: Today's breakthrough is tomorrow's legacy technology. A common language can enable leaders to think flexibly across organizational and technology needs, without having the business strategy reliant on any single technology.

Increased innovation: A common language can help promote innovation by facilitating the sharing of ideas and knowledge across different teams and departments. This can lead to new insights and approaches that might not have been possible without a shared language.

Creating greater strategic value: The obvious advantages that come from an improved capacity to change, binding organization strategy, people, and technology.

Enhanced efficiency: When everyone involved in a digital transformation project uses a common language, it can streamline processes and reduce the time and effort required to complete tasks.

Greater consistency: A common language helps ensure that everyone is on the same page when it comes to the goals, objectives, and processes involved in a digital transformation. This consistency can help reduce errors and improve outcomes.

Identify Your Champions

Creating your digital transformation coalition is critical to your success. These are your champions who enthusiastically advocate for the vision and help create momentum.

Typically, early adopters make themselves known, they want to get involved. It is always fascinating to us that all the organizations we support, the natural change ambassadors were already somehow involved.

Here are some reasons why the guiding coalition is important:

Collaboration: Your champions bring together stakeholders from across the organization, including business units, IT, and other departments. By collaborating, you can ensure that everyone is aligned towards the same goals and working together to achieve them. You also create a more comprehensive and holistic vision for the future.

Increased buy-in: By involving stakeholders in the process, you increase their buy-in, sense of ownership and commitment to the initiative. This can help to overcome resistance and increase the chances of successful implementation.

Improved decision-making: A digital transformation coalition can improve decision-making by bringing together diverse perspectives and experiences. By considering a variety of viewpoints, you can make more informed and strategic decisions.

Faster implementation: By working together with early adopters, you can streamline the implementation process and reduce the time required to achieve your goals. This can help to accelerate the benefits of the transformation and achieve ROI more quickly.

Change management: A digital transformation coalition can help to manage change more effectively by reducing resistance to change in their respective teams and communicating progress, therefore increasing the likelihood of successful adoption.

So you are convinced... Here is what to look out for

Look for curiosity. Early adopters are often curious and open to new ideas and technologies. They are always looking for ways to improve their work and are willing to try new things.

Identify opinion leaders. Opinion leaders are individuals who have a strong influence on others in the organization. Look for individuals who are respected and trusted by others and who are often sought out for advice.

Observe technology use. Look for individuals who are already using technology in innovative ways or who are early adopters of new tools and platforms. These individuals are often eager to experiment with new technologies and are quick to identify the benefits.

Seek out feedback. Early adopters are often willing to provide feedback on new technologies or processes. Look for individuals who are vocal about their opinions and who are willing to share their experiences with others.

Monitor social media. Social media can be a useful tool for identifying early adopters. Look for individuals who are active on social media and who are sharing information about new technologies or processes.

Consider generational differences. Millennials and Gen Z are often more comfortable with technology and more likely to be early adopters. Consider targeting these groups when looking for early adopters.

By identifying and engaging these individuals, you can help to drive adoption and acceptance of new technologies and processes. Often, we work with clients to not only identify, but initially engage them with a workshop or even better our **Certified Digital Change Practitioner / Leader** programmes.

REFLECTION SECTION

1. Who are the key stakeholders in your organization that would have influence over the success of your transformation? Think department heads, Subject matter experts, leaders of large teams, key partners etc

2. Who are your champions? And have you done enough to prepare them for what is coming? i.e. do they understand the full context for change, the key benefits and the appropriate digital literacy to spread the word confidently?

3. Could you organise a series of workshops to bring potential influencers together for a collective sense of ownership?

4. What training and development do you think would serve your champions?

5. What is your North Star?

We can help with the above with not only specific and certified training programmes, but also ongoing innovation initiatives to start identifying early opportunities.

REMEMBER: You can visit www.Everyday-Transformation.com for the **Transformation Insight Assessment™** which includes more questions to guide you.

Placing the Customer at the Centre of Everything

Another area for philosophical alignment is around putting the customer at the centre of everything in digital transformation. This means focusing on understanding and meeting the needs and expectations of customers in every aspect of the transformation process. This is essential because digital transformation is all about improving the way that companies interact with their customers in the digital age.

We believe Customer Experience (CX) today is where the battle for market share is won and lost!

By prioritizing CX in digital transformation initiatives, companies can:

Identify customer needs: Collecting and analysing customer data to gain insights into their needs, preferences, and behaviours. This can help to inform digital transformation initiatives and ensure that they are aligned with customer needs.

Customer journey mapping: Understanding the customer journey and identifying pain points and areas for improvement. This can help to prioritize digital transformation initiatives that will have the greatest impact on the customer experience.

Focus on customer-centric design: Using design thinking and other customer-centric design methodologies to develop digital products, services, and experiences that are easy to use and meet customer needs.

Increase agility: By focusing on CX, companies can become more agile and responsive to changing customer needs and preferences. This can help companies to stay competitive in a rapidly changing digital landscape.

Foster innovation: By focusing on CX, companies can foster a culture of innovation that is focused on meeting the needs of customers in the digital age. This can lead to the development of new and innovative digital products and services that better meet customer needs.

Measure success: By focusing on CX, companies can measure the success of their digital transformation initiatives in terms of customer satisfaction, loyalty, and retention. This can help companies to ensure that their digital transformation initiatives are delivering value to customers.

Collect feedback: Collecting and incorporating customer feedback throughout the digital transformation process. This can help to ensure that digital products, services, and experiences are meeting customer needs and expectations. Remember you cannot transform something you don't understand. If you don't know the current state of your customer's experience, how can you possibly design the future state?

Personalize: Using customer data to personalize digital experiences and interactions. This can help to improve customer engagement and loyalty.

Continuous improvement: Continuously monitoring and improving the customer experience through ongoing data collection and analysis. This can help to ensure that digital transformation initiatives are delivering value to customers over time.

Case Study – BT: One great case study for customer centricity in the context of digital transformation is the transformation of the British multinational telecommunications company, BT. Their digital transformation journey clearly demonstrates why to prioritize customer centricity is driving business success in the digital age.

By focusing on their customer and implementing customer-centric digital initiatives, they improved the customer experience and became more competitive in a rapidly changing digital landscape. Back in January 2017, the CEO at the time, Gavin Patterson, committed to turning BT's reputation around and announced that delivering a brilliant customer experience was going to form one of BT's key strategic pillars. He shared their ambition was not just to become a CX market leader in telecoms, but to be a global role model for exceptional CX. Whilst still on their digital journey, BT is now a multi-award winner in CX.

They acknowledged that disruption was transforming the telecommunications industry and that they needed to adapt their business to remain competitive. They embarked on a digital transformation initiative with a focus on putting the customer at the centre of everything they do.

To achieve this, BT implemented several customer-centric digital initiatives, including:

Self-service portals: BT developed self-service portals for their customers, allowing them to manage their accounts, pay bills, and access customer support online.

Mobile apps: BT developed mobile apps that allowed customers to manage their accounts and access customer support on their mobile devices.

Social media engagement: BT used social media to engage with customers and provide customer support.

Personalized experiences: BT used customer data to personalize customer experiences, such as providing customized recommendations for products and services.

Customer feedback: BT collected and analyzed customer feedback to improve the customer experience and inform ongoing digital transformation initiatives.

As a result of these initiatives, BT was able to improve the customer experience and drive business success. They reported a 95% increase in the number of customers using their self-service portals and a 20% reduction in customer complaints.

When you make customer experience your priority, you must invest in bringing it to life, putting your people at the heart of your plans and ensuring that they are proud of your purpose (all part of philosophical alignment), only then will you be on the way to building a customer centric culture.

If you can do this, your people will start to bring your vision to life for your customers with small changes, every single day. And like in the BT example, your customers will start telling you they can feel the difference... that is when you know you are on the right track.

The Opportunity of Change

The opportunity of change in the context of digital transformation refers to the potential benefits and positive outcomes that can arise from the adoption of digital technologies in various aspects of business and society. These benefits can include increased efficiency and productivity, improved customer experiences, enhanced communication and collaboration, and new opportunities for innovation and growth.

By embracing digital transformation, organizations can streamline processes, automate tasks, and gain access to valuable data insights that can inform better decision-making. They can also leverage digital technologies to create new products and services, expand their reach and market share, and stay ahead of the competition.

However, digital transformation also involves significant changes in organizational culture, processes, and skill sets. Organizations must be willing to invest in training and development to ensure that their employees have the necessary digital literacy and technical skills to effectively leverage new technologies. Additionally, they must be willing to adapt their business models and processes to take advantage of the opportunities presented by digital transformation.

Here's the major upside of this type of culture shift. You are in effect creating a workforce who are more agile and less resistant to change when future disruption happens. An organization fit for the future.

The risks of doing nothing in regard to digital transformation can be significant for organizations and society as a whole. Here are a few potential risks:

Falling behind the competition: As more and more businesses embrace digital transformation, those that fail to do so risk falling behind their competitors. They may struggle to keep up with evolving customer expectations and market trends and may find it difficult to innovate and bring new products and services to market.

Missed opportunities: Digital technologies can open up new opportunities for organizations to create value, whether that's through improved efficiency, enhanced customer experiences, or new revenue streams. By failing to embrace digital transformation, organizations may miss out on these opportunities.

Cybersecurity risks: With more business processes and data moving online, organizations face an increased risk of cyber-attacks and data breaches. Failing to invest in cybersecurity measures can leave organizations vulnerable to these risks.

Inefficient processes: Digital transformation can help organizations streamline processes and reduce costs. By failing to embrace these technologies, organizations may be stuck with inefficient and outdated processes that are costly and time-consuming.

Reduced resilience: The COVID-19 pandemic has highlighted the importance of digital technologies for maintaining business continuity. Organizations that fail to embrace digital transformation may be less resilient in the face of future disruptions or crises.

Everything to lose and much to gain. Overall, the risks of doing nothing can be significant, but remember, disruption is going to either happen to you.... Or because of you.

Here are just some examples of disruption in the last 40 years and the opportunities they created.

Tesla – Disrupted the automotive industry by creating electric cars with advanced digital features.

Amazon – Created a seamless online shopping experience, allowing customers to purchase products with just a few clicks.

Uber – Revolutionized the transportation industry with its ride-sharing platform.

Netflix – Disrupted the traditional entertainment industry by offering on-demand streaming services.

Airbnb – Disrupted the hospitality industry with its online platform that connects travellers with unique lodging options.

Spotify – Disrupted the music industry by offering a personalized music streaming service.

Apple – Revolutionized the smartphone industry with the introduction of the iPhone.

Shopify – Enabled small businesses to create online stores and compete with larger companies.

Bank of America – Enhanced customer experience through its mobile banking app and digital services.

Walmart – Streamlined supply chain and improved efficiency through digital inventory management systems.

Nike – By leveraging digital technologies to create personalized customer experiences and engage with customers through social media, Nike has established itself as a leader in the sportswear market.

Google – Revolutionized the search engine industry with its advanced algorithms and personalized search results.

META – Created a new era of social networking, enabling people to connect and share information with each other.

Instagram – Disrupted the photo-sharing industry, allowing users to easily edit and share photos with a global audience.

YouTube – Enabled people to create and share video content with a global audience.

Zara – Used digital technology to streamline its supply chain and bring new fashion designs to market more quickly.

Starbucks – Created a seamless mobile ordering and payment system for customers.

Dominos – Enabled customers to order pizza online and track their delivery in real time.

Coca-Cola – Used digital technology to personalize marketing messages and engage with customers in real time.

Virgin Atlantic – Disrupted the airline industry with its innovative in-flight entertainment system.

Sephora – Created a personalized shopping experience for customers, using digital technology to recommend products based on their preferences.

Amazon Web Services – Enabled businesses to easily and cost-effectively host their websites and applications in the cloud.

McDonald's – Used digital technology to improve the ordering experience for customers, introducing self-service kiosks and mobile ordering.

And Specifically for our Friends and Clients in the Middle East

Souq.com – Disrupted the e-commerce industry in the Middle East, offering a wide range of products and services online.

Careem – Revolutionized the transportation industry in the Middle East with its ride-hailing platform.

Noon.com – Disrupted the e-commerce industry in the Middle East, offering a variety of products at competitive prices.

Emirates – Used digital technology to offer a seamless travel experience for customers, from booking to arrival.

Talabat and Hungerstation – Disrupted the food delivery industry in the Middle East, offering a wide range of restaurant options to customers.

Ounass – Used digital technology to offer luxury fashion and beauty products to customers in the Middle East.

Etisalat – Used digital technology to offer a range of telecom services, from mobile phones to high-speed internet.

Dubai Electricity and Water Authority (DEWA) – Used digital technology to improve the efficiency and sustainability of energy and water services in Dubai.

Aramex – Used digital technology to streamline logistics and delivery services, offering faster and more reliable shipping options.

Bayut – Disrupted the real estate industry in the Middle East, offering a range of property listings and search tools.

Emirates NBD – Used digital technology to offer mobile banking services to customers, from account management to bill payments.

CareShield – Used digital technology to offer health insurance products to customers in the Middle East.

The Entertainer – Used digital technology to offer discounts and deals on a range of products and services to customers in the Middle East.

Nana – Used digital technology to offer on-demand home services, from cleaning to plumbing, to customers in the Middle East.

Al Tayer Group – Used digital technology to offer a range of luxury fashion and beauty products to customers in the Middle East.

Meraas – Used digital technology to offer immersive and interactive experiences for customers, from entertainment to hospitality.

Saudi Aramco – Used digital technology to improve the efficiency and safety of its operations in the oil and gas industry.

Abu Dhabi National Oil Company (ADNOC) – Used digital technology to improve the efficiency and sustainability of its operations in the oil and gas industry.

Careem NOW – Used digital technology to disrupt the food delivery industry in the Middle East, offering fast and reliable delivery services to customers.

REFLECTION SECTION

1. What are the common attributes to the opportunities listed above and how does this apply to your organization?
2. How have your customers' expectations changed in the last 10 years and what have you done to exceed them?
3. Who in your industry is leading the charge to disrupt using technology and likely to raise the bar of customer expectation?
4. What comparable industries or sectors could you look to for inspiration when it comes to product/service innovation and the role of technology in delivery?

> **REMEMBER:** You can visit www.Everyday-Transformation.com for the **Transformation Insight Assessment™** which includes more questions to guide you.

New Values Required

Organizational values are critically important because they provide a foundation for the culture and behaviour of an organization. They define what an organization stands for, what it believes in, and how it operates. Values guide decision-making, actions, and interactions with stakeholders, including customers, employees, partners, and communities.

It might be time to re-consider your organizational values in a fast-changing digital world because the values that were relevant in the past may no longer be sufficient or applicable moving forwards.

Re-visiting organizational values can help ensure that they align with the current realities and future trends and provide a clear direction for the organization in the face of rapid change. Values such as innovation, agility, and customer-centricity may become more important in a digital world, while traditional values such as hierarchy and control may become less relevant.

In addition, re-visiting organizational values can help foster a culture of continuous learning and improvement, which are likely to serve you better as you progress through your journey. By regularly reviewing and updating organizational values, leaders can ensure that their organizations are equipped to thrive in a constantly evolving landscape. But make no mistake over the importance of this exercise when it comes to philosophical alignment as the values of the organization are often used to justify arguments for and against initiatives.

A common set of values we regularly see in clients embracing change include:

- **Open-mindedness** – Being receptive to new ideas and different ways of doing things.

- **Flexibility** – Being able to adapt to changing circumstances and requirements.

- **Resilience** – Being able to bounce back from setbacks and challenges.

- **Collaboration** – Being able to work effectively with others towards a common goal.

- **Learning orientation** – Having a willingness to continuously learn and improve.

- **Creativity** – Being able to think outside the box and produce innovative solutions.

- **Initiative** – Being proactive and taking the lead in driving change.

- **Empathy** – Being able to understand and relate to others' perspectives and feelings.

- **Accountability** – Taking responsibility for one's actions and decisions.

- **Vision** – Having a clear sense of direction and purpose for the organization and being able to communicate this to others.

- **Influence** - Understanding how to position ideas for maximum adoption and cooperation.

We believe that organizations that not only define their values, but actively promote living the values, attract like-minded talent in the recruitment process and ultimately create a cultural experience congruent with those values.

Typically, in most organizations the cultural experience becomes the customer experience, which in turn becomes the brand experience.

Case Study – NEOM: One case study which demonstrates the power of unification through values is NEOM, a place where both of us (the Warrens) have spent some time. For those unfamiliar with NEOM it is a region in the northwest of Saudi Arabia combining 468 km of coastline on the Red Sea, with snow-capped mountains in land.

NEOM is a series of individual giga projects focussed on creating the land of the future, where the greatest minds and best talents are empowered to embody pioneering ideas and exceed boundaries

FAIL
FAST
LEARN
QUICK

in a world inspired by imagination. To do this they use very specific language and values to attract both talent and investment to realise the vision.

Their 'future loop' represents the spirit of their mission – to create a 'new future' based upon five core principles: nature, technology, liveability, sustainability, and community. They are their guiding lights, as they build and activate their project.

The name NEOM is derived from two words. Envisioned by His Royal Highness Mohammed bin Salman, Crown Prince, and Chairman of the NEOM Company Board of Directors, the first three letters come from the Ancient Greek prefix neo – meaning 'new'. The 'M' is the first from 'Mustaqbal', an Arabic word meaning 'future'.

"If we are to solve the challenges of tomorrow, we must face up to them today, no matter how difficult they may seem. At NEOM, we are addressing some of the most pressing challenges facing humanity by bringing together a community of the brightest minds committed to reimagining what a sustainable future will look like in 20 to 30 years, and building it today. We are redefining the future now. NEOM is open for business."

NEOM Chief Executive Officer
Nadhmi Al-Nasr

Failure Is Actually an Option...

...But not really. It's part of the strategy in an agile business, the practice of empiricism.

Empiricism is a philosophical approach that emphasizes the importance of evidence and experience in acquiring knowledge. According to empiricists, knowledge comes primarily from sensory experiences and observations, rather than innate ideas or concepts.

Empiricists believe that knowledge is gained through a process of observation, experimentation, and reflection. They value empirical evidence over theoretical speculation or abstract reasoning, and they emphasize the importance of testing hypotheses and theories against real-world data.

In the context of agile methodology, empiricism is a key principle that underpins the iterative, feedback-driven approach of development. Agile

There is no innovation and creativity without failure. Period.

Brené Brown

teams rely on empirical data and feedback to inform their decision-making and adapt their approach over time. This can include data on user behaviour, product performance, and team productivity, which is used to inform continuous improvement and optimize outcomes.

Overall, empiricism is a fundamental approach to acquiring knowledge and making decisions based on evidence and observation, which is closely aligned with the principles of agile methodology.

One of the core principles of agile methodology is that "fail fast, learn quick" - in other words, it is acceptable to fail as long as the team learns from it and adapts quickly. This is because agile values the iterative process of development, where small, incremental changes are made based on continuous feedback and testing.

Agile recognizes that not all ideas will work out, and that failure can be a valuable learning experience that helps the team improve and iterate on their approach. By embracing failure as an option, teams can take more risks and experiment with new ideas, which can lead to breakthrough innovations and improved outcomes.

However, it's important to note that agile does not encourage reckless or irresponsible behaviour, and teams are still expected to prioritize quality and adhere to best practices. The goal is not to fail for the sake of failing, but to be willing to take calculated risks in pursuit of continuous improvement.

It is also worth noting that not all consequences of risk taking are equal. Some sectors are more regulated than others and some customers more forgiving depending on the context of your products and services. These are all conversations to be had when defining values and philosophy for the road ahead.

In summary, while failure is not the end goal in agile, it is viewed as an acceptable outcome if the team learns from it and can use those insights to improve their approach moving forward.

The Sailing Metaphor Exercise

Before we move onto the rest of the framework, we wanted to introduce you to an exercise we often facilitate with clients to help achieve a common understanding of direction and move in the direction of philosophical alignment.

To illustrate this exercise and fire up the creative juices we introduce the power of the metaphor to evoke divergent thinking.

Human beings paint pictures with words and use metaphor for storytelling, ideation, communication, and knowledge transfer. But what is a metaphor and how do they help us? A metaphor compares two apparently dissimilar things by equating one thing as the other. Through this association, our minds can bring one idea into the conceptual space of another idea.

Whenever you compare two objects this way, one of them is instantly seen in a different light, illuminated, and re-configured through the comparison. The concrete becomes abstract, the ephemeral grounded momentarily, the unknown connected to the known in a way that helps us understand.

This tendency to compare two dissimilar things is a very human. In fact, our brains are designed to think in metaphorical constructs. One of the fundamental findings of cognitive science is that people think in terms of frames and metaphors. The frames are in the synapses of our brains, physically present in the form of neural circuitry. When the facts don't fit the frames, the frames are kept and the facts ignored.

Simply put we see things differently when we look through the lens of metaphor.

Such metaphor – both verbal and visual – is without doubt one of the most powerful tools to help people communicate and understand the complex, abstract principles of business. For The Storytellers, it's a fundamental method of illustrating our clients' stories, figurative retellings of the world, laying a fabric of imaginative story over raw reality and thus transforming that reality.

Sailing as a Metaphor for Business

Sailing metaphors are common in the workplace, appearing countless times in the language used by leaders. They often speak of "navigating through troubled or stormy waters" or "re-charting the course" when discussing business challenges. Stories are often employed as anchor to a key point or a compass to guide the organization. Other references include "the winds of change" and the importance of "a strong hand on the tiller", 'maintaining a business on an even keel", conducting oneself in an "above-board" manner, "staying afloat", "battening down the hatches", and "sailing close to the wind" are just a few examples of the nautical expressions that litter business discourse.

Yacht racing serves as a compelling metaphor for managing a business, as it encompasses shared fundamental elements. In both realms, a team of individuals must harness speed, tactics, strategy, timing, and diverse resources to attain a destination and accomplish goals. This pursuit takes place amidst a fleet of competitors, within an unpredictable and ever-changing environment. The parallels between yacht racing and business management highlight the need for adaptability, teamwork, and a keen understanding of the dynamic landscape to navigate towards success.

Yacht racing stands apart from other forms of racing due to a key distinction: the boats involved do not sail the same course. While there is a defined starting point and a clear endpoint for the race, the paths taken by individual boats can differ widely in terms of route and distance covered. In contrast, a business may have a definitive beginning and a defined goal, but its race is an ongoing endeavour that often encompasses multiple and diverse racecourses simultaneously. This highlights the dynamic and ever-evolving nature of business, where the journey towards success involves navigating through varied routes and challenges while aiming to achieve overarching objectives.

Both yacht racing and business operations exist within constantly changing environments. Yacht racing entails navigating the physical elements of wind, waves, and weather, as well as adapting to the competitive landscape. Similarly, businesses must contend with dynamic shifts in economic conditions, regulatory frameworks, societal trends, and technological advancements. In both realms, the individuals in charge, be it the boat skipper or the business owner, must make choices and exercise control over certain aspects. However, they also need to adapt and adjust to elements beyond their control.

Similar to skilled sailors, effective business managers possess the ability to anticipate changes in conditions. The winning skipper needs to demonstrate superior foresight and adjust for these changes better than the competition. Both the company and the crew must continually develop and execute a series of tactics, encompassing short-term strategies for individual races, medium-term strategies for weekend regattas, and long-term strategies for an entire racing season. Without a well-defined and clearly articulated strategy, a boat or business simply reacts to whatever circumstances arise, lacking the proactive approach needed for sustained success. Just as a sailor navigates the unpredictable seas, a business manager must steer their organization with strategic intent, making calculated decisions based on a thoughtful understanding of the competitive landscape and future trends.

Both businesses and race boats rely on essential elements such as leadership, teamwork, and swift decision-making to achieve success. They also require innovative problem-solving, clear objectives, and effective communication to function effectively. It is important to note that speed alone cannot guarantee victory if the wrong strategic choices are made or if the boat or business veers off in the wrong direction. Conversely, even the most impeccable strategy and tactics cannot compensate for slow speed. To secure victory, a mastery of all these elements is required: meticulous preparation, strategic planning, proficient boat handling, swiftness, and tactical acumen. In both the racing arena and the business world, triumph hinges upon a holistic approach that encompasses a range of interconnected factors, each playing a vital role in achieving the desired outcome.

So, let's take a look at your boat...

Sailboat Exercise

The following exercise plays to metaphor and can be used for leadership teams throughout the organization... i.e., the boat can represent your department, division, or the business as a whole.

Setting up the Exercise

Explain that the sailing boat represents the organization, and the boat currently has an agreed destination (vision).

Every boat experiences two types of forces... forces of momentum (i.e. the wind that fills the sails) and forces of resistance (the water and currents that create drag). The point of this exercise is to brainstorm and provoke discussion about those forces in your organization... what moves you forward? And what slows you down?

Instructions:

1. Organise people into small enough groups where everyone is heard in discussion.

2. Ensure each group has a flip chart and is standing for the exercise.

3. Ask each group to nominate a scribe to write ideas and a spokesperson to present their thoughts after.

4. Now get the teams to draw a small boat on the paper and list as many forces of momentum above the boat as they can. Essentially things that drive the organization forwards, that enable progress or create demand.

5. Next identify forces of resistance and list them below the boat. This are the factors that slow you down (and might be totally necessary like regulatory or compliance related issues).

6. Encourage brainstorming initially followed by challenge and discussion.

7. Finally bring all groups back together and take turns to present your ideas.

This discussion will put the purpose and vision front and centre, whilst allowing the participants to see the organization through the eyes of their colleagues, taking on new perspectives.

When we facilitate this exercise for clients, we broaden the metaphor to identify risks, values and capabilities… amongst other things. You can even broaden the exercise by appraising the environment you sail in. This is beautifully explored in 'Blue Ocean Strategy,' by W. Chan Kim and Renée Mauborgne

According to the authors', the majority of markets can be characterized as "red oceans" - highly competitive and saturated with numerous players vying for the same limited opportunities. In such environments, it is akin to sharks feeding on the same pool of fish, resulting in intense competition, commoditisation, and often minimal differentiation.

Over time, submarkets emerge in response to these fiercely competitive red oceans where there is a step up in value or a niche being served. To truly stand out from competitors and carve a unique position, it becomes imperative to create a "blue ocean". By venturing into uncharted waters and creating an uncontested market space, businesses can find renewed growth and success by offering something truly distinct and irresistible to their target audience.

The key takeaway here is to avoid trying to beat competitors. Instead, focus on making them irrelevant by creating a leap in value for buyers and your company.

But we can extend this metaphor even further by assessing the conditions. Are you fishing in rough seas? Are you on the correct course to arrive at your destination ahead of the competition?

Let us know how you get on with this exercise, or if you prefer to work with an independent facilitator... let's talk!

REFLECTION SECTION

1. What are your organizational values and do they serve where you want to go?
2. Who needs to be involved in any conversation about brand values?
3. On a scale of 1 to 10 how agile is your organization?
4. What are the forces that enable opportunity for you? What advantages do you have over your competition? What disadvantages do you have?
5. What are the forces of resistance in your organization i.e. the things that slow you down and reduce your ability to adapt or deploy quickly?
6. Does any part of your organization work in an agile way today?

REMEMBER: You can visit www.Everyday-Transformation.com for the **Transformation Insight Assessment™** which includes more questions to guide you.

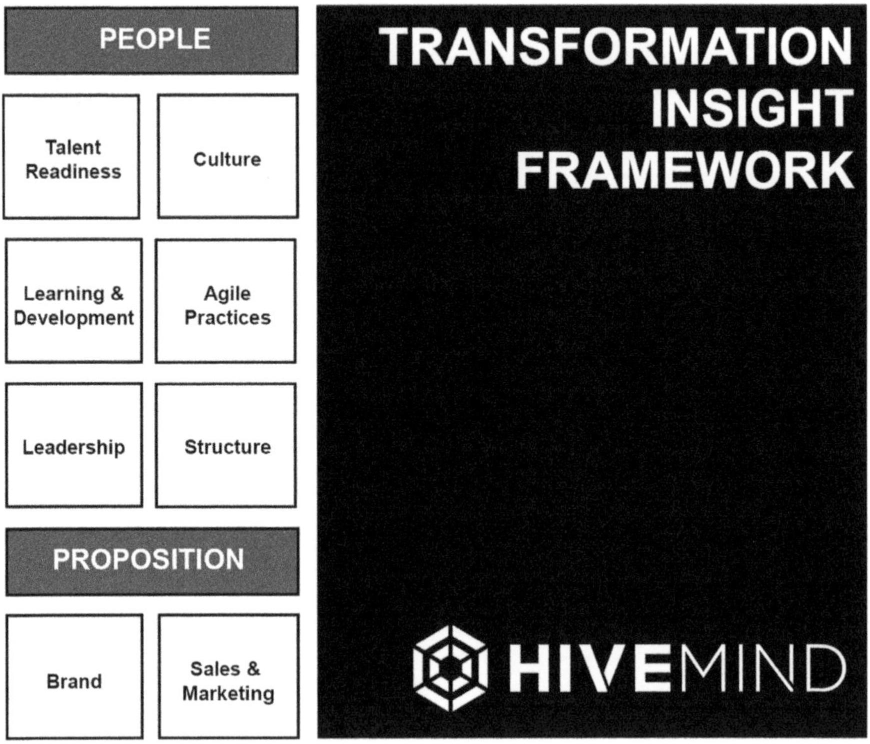
PEOPLE
Talent Readiness
Culture
Learning & Development
Agile Practices
Leadership
Structure
PROPOSITION
Brand
Sales & Marketing
TRANSFORMATION INSIGHT FRAMEWORK
HIVEMIND

PEOPLE ALIGNMENT

The People component of the **Transformation Insight Framework™** focusses on the humans who essentially make things happen. We are not particularly fans of the term "human resources" as it reduces human beings to mere resources or assets that can be used by a company for its own purposes. Think about it, you are asking people to be passionate about the organization and the change journey you are about to embark on... then dehumanize them by calling them a resource.

It can also be seen as suggesting that people are interchangeable and can be easily replaced, which can be degrading and demotivating for employees. Additionally, it may imply a focus on the company's needs rather than the needs of the employees.

Some organizations have started to use alternative terms like 'Human Capital Management' or 'Talent Management,' to shift the focus towards a more human-centred approach. Our particular favourites are;

"Happiness Department" – This alternative name is used by the Brazilian company Havaianas, which is known for its fun and playful culture. The term reflects the company's focus on creating a positive and enjoyable workplace environment.

"Unicorn Department" – This alternative name is used by the online retailer Zappos, which is known for its unique corporate culture. The term is meant to reflect the company's focus on finding and nurturing rare and valuable talent.

"People Operations" – This term is used by Google to describe its HR department. It suggests a focus on people rather than resources and reflects the company's emphasis on data-driven decision-making.

"Talent Team" –This alternative name is used by the software company HubSpot. It suggests a focus on attracting and developing top talent, rather than simply managing resources.

*Get the culture
right, and
everything else
just falls
into place*

Tony Hsieh

Ultimately, the language we use can have a significant impact on how we perceive and interact with the world around us, including the people we work with. It's important to use language that accurately reflects our values and priorities, and that treats people with the respect and dignity they deserve.

Forgive the slight tangent... but if you want the best from your people, details matter. Or to quote Simon Sinek, *"Happy employees ensure happy customers. And Happy customers ensure happy shareholders - In that order."*

Crafting an organizational culture optimized for digital transformation is what this section of the book is all about. When it comes to culture, it is often the little things that make a big difference.

But before we specifically examine the part culture plays in an organizations ability to embrace and adapt to change, let us agree what it is.

What Is Organizational Culture? And Why Should We Care?

If we were to ask you to close your eyes and think about the culture at Google (yes, we know it is hard to read with your eyes closed lol), what words would come to mind? You would probably use words like creative, fun, flexible and innovative, right? Alternatively, if we asked you to think about the military you might say orderly, organised, disciplined and chain of command.

Every organization has a culture, whether company leadership builds and maintains it purposefully or allows it to grow on its own. An organization's culture defines how individuals work and function within a company, making organizational culture a crucial element of a company's ultimate success.

If you want to provoke a lively debate, simply start a conversation on organizational culture and grab some popcorn.

There is universal consensus that it both exists, and that it plays a crucial role in shaping behaviour. There is however little agreement on what organizational culture actually is, what influences it, and how it influences behaviour. The most important question for us today is, can you, as a leader, change it.

This is a challenge, because without a reasonable definition of culture, we cannot hope to understand its connections to other key elements of the organization, such as structure, systems/processes, or team dynamics. Nor can we develop a good approach to analysing, maintaining, or transforming. If we can define what organizational culture is, it gives us an understanding on how to diagnose problems and even to design and develop better cultures.

"The only thing of real importance that leaders do is to create and manage culture. If you do not manage culture, it manages you, and you may not even be aware of the extent to which this is happening." **Edgar Schein**

We would add this point to Edgar's quote, if you don't think your organizational culture is part of your remit, yet you play a part in your organization's digital transformation... Then we might suggest you haven't fully comprehended your task.

You may have heard people simplistically say, "culture is the way we do things around here". Actually, it was Aristotle who said, "We are what we repeatedly do".

This view elevates rituals, repeated behaviour, or habits as the core of culture and gives less attribution to what people feel, think, or believe. It also focuses our attention on the forces that shape behaviour in organizations, and so highlights an important question: are all those forces (including structure, processes, and systems) "culture" or is culture simply the behavioural output?

A common challenge we see when clients approach a digital transformation... They recognise they need to shift the culture to ensure the best chance of success, so they define the desired culture, communicate it to employees, and expect behavioural change. It doesn't happen.

The problem is that they don't address the systems, processes, and structures to enable behavioural change. For example, you cannot call yourself an agile organization if it still takes 12 months to get budget approval on a small project. Maybe an exaggeration but you get the point.

Maybe you operate in a highly regulated industry, and it is compliance that slows things down? The fact is culture sets the intention, but your systems enable the behaviour.

We define organizational culture as the collection of beliefs, values and methods of interaction that create the environment of an organization. Culture encompasses the foundational values of a company and the consistent, observable patterns of behaviour. It also reflects an organization's expectations, its philosophy, and the experiences of all employees from the bottom to the top. Often influencing the future direction of the company and their chances of success.

Culture is powerfully influenced by incentives. The best predictor of what people will do is what they are incentivized to do. By incentives, we mean financial rewards, and non-financial rewards such as status, recognition, training, and other staff rewards schemes (i.e. car, gym membership etc.).

One thing is for sure… It is difficult to name even a single successful company, one that is a respected leader in their field, that does not have a distinct, readily identifiable culture. Think of the most successful companies you know, from huge corporations like Google, Dyson, Coca-Cola, Disney, Apple, McDonald's, and Tesla to smaller entrepreneurial start-ups. Almost everyone, small or large, has developed a distinctive culture that is easily identifiable by its employees.

Sometimes it is created by the original founder (such as Apple). Sometimes it evolves over time as they overcome challenges. More often it is deliberately developed by leadership teams who decide to systematically improve performance.

How Does Organizational Culture Evolve?

Organizational culture evolves over time, shaped by a variety of factors including the organization's history, its leadership, and the employees who work there. Culture can also be influenced by external factors such as the wider societal culture, economic conditions, and technological change. So, trying to assess organizational culture is complicated by the reality that you are trying to hit a moving target. But this opens the possibility that culture change can be managed as a continuous process rather than through big shifts (often in response to crises). Additionally, it emphasizes the idea that an optimum 'destination' may never (and maybe should never) be reached.

This perspective provides the kind of holistic, nuanced view of organizational culture that we believe is needed by leaders today in order to truly understand their challenge, and to have any hope of changing their culture for the better.

External Positioning

TRANSFORMATION

FAST CHANGE

Individuality Flexibility

Stability Control

ADHOCRACY CULTURE

Orientation:
Create

Leadership:
Innovator, entrepreneur, visionary

Value Drivers:
Agility, transformation, Innovation

MARKET CULTURE

Orientation:
Compete

Leadership:
Hard driver, competitor, producer

Value Drivers:
Market share, profitability, goal achievement

COMPETING VALUES FRAMEWORK

CLAN CULTURE

Orientation:
Collaborate

Leadership:
Facilitator, mentor, team builder

Value Drivers:
Commitment, communication, development

HIERARCHY CULTURE

Orientation:
Control

Leadership:
Coordinator, monitor, organizer

Value Drivers:
Efficiency, timeliness, consistency

LONG-TERM CHANGE

INCREMENTAL CHANGE

Internal Maintenance

A Useful Framework for Evaluating Organizational Culture

Understanding your own corporate culture is important because it will affect the decisions you make, the processes you want to implement, and the results you can expect from your teams. But correctly identifying a corporate culture can be tricky!

This is where the **Competing Values Framework** comes in. The Competing Values Framework (CVF) is a model that helps explain the different types of organizational culture and how they relate to performance. The framework was developed by Robert Quinn and John Rohrbaugh in the 1980s based on their research into organizational effectiveness.

Their empirical studies identified two dimensions that enabled them to classify various organizations' "theory of effectiveness". See illustration.

The first dimension is represented on the vertical axis and shows where the organization's culture sits between the two extremes of being flexible and absolutely stable. Google, for example, would sit well towards the "flexible" end of this axis, in contrast to an organization like a bank, which is reassuringly bureaucratic and consistent.

The second dimension is represented on the horizontal axis and shows whether the organization is more internally or externally focused. Those with a strong, internally focused culture benefit from effective relationships between team members, and clearly defined processes. Zappos for example, is renowned for its internal focus. This online shoe retailer prioritizes collaboration, teamwork, and employee satisfaction encouraging employees to be themselves. In externally focused organizations, such as Apple, the culture puts strong emphasis on valuing customer satisfaction and competitiveness.

As you can see in model illustrated, these two intersecting axes result in four quadrants, each representing sets of values and typical activities. Organizations in each quadrant are described as follows:

COLLABORATE (Clan Culture): Clan cultures are characterized by a family-like atmosphere where employees have a strong sense of belonging and loyalty to the organization. The focus is on collaboration, teamwork, and employee development. These organizations prioritize employee satisfaction and retention and often have a long-term outlook.

CREATE (Adhocracy Culture): Adhocracy cultures are innovative and creative. These organizations encourage risk-taking, experimentation, and the development of new ideas. The focus is on growth and innovation, and these organizations are often found in fast-paced industries such as technology and advertising.

COMPETE (Market Culture): Market cultures are results-driven and competitive. The focus is on achieving specific goals and targets, and employees are often motivated by financial incentives. These organizations prioritize efficiency, productivity, and market share.

CONTROL (Hierarchy Culture): Hierarchy cultures are structured and stable. These organizations have clear rules and procedures, and there is a strong emphasis on efficiency and control. The focus is on maintaining stability and achieving predictability.

There is no "best" or "worst" quadrant to be in. Most organizations will show all of these characteristics to some degree. But what matters is that the characteristics of one, or perhaps two, of the quadrants will be clearly dominant. The "right" quadrant for an organization at a particular time will depend on what it produces or does, where it is in its lifecycle, the conditions in which it operates, its position within the marketplace, and its source of competitive advantage.

The CVF suggests that organizations can benefit from balancing these competing values. For example, a clan culture can benefit from incorporating elements of adhocracy or market culture to encourage innovation and competitiveness. Similarly, a market culture can benefit from incorporating elements of clan or adhocracy culture to promote employee engagement and creativity.

One recent case study that demonstrates the competing values framework is the transformation of Ford Motor Company under the leadership of CEO Alan Mulally.

Before Mulally's arrival in 2006, Ford was struggling with declining market share, high costs, and low morale. Mulally recognized that Ford needed to undergo a significant transformation to become a more competitive and successful company.

To guide this transformation, Mulally used the competing values framework. He identified four key values that were necessary for Ford's success: a focus on results, a commitment to customer satisfaction, a focus on teamwork and collaboration, and a willingness to embrace change.

Mulally implemented these values throughout the organization, using them as a guide for decision-making and cultural change. He created regular meetings where senior leaders from different departments could collaborate and share information, breaking down silos and promoting teamwork. He also focused on improving quality and customer satisfaction, using data-driven methods to identify and address customer concerns.

Through these efforts, Mulally was able to turn around Ford's fortunes. The company became more competitive, with higher market share and profits. The culture of the organization also shifted, with a greater emphasis on collaboration, innovation, and continuous improvement.

This case study demonstrates the power of the competing values framework to guide organizational change and transformation. By identifying and prioritizing key values, leaders can create a roadmap for change and align the organization around a shared vision.

Using the Competing Values Framework

The CVF can be used as a diagnostic tool to assess an organization's current culture and to help identify areas for improvement. By understanding the different cultural dimensions and their impact on organizational performance, leaders can develop strategies to promote a more balanced and effective organizational culture.

You may discover that your current culture is leading to problems, and in this scenario, you may want to pay attention to the qualities of the diagonally opposite quadrant. By incorporating some of these into your company or your team's practices, you may be able to bring about positive change. However, you need to be aware that you'll have to make trade-offs in the opposite quadrant. If you need to encourage creativity, for example, expect to lose a bit of control. On the other hand, if you want your organization to focus on being competitive, you may find there's less scope in your team for caring and collaborative relationships. If you use the CVF to anticipate these kinds of outcomes, you should find it easier to handle them.

DOWNLOAD: If you would like to download the Competing Values Framework Assessment to enable you to self-assess where your culture is today and where you would like it to be in the future... Visit www. Everyday-Transformation.com.

When considering the People aspect of the framework, there are several key considerations below to keep in mind, we will be going into more detail on these in the next section:

Skillset and knowledge: The first consideration is to ensure that people have the necessary skills and knowledge to perform their jobs effectively. This may involve providing training and development opportunities to enhance their skills and knowledge.

Communication and collaboration: Another key consideration is to promote effective communication and collaboration among employees. This can be achieved through team-building activities, open-door policies, and creating a supportive work environment.

Motivation and engagement: It is essential to keep employees motivated and engaged in their work to ensure their productivity and job satisfaction. This can be achieved by recognizing and rewarding their efforts, providing opportunities for career advancement, and offering a positive work-life balance.

Diversity and inclusion: Diversity and inclusion are crucial considerations for the people component of the Transformation Insight Framework™. It is important to promote a culture of diversity and inclusivity to ensure that employees feel valued and respected.

Leadership and management: Effective leadership and management are critical for the success of any organization. It is important to ensure that the leaders and managers of the organization have the necessary skills and experience to manage the workforce effectively.

Putting Humans First (Internal Workforce and External Customer)

Putting humans first in a digital transformation means prioritizing the needs and experiences of people throughout the process of implementing new digital technologies or ways of working. This is important because digital change can often have significant impacts on employees, customers, and other stakeholders and as previously mentioned, according to Gartner, culture is the largest contribution to project failures.

But it is not just a lip-service exercise, there are numerous benefits. Putting people first in an organizational context can lead to a more engaged, productive workforce, satisfied customers, better financial performance, and a stronger reputation and brand image.

Some stats we picked out from numerous studies:

- **46%** of job seekers say that company culture is an important factor.

- **94%** of entrepreneurs and 88% of job seekers say that a healthy culture at work is vital for success.

- **69%** of employees would work harder if they received more recognition.

- **86%** of job seekers avoid companies with a bad reputation.

- Millennials prioritize 'people and culture fit' above everything else.

- Team leaders have the highest impact on company culture.

- Having highly engaged employees can lead to a **202%** increase in performance.

- A culture that attracts high-calibre employees leads to a **33%** revenue increase.

- Married candidates value culture more than their single colleagues.

- Around **63%** of US companies find it harder to retain than to hire workers.

Improved employee engagement and productivity: When employees feel valued and supported, they are more likely to be engaged and productive. By putting people first, we create a positive work environment that fosters collaboration, creativity, and innovation.

Enhanced employee retention: Employees are more likely to stay with an organization that values their contributions and supports their growth and development. By prioritizing people, we create a workplace culture that attracts and retains top talent. It is estimated that employee turnover is costing the US alone $160bn a year... and the likelihood is that you are losing your best and your brightest, with high performers delivering approximately 400% in productivity when compared to the average.

Increased customer satisfaction: As mentioned previously, when organizations prioritize the needs and experiences of their employees, they are better equipped to deliver products and services that meet the needs and expectations of their customers. By focusing on user experience and feedback, we can improve the quality and effectiveness of the business offerings.

Improved financial performance: Organizations that prioritize people tend to see better financial performance over the long term. This is because engaged, productive employees and satisfied customers can help to drive revenue growth, reduce costs, and increase profitability.

Enhanced reputation and brand image: By putting people first, organizations can enhance their reputation and brand image, which can help to attract new customers and talent. Organizations that prioritize social responsibility, diversity and inclusion, and employee well-being are often seen as more attractive to consumers and employees alike.

Case Study – Microsoft: One example of an organization that puts people first in its digital transformation is Microsoft, who underwent a significant transformation in recent years, shifting its focus from being a traditional software company to being a cloud-based services company. This transformation has been driven by a deep commitment to putting people first and fostering a culture of continuous learning and growth.

To achieve this, Microsoft took several steps:

Emphasizing employee well-being: Microsoft has implemented a number of policies and programs aimed at promoting employee well-being, including flexible work arrangements, mental health resources, and on-site health clinics. The company also encourages employees to take breaks and prioritize their well-being and has implemented a "healthy habits" program that encourages healthy eating, exercise, and sleep.

Providing training and support: Microsoft has invested heavily in training and support programs to help employees develop new skills and adapt to new technologies. The company offers a range of training resources, including online courses, in-person training, and mentorship programs. Microsoft also provides ongoing support to help employees stay up to date with the latest technologies and industry trends.

Fostering a culture of continuous learning: Microsoft has embraced a culture of continuous learning and growth, encouraging employees to take risks, experiment, and learn from failures. The company also values diversity and inclusion and has implemented programs to support and promote diversity across the organization.

Prioritizing user experience: Microsoft has made user experience a top priority in its digital transformation, emphasizing the importance of creating intuitive, user-friendly products and services. The company has also implemented a range of user testing and feedback programs to ensure that its products meet the needs and expectations of customers.

By putting people first in its digital transformation, Microsoft has been able to create a more positive and supportive workplace culture, attract and retain top talent, and deliver innovative products and services that meet the needs of customers.

Rest assured, many of these areas Microsoft focussed on we are going to explore in more detail in the pages that follow.

Involve People in the Process!

Employees are the ones who will be most directly affected by changes in technology and processes, so it's important to involve them in the planning and implementation process. This can help to identify potential issues or concerns early on and ensure that the new technologies or processes meet their needs.

Most importantly though, getting them involved reduces their anxiety around change and once contextualised can increase engagement and motivation in the process.

We believe developing ideas from the people that actually engage the customer is essential with Everyday Transformation™. This thinking is supported by the 'Iceberg of Ignorance'.

The Iceberg of Ignorance is a concept that highlights the fact that senior managers and executives are often unaware of the true extent of problems within their organizations. The concept was developed by consultant Sidney Yoshida in the 1980s, and it suggests that only a small percentage of problems are visible to senior management, while the vast majority remain hidden.

The iceberg analogy is used to illustrate this concept, where the tip of the iceberg represents the visible problems that are known to management, while the larger, unseen portion of the iceberg represents the problems that are not known or understood by management.

According to Yoshida, the top layer of the iceberg (i.e., the visible problems) represents only 4% of the total problems in an organization, while the other 96% are hidden beneath the surface. These hidden problems can be caused by a range of factors, such as ineffective communication, lack of employee involvement, and a failure to collect and analyze data.

The model highlights the importance of engaging employees at all levels of the organization in problem-solving and decision-making. By involving employees in the identification and resolution of problems, organizations can tap into the knowledge and expertise of their workforce and improve the overall performance of the organization.

As part of our Everyday Transformation™ Programs we give staff of all levels a new lens with which to see their day to day roles. By taking them through a process of understanding the possibilities (technology) when it comes to automation or (methodology) in regard to process improvement, we actively work on ideation and implementation.

Remember 'Everyday Transformation™' includes every role, every process, every customer interaction. More on Innovation Management in 'Process'

Other strategies we have used include;

Celebrating the wins – Sharing success stories throughout the process inspires participation from others, but also acts as a great way to recognise contribution. It is especially powerful to track the metrics, i.e. hours saved, productivity increased, customer satisfaction and of course ROI.

Incentive Schemes – You may also take recognition to the next level by rewarding ideas that are actually brought to fruition. One client even used gamification by introducing departmental leader boards for both ideas submitted and implemented.

Staff Newsletter – A regular update to communicate all initiatives and recognise efforts.

Host lunch and learn sessions or town halls – where employees can share knowledge and best practices related to the digital transformation.

Conduct regular surveys or polls – to gather feedback on the digital transformation process.

Create digital transformation roadshows – especially useful if your organization spans multiple sites in multiple geographical regions, with a focus on sharing the progress and benefits of the transformation.

Create a "digital champions" program – as previously discussed to identify and reward employees who are actively involved in the transformation.

Create focus groups with employees – either departmental or cross functional to gather feedback on the digital transformation process.

Set up online communities or social media groups –Again great for a distributed workforce so employees discuss and share ideas about the journey.

Monitor and address employee feedback – It's important to monitor employee feedback throughout the digital transformation process and address any concerns or issues that arise. This can help to ensure that the new technologies and processes are effective and that they meet the needs of everyone involved.

Use this information to make adjustments to the plan and ensure that the transformation meets the needs of the organization and its employees.

Feedback Improves Change Management:

Monitoring employee feedback can help managers identify areas of resistance or concern early in the change process, allowing them to address these issues proactively or even adjust the plan. This can help to prevent delays and disruptions to the change process, and ultimately improve the success of the change initiative.

Enhanced Employee Retention:

The case for retention was made before, but when employees feel that their concerns are being heard and addressed, they are more likely to feel valued and committed to the organization. This can improve employee retention rates, and reduce the costs associated with employee turnover.

Better Decision Making

Gathering and analysing employee feedback can provide valuable insights into the effectiveness of change initiatives. This information can help managers make more informed decisions, and adjust their strategies as needed to improve the success of the change process.

Better still, if you aspire to be more agile encourage decision making at the point of information flow, which refers to the process of making decisions as information becomes available, rather than waiting for all the information to be collected and analyzed. This approach allows organizations to be more responsive, as decisions can be made more quickly and effectively.

Traditionally, decision making has been a hierarchical process, where information flows from lower-level employees up to higher-level managers, who then make decisions based on that information. However, this approach can be slow and cumbersome, as information may get delayed or filtered as it moves up the hierarchy.

In contrast, decision making at the point of information flow involves empowering employees at all levels to make decisions based on the information they have available.

One example of this approach is in supply chain management. Rather than waiting for all the information about a supply chain disruption to flow up to top management, companies can empower lower-level employees to make decisions about alternative suppliers or shipping options based on the information they have available. This allows companies to respond quickly to disruptions and minimize the impact on their operations.

If you are going to empower this approach though, ensure accountability is high and understood. Sure, trust your people to think, evaluate and act... as if the CEO of the company was looking over their shoulder.

Involving staff in the process and actively seeking feedback is critical to ensure that employees understand the changes and benefits of the process, feel engaged and motivated to participate, and have the skills and knowledge needed to support the transformation.

The Compelling Case for Business Agility

Business agility refers to an organization's ability to respond quickly and effectively to changing market conditions, customer needs, and technology trends.

In today's fast-paced business environment, agility has become a critical factor for success and one of the top three subjects we are asked to train on with courses on Agile Mindset and Agile Leadership in high demand.

First and foremost, business agility is essential because of the rapidly changing business environment previously discussed. Companies must be able to quickly adapt to changes in the market, including shifts in customer needs, new technology trends, and changes in the competitive landscape.

Let's take the COVID-19 pandemic to illustrate this point. Afterall for most of us it was the biggest disruption in our lifetime. The pandemic impacted many industries, requiring companies to quickly adapt to remote work and new health and safety protocols. Companies that were agile were better able to respond to these changes and maintain their operations, while those that were not agile struggled to keep pace.

Another reason that business agility is important is that it helps companies stay ahead of the competition. In a fast-paced business environment, companies that can quickly adapt and respond to changes are more likely to be successful than those that are slow to respond. For example, companies that were able to quickly transition to online sales and delivery during the COVID-19 pandemic were better able to remain competitive, while those that were slow to respond lost market share.

Business agility also drives innovation and growth. Companies that are agile are better able to identify new opportunities for growth and innovation and respond quickly to changing customer needs and market trends. For example, companies that were able to quickly pivot to new products and services during the COVID-19 pandemic were better able to maintain their operations and grow their businesses, while those that were slow to respond fell by the wayside with serious consequences.

To achieve business agility, companies must adopt a culture of continuous improvement and innovation. This requires a willingness to experiment and take risks, as well as a focus on encouraging collaboration and teamwork. Initiatives that empower people to network, working together to find new and innovative solutions to complex problems.

"

In today's era of volatility, there is no other way but to re-invent. The only sustainable advantage you can have over others is agility, that's it. Because nothing else is sustainable, everything else you create, somebody else will replicate.

Jeff Bezos

In addition, companies must adopt the right tools and technologies to support their business agility efforts. For example, cloud computing, mobile technologies, and advanced analytics can all help companies respond quickly to changing market conditions and customer needs. These technologies also enable companies to collect and analyze vast amounts of data on their customers and operations, providing insights into new opportunities for growth and innovation.

Finally, companies must be willing to invest in their people. This means providing training and development opportunities to help employees stay current with new technologies and business practices. Investment in leadership is essential, providing them with the skills and knowledge they need to get the best out of people by fostering a culture of collaboration, innovation, and performance. Improving their emotional intelligence and ability to coach, support and motivate their teams.

Everyday Transformation™ is about incorporating agility, so these traits become daily habits, embedded in the culture, and the default approach to every situation. To have an agile mindset is to have an instinctive reflex in response to challenges, solution and collaboration focused.

Case Study – LEGO: One great recent example of a company introducing agile at a team level is LEGO. Initially focussed on transforming 25% of their product teams into self-organizing Scrum teams.

The result of the initial change was that the other 75% of teams followed quickly behind with developers empowered to manage their own work, and a farewell to the army of "managers with spreadsheets."

The results... Developers now give more accurate estimates, with more predictable outcomes. They stopped doing excessive documentation and other unproductive practices and were better able to prioritize work. Previously, the person who shouted the loudest got their work done first. Now, with transparency taken to another level, decisions are based on real necessity.

Nothing beats face-to-face communication, and the positive effect it has on team morale was palpable. Especially the communication that occurs during LEGO's big room events. During these meetings, teams showcased their work, worked out the dependencies, estimated risks, and planned for the next release period.

The Agile approach was a key factor in forming autonomous teams. Within them, people have been able to transform the way they work by making it more transparent, so now each team member knows what the others are doing, and their purpose is shared. This also allows for consistent productivity and improved management of expectations. More importantly, business objectives are met within the timeframe driven by business strategy.

Business agility can be achieved through a combination of several building blocks. Here are some of the key components that are essential to building a culture of agility within an organization:

1. **Empowered Teams:** Teams should be given the autonomy to make decisions, take ownership of their work, and be held accountable for their results. This helps to create a culture of trust and empowerment that drives innovation and creativity.

2. **Flexible Processes:** Organizations should adopt flexible processes that can be adapted quickly to changing circumstances. This includes embracing Agile methodologies, which prioritize iterative and incremental approaches to problem-solving.

3. **Customer-focused:** Organizations must be customer-focused and always seek to understand the needs and wants of their customers. This requires a deep understanding of customer behaviour and the ability to respond quickly to changes in the market.

4. **Data-driven decision-making:** Organizations should use data to inform their decision-making processes. This helps to ensure that decisions are based on facts and evidence, rather than assumptions or gut feelings.

5. **Cross-functional collaboration:** Agile organizations require close collaboration between teams and departments. This enables them to share knowledge, ideas, and perspectives, and to work together to solve complex problems.

6. **Continuous improvement:** Agile organizations embrace continuous improvement, which involves regularly reviewing and refining processes and practices to ensure that they are always delivering the best possible results.

7. **Continuous learning:** Agile organizations are committed to continuous learning and development. This requires a culture of experimentation, where failure is seen as an opportunity for learning and growth.

8. **Clear Communication:** Clear and effective communication is essential to building a culture of agility. Organizations should foster open and honest communication channels that allow teams to share information, ideas, and feedback.

9. **Adaptability:** Business agility requires organizations to be flexible and adaptable, able to quickly respond to changes in the marketplace, and to embrace new technologies and approaches as they emerge.

10. **Embracing Failure:** Agile organizations recognize that failure is an inevitable part of innovation and experimentation. They embrace failure as an opportunity for learning and growth, and use it to drive continuous improvement.

11. **Employee Engagement:** Employee engagement is critical to building a culture of agility. Organizations should prioritize employee engagement, creating a workplace that values, supports, and rewards its employees.

12. **Leadership Support:** Strong leadership support is essential to building a culture of agility. Leaders must lead by example, embracing change and innovation, and creating a supportive and empowering work environment.

13. **Innovation Culture:** Organizations must foster a culture of innovation, where creativity and experimentation are encouraged, and employees are empowered to drive change and bring new ideas to the table.

14. **Flexible Technology:** Organizations should embrace technology that is flexible, scalable, and able to adapt to changing needs. This includes leveraging cloud computing, software-as-a-service (SaaS) solutions, and other emerging technologies.

15. **Cultural Alignment:** Organizations should align their culture with their strategic objectives, ensuring that their values, beliefs, and practices are in line with their business goals.

16. **Talent Management:** Agile organizations prioritize talent management, investing in the development and training of their employees, and creating opportunities for career growth and advancement.

17. **Customer Feedback:** Organizations should seek and incorporate customer feedback into their decision-making

processes, using it to inform their product and service offerings, and to drive continuous improvement.

18. **Collaborative Decision-making:** Organizations should embrace collaborative decision-making, bringing together teams and departments to make decisions together, and leveraging the diverse perspectives and skills of their employees.

Provide Training and Support

Digital transformation involves using technology to fundamentally change the way a business operates and interacts with its customers, employees, and partners. It requires a broad range of skills across different disciplines.

New technologies and processes will obviously require new skills and knowledge for the technologists and practitioners expected to use them. However, there is a wider set of skills required across the organization to realize culture change, especially towards more agile practices.

Here are some key skills that are required in a digital transformation:

- Agile Mindset and Soft Skills which improve collaboration across the whole organization oiling the wheels of cooperation and helping to break down silos.

- Agile Leadership Skills - Improving situational awareness and adaptability, as well as emotional and political intelligence.

- Strategic thinking: The ability to understand the big picture and create a clear vision for the digital transformation initiative.

- Technology expertise: Knowledge of emerging technologies and their potential applications, as well as the ability to evaluate, select, and implement technology solutions.

- Change management: The ability to manage change and effectively communicate the benefits and challenges of digital transformation to stakeholders.

- Data analysis: The ability to collect, analyze, and interpret data to inform decision-making and drive business outcomes.

- Design thinking: The ability to use human-centred design principles to create customer-centric solutions that meet user needs.

- Agile methodology: Knowledge of agile project management methodologies to enable rapid prototyping, testing, and iteration.

- Cybersecurity: Awareness of cybersecurity risks and the ability to implement appropriate security measures to protect against cyber threats.

- Collaboration and teamwork: The ability to work collaboratively with cross-functional teams and stakeholders to drive the digital transformation initiative forward.

- Creativity and innovation: The ability to think creatively and develop innovative solutions that disrupt traditional business models.

So, it's important to provide your talent with the training and support they need to be successful in their roles. This can help to reduce stress and frustration, improve their sense of how they are valued and increase their confidence in their ability to deliver. Whilst there will be key staff who will need to be prioritized for the specific areas above, the most successful organizations make upskilling available to all, ensuring that everyone is able to adapt to the changes.

Creating a Culture of Continuous Learning

A learning culture is a culture that values learning and encourages continuous improvement. It is a culture that recognizes that learning is not a one-time event, but a lifelong process and the benefits of a learning culture are numerous. It leads to improved job performance, increased productivity, higher job satisfaction, and lower turnover rates. A learning culture also fosters innovation, creativity, and a growth mindset.

Here are 21 top tips for getting started

1. **Start at the top** – Leaders must lead by example and demonstrate a commitment to learning and continuous improvement.

2. **Create a learning culture mission statement** – Define what a learning culture means to your organization and communicate it to everyone.

3. **Provide access to learning resources** – Ensure employees have access to books, online courses, workshops, seminars, or conferences.

4. **Encourage continuous learning** – Provide opportunities for employees to learn new skills, take on new challenges, and work on different projects.

5. **Provide feedback and recognition** – Regularly provide feedback and recognition to employees to promote growth and development.

6. **Lead with curiosity** – Encourage curiosity and questioning to foster a culture of learning.

7. **Encourage a growth mindset** – Foster a belief that abilities and intelligence can be developed through hard work, dedication, and a willingness to learn.

8. **Build a culture of trust** – Create an environment where employees feel comfortable sharing their ideas and opinions.

9. **Foster open communication** – Encourage open communication and collaboration to promote learning and growth.

10. **Encourage experimentation** – Provide opportunities for employees to experiment and learn from their mistakes.

11. **Provide mentorship opportunities** – Encourage employees to seek out mentors to help guide them in their learning and development.

12. **Provide ongoing training** – Offer regular training opportunities to ensure employees are continuously developing their skills and knowledge.

13. **Encourage peer learning** – Encourage employees to learn from each other by sharing their knowledge and experiences.

14. **Celebrate learning achievements** – Recognize and celebrate employees who achieve learning goals and milestones.

15. **Provide career development opportunities** – Offer opportunities for career development and advancement to keep employees engaged and motivated.

16. **Measure learning outcomes** – Measure the effectiveness of learning initiatives to ensure they are having the desired impact.

17. **Reward curiosity and learning** – Reward employees who demonstrate curiosity and a willingness to learn.

18. **Create a positive learning environment** – Create an environment that is conducive to learning, such as providing comfortable spaces for reading and studying.

19. **Embrace technology** – Embrace new technologies and tools that can support and enhance learning initiatives.

20. **Make learning part of the company culture** – Make learning a fundamental part of the company culture and values and integrate it into the daily operations of the organization.

21. **Encourage employees to attend industry events** and conferences to learn about new digital trends and innovations.

Imagine leading an organization where everyone demonstrates a willingness to learn and adapt to new technologies, tools, and processes. Where everyone is keen to stretch their thinking and approaches every new situation with an open mind. Imagine a whole workforce un-intimidated by change or the unknown, as it simply provides an opportunity for new experience and growth. Now that's a culture which attracts talent.

Applied Learning

One of the things we do wherever possible is encourage clients to introduce an applied learning strategy for their employee training programs. It's a type of learning that involves taking knowledge and skills and putting them into practice.

Real-world relevance: Applied learning is based on the idea that the best way to learn is by doing. It allows learners to apply theoretical knowledge to real-world scenarios, which helps them understand the relevance of what they are learning.

Enhances retention: When delegates apply knowledge in real-world settings, they are more likely to remember it because they are actively engaged in the learning process.

Develops problem-solving skills: Applied learning encourages people to think critically and creatively to solve problems.

"

I hear, and I forget. I see, and I remember. I do, and I understand.

Confucius

Builds practical skills: Applied learning helps learners develop practical skills that are valuable in the workplace. These skills can include communication, teamwork, decision-making, and time management.

Increases motivation: Applied learning is more engaging and motivating than traditional classroom learning because it is typically contextualised and therefore appreciated due to the relevance.

One of the ways we like to finish off significant programs is with a capstone project (often called an applied learning project)...

The term "capstone" comes from the building industry, where it refers to the final stone or brick placed at the top of a structure to complete it as the finishing touch and provide the structural integrity and stability.

The use of the term "capstone" in education is a metaphorical extension of this concept. A capstone project is the final assignment that a delegate completes to apply the learning. Like the capstone in construction, it's the final piece that completes the educational structure and embeds the new knowledge or skills.

A good capstone project in corporate learning should be designed to provide learners with an opportunity to apply the knowledge, skills, and competencies they have acquired during their training to a real-world problem or challenge in their workplace. Here are some key elements of a good capstone project:

1. **Relevance:** The project should be relevant to the learner's job role and should address a real business problem or opportunity.

2. **Complexity:** The project should be challenging enough to require learners to apply critical thinking, problem-solving, and decision-making skills.

3. **Interdisciplinary:** The project should require learners to draw upon knowledge and skills from different areas of their training.

4. **Teamwork:** The project should require learners to collaborate with others in their organization to develop a solution.

5. **Creativity:** The project should allow learners to think creatively and develop innovative solutions to the problem.

6. **Practicality:** The project should result in a tangible outcome or solution that can be implemented in the workplace.

7. **Feedback:** Delegates should receive feedback from their instructors throughout the project (project check-ins) to help them improve their work.

8. **Reflection:** Learners should be encouraged to reflect on their project and their learning throughout the process.

9. **Presentation:** Learners should have the opportunity to present their project to others in their organization to share their findings and recommendations.

Overall, a good capstone project should provide your talent with a meaningful and challenging experience that allows them to demonstrate their mastery of the skills and knowledge they have acquired in their training program.

Our signature Everyday Transformation™ Program is essentially applied learning, embedding innovation and digital literacy throughout the organization, creating relevant and genuine initiatives to generate new income streams, save money, improve efficiency and enhance customer experience.

Assessing the Skills Shortage

Assessing the skills gap for employees when going through a digital transformation is crucial to identify the right training for the right roles.

STEP ONE – Identify Skills required.

Based on the above we know what we need to have in place to assure success... but how do we get there?

STEP TWO – Current skills analysis

Assess the current skills and knowledge of employees to identify areas of strength and areas for improvement. This can be done through surveys, assessments, or performance reviews.

STEP THREE – Skills gap analysis

Determine the gap between the skills and knowledge employees currently possess and the skills and knowledge needed to support the digital transformation. This will help you identify the areas where employees need training and development.

STEP FOUR – Develop a training plan.

Develop a training plan to address the skills gap identified in step 3. This may include online courses, in-person training sessions, coaching, and mentoring.

STEP FIVE – Evaluate training effectiveness.

Evaluate the effectiveness of the training by assessing the skills and knowledge of employees after they have completed the training. This will help you determine whether the training has been effective in addressing the skills gap.

STEP SIX – Continuously update the training plan.

As the digital transformation progresses and new technologies and processes are introduced, continue to assess the skills gap and update the training plan as needed to ensure that employees have the skills and knowledge needed to support the transformation.

Attracting New Talent

Not every skills shortage can be solved though with training. There will be time critical projects, or times when experience is required to steady the ship. Your organization's ability to attract new talent might be critical for growth and staying competitive in the market.

When an organization cannot recruit the skills they need, they may experience a number of negative consequences, including;

- **Reduced productivity:** The inability to recruit the necessary skills can lead to decreased productivity as existing employees may be required to take on additional responsibilities or work outside of their area of expertise.

- **Increased costs:** Organizations may have to pay higher salaries or offer more attractive benefits packages to attract qualified candidates, which can increase labour costs.

- **Decreased innovation:** Without the necessary skills, organizations may struggle to innovate and keep up with competitors who are able to recruit the talent they need.

- **Stagnation:** The inability to recruit the necessary skills can lead to stagnation, where the organization is unable to grow and evolve.

- **Increased turnover:** Employees may become frustrated if they are required to take on additional responsibilities outside of their area of expertise, leading to increased turnover.

There are other strategies for solving some of these problems which we will discuss in the Partner section of the book. In the meantime, here are some steps you can take to be a more attractive prospective employer.

Develop a strong employer brand: A strong employer brand can help differentiate your organization from competitors and attract top talent. This can be achieved by showcasing your company's mission, values, and culture through your website, social media, and other marketing channels.

Offer competitive compensation and benefits: Offering competitive compensation and benefits can make your organization more attractive to job seekers. Research what similar organizations in your industry are offering and ensure that you're competitive.

Provide opportunities for growth and development: Offering opportunities for growth and development can be an excellent way to attract top talent. This can include offering training programs, mentorship opportunities, and career advancement opportunities.

Use social media and job boards: Use social media platforms like LinkedIn and Twitter to promote your organization and job openings. Additionally, posting job openings on popular job boards like Indeed or Glassdoor can help you reach a wider audience.

Create a positive candidate experience: Providing a positive candidate experience can make a significant impact on how candidates view your organization. This can include responding to applications promptly, being transparent about the hiring process, and providing feedback to candidates throughout the process.

Develop a diverse and inclusive workplace: Creating a diverse and inclusive workplace can attract talent from a wide range of backgrounds and experiences. This can be achieved by promoting diversity and inclusion in your job postings, actively recruiting diverse candidates, and providing training on unconscious bias to employees.

By following these steps, you can attract new talent to your organization and create a strong team that can help drive success and growth.

Retaining Existing Talent

The bigger challenge for many organizations today is how to retain good people? We are seeing this all the time with clients who run graduate programs, bring in fresh faces and within six to twelve months after their training (or sometimes during), they leave for a better offer... and we are not necessarily talking financial incentives only.

With the work we are doing in Saudi Arabia we train everyone from C-Suite to Graduate. On more than one occasion we have delivered a graduate development programme for one company, then delivered for another company a little later, only to encounter a delegate we have worked with before at the previous company.

In order to address this some are looking at some kind of a retainership or minimum service contract, but these simply won't work, and here is why...

To help you make sense of this let us explain what is motivating people in the workforce today. If you think about it, the world of business has seen three distinct generational changes over the last 100 years or so. The **industrial revolution**, the **information revolution** and currently we are in the **social revolution**.

During the **industrial revolution** people's motivation for work was for survival. They wanted basic necessities like a roof over their heads, food on their plates and basic amenities. They were tolerant of all working conditions including situations of abuse, and would never leave, because opportunities were less commonplace. You had made it if you found a 'job for life.' People nostalgically remember this generation as more loyal, but we would argue this was a myth, they simply had less options and more basic needs (on the Maslow hierarchy of needs). Consider these people the grand parents of today's workplace.

Next came the **information revolution**, technology companies started to flourish, and companies focussed on brand building. The work force in this era had different motivations, no longer pre-occupied with simply surviving (their parents took care of that), they aspired for a better standard of living. Opportunity was more abundant, so they had a little more choice and sought out a better salary to afford their own home, a nice car or even to save for private education for their children. Their desire for a better standard of living extended into the workplace, they wanted an improved working environment and a better relationship with colleagues (culture).

Right now we are in the **social revolution**, and it is a different matter. Employees today are perceived as being less loyal, which is still a myth btw, they simply have more options than ever before, and more considerations when making their decisions. Values play a bigger part in where you work, and people operate higher up the Maslow Hierarchy of needs. Which means today's workforce, in the developed world at least, don't care about simply survival, grandparents took care of that, and their parents took care of standard of living. Even the labour workforce have widescreen TV and many of the niceties.

Today information is freely available, and people can literally learn to do anything online (inexpensively) and it has never been easier to start your own business and be in charge of your own destiny. So, we all need to understand, we live in the social revolution (or digital) where everything is human centric, and Identity has never been more important.

So, coming back to our point... if you threaten a pay cut or some form of retaining contract, they will respond with "thanks, but no thanks, I'll find another job".
Today's workforce needs something else. They want quality of life, not standard of life. Which means quality of workplace, which means quality of job, quality of environment, quality of role, opportunities to learn and grow, all of it!

The interview process today is no longer "tell me why we should hire you" but rather "Let us tell you why you should want to work here". Unless you don't have a solution for that, you will always struggle to retain talent.

Here is one example from one of our Saudi clients (who shall remain nameless) where we worked on a Tech Graduate program, predominantly cyber security. When the program started, they were joining a team of 20 experienced cyber professionals. By the time it had finished, 80% of their experienced colleagues had been head hunted, meaning they were entering an environment where there was far more expectation on their shoulders.

Embracing Diversity and Inclusivity

Striving to increase workplace diversity should not just be empty rhetoric it is an evidence backed, sensible business decision. A 2015 McKinsey report on 366 public companies found that respondents in the top quartile for ethnic and racial diversity in management, were 35% more likely to achieve financial returns above average when compared to their industry, and those in the top quartile for gender diversity were 15% more likely to have returns above the industry average too.

Another study by Credit Suisse of 2,400 companies showed that organizations with at least one female board member yielded higher return on equity and higher net income growth than those without.

Research consistently shows us that nonhomogeneous teams are simply smarter. When we Work with people who are different from us, we are challenged with new perspectives and our brains are stretched by new ways of thinking, sharpening its performance. Let's explore why diverse teams are smarter.

They Focus More Attention on the Facts

In a study published in the Journal of Personality and Social Psychology, researchers assigned 200 participants to mock jury panels of six people each. The panels comprised of all white panels, or split white and black panels (4 white and 2 black). The jurors were shown a video of a trial featuring a black defendant, and white victims. They were then asked to decide whether the defendant was guilty or not guilty.

The results showed that the diverse panels raised more facts related to the case than homogenous panels and made fewer factual errors while discussing the evidence. When errors did occur, they were more likely to be corrected during deliberation. One possible reason for this difference was that white jurors on diverse panels recalled evidence more accurately.

The results suggest that people from diverse backgrounds appear to alter the behaviour of a group's social majority in ways that lead to improved and more accurate group thinking. Essentially by bringing more awareness to potential subconscious bias.

Diverse teams are more likely to re-examine facts and remain objective. They may also encourage greater scrutiny of each member's actions with more accountability, keeping their combined cognitive resources sharp and alert. By breaking up workplace homogeneity, you allow employees to become more aware of their own potential biases which are entrenched ways of thinking that can blind them to key information and even lead them to make mistakes in the decision-making processes.

They Are More Innovative

As previously discussed in this book, to stay competitive, we should always continue to innovate. Research suggests that one of the best ways to boost our capacity to transform ourselves and our products or services, may involve hiring more women and culturally diverse team members. In a study published in Innovation: Management, Policy and Practice, the authors analyzed 4,277 organizations in Spain and their levels of gender diversity in research and development. Using statistical models, they found that companies with more women were more likely to introduce radical new innovations into the market over a two-year period.

Another study, published in Economic Geography, concluded that increased cultural diversity is a huge benefit to innovativeness. They combined data from the London Annual Business Survey for 7,615 firms and the results revealed that organizations run by culturally diverse leadership teams were more likely to develop new products than those with homogenous leadership.

The point is, although people might feel more comfortable working with people who have cultural similarities, when we embrace diversity we avoid the costly pitfalls of conformity, which in turn discourages innovative thinking.

Simply put, when you enrich your talent pool with representatives of different genders, races, and nationalities, you increase company's joint intellectual potential. By creating a more diverse workplace we help to keep our biases in check and make people question their assumptions. Additional to this, we need to ensure we have inclusive practices so that everyone feels they can participate and be heard. All of this can make your teams smarter and, ultimately, make your organization more successful.

How This Can Drive Digital Transformation

In the context of Everyday Transformation™, embracing diversity and inclusivity is critical for organizations looking to successfully navigate change because of this impact on innovation, problem-solving, and collaboration. So where should we focus our efforts?

Recognizing the Importance of Diversity and Inclusivity

The first step in building a culture that is inclusive and respectful of diversity is recognizing the importance of these values. Organizations must understand the positive impact that diversity and inclusivity can have on the workplace as mentioned above and proactively create a more supportive and inclusive environment.

Building an Inclusive Workplace

To build a culture that is inclusive and respectful of diversity, organizations must create a workplace that is welcoming and supportive of all employees. This means actively promoting diversity, creating opportunities for employees from different backgrounds to work together, and providing training and support to help employees understand and embrace inclusivity.

Encouraging Diverse Perspectives

Another key component of building a culture that is inclusive and respectful is encouraging different perspectives. Organizations must create an environment where all employees feel comfortable sharing their ideas and experiences, and where their contributions are appreciated. By doing so, organizations can tap into the creativity and expertise of employees from diverse backgrounds, leading to better problem-solving and innovation.

Fostering a Culture of Respect

Respect is critical for building a culture that is inclusive and values diversity. But more importantly it smooths the waters for grown up conversations essential for the journey ahead.

Change Hurts, but It Is Worth It

Change is the only constant that surrounds us, but for employees, this can be difficult to manage and upsetting. When striving for a successful transformation we must consider the different perceptions of those initiating change, implementing it, and being impacted by it.

"

What I feel is the sound of a change echoing through me

Status Quo

In this section we want to discuss the psychology behind resistance and some techniques to overcome it. We will also explore the types of change, discuss why people react the way they do during transformation, and share tactical approaches to overcoming resistance to change in the workplace.

Human beings love certainty. There is great comfort in the status quo. We naturally resist change because change represents uncertainty, which our brains see as a threat.

In times gone by there were life and death consequences to threats, and whilst not all situations today have the same consequences, our amygdala (lizard brain) still protects us as if they do. This causes anxiety about the future and makes us worry about how things will turn out, or whether we'll be able to cope with the new situation.

When we feel anxious, our self-preservation mechanisms (fight or flight) are mobilised. Our thinking moves from the frontal lobe area, (used for higher-level intellectual functioning), and becomes instead focussed on survival. When this happens, we experience a diminished capacity for rational thinking even when the change is advantageous for us, therefore we still resist it.

Change can also be difficult and uncomfortable because it disrupts our sense of familiarity and routine. When we're used to a certain way of doing things, it can be challenging to adjust to new circumstances or a new environment. Additionally, change often involves a sense of loss or the need to let go of something we're attached to. This could be a job, a relationship, a home, or any other aspect of our lives that we're accustomed to.

However, it's important to remember that change can also bring new opportunities for growth and development, and that we can learn to embrace and even welcome change as a natural part of life.

Why do we love routine?

Routine activities use an area of the brain called the basal ganglia which is strongly interconnected with the cerebral cortex, thalamus, and brainstem, amongst others. This area is associated with a variety of functions including control of voluntary motor movements, procedural learning, routine behaviours, and habits. The basal ganglia are activated by familiar and repetitive activity which no longer require close attention, therefore using much less energy than our working memory (used to pay attention to new information).

Activities that are repeated eventually become controlled by the basal ganglia, thereby freeing up the prefrontal cortex to focus on fresh stimuli. Routine therefore becomes hardwired into our brain and any habit, good or bad, is difficult (not impossible) to override. I am sure you can relate, how much concentration did it take to learn to drive? Now though I bet you can take whole journeys without having to think about it.

> *"Without conscious and deliberate effort, inertia always wins"*
> **Tony Hsieh**

As humans, we naturally experience inertia: an inherent laziness. Studies demonstrate that when we physically move, we will find the most energy efficient way to do it and burn as few calories as possible. On a psychological level, this laziness underlies why we find it difficult to change and this is known as cognitive inertia.

Cognitive inertia is the reason we find it easier to stick with the status quo. We stick to what we know: we eat the same food, we wear the same clothes and we have the same friends. On a positive level, cognitive inertia prevents us from suffering from decision fatigue and it frees up our brain to take on other matters. But there are times when we need to break this inertia, when what we are doing no longer serves us or is no longer relevant.

How Does the Brain Make and Change Decisions?

Decision-making can happen fairly quickly in the brain. When we are faced with different choices our brain considers the potential outcome for each option. The larger the difference in value, the faster we make the decision. But when the options are similar in value, it can take much longer. Or in other words it relates to the amount of certainty we need... the more certain of an outcome we are, the more likely we are to commit to a decision. We don't all have the same risk threshold either, so the level of certainty required varies from person to person.

A point worth noting... Providing too many choices also reduces decision making time. If you want people to commit to change, present one compelling vision with a better outcome than the status quo.

Operational Change vs Social Change

There are two parts to organizational transformation. The first is operational (or technical) and the second is social. It is important that we understand the difference between the two if we want to manage or reduce resistance.

Operational change refers to changes made to the processes, procedures, or systems of an organization to improve its efficiency, effectiveness, or productivity. i.e. what we do and how we do it. These changes are usually focused on improving the internal operations of an organization and may include things like streamlining processes or adopting new technologies.

On the other hand, social change refers to changes in the beliefs, attitudes, behaviours, and values of individuals or groups within a society. Social change can result from a variety of factors, including changes in technology, economic conditions, political systems, and cultural norms. While operational change and social change are different, they can sometimes be related. For example, an organization that adopts new technologies may also be contributing to social change by changing the way people interact with technology or by disrupting existing industries. Similarly, social changes can also drive operational changes within organizations, such as changes in consumer preferences or societal expectations that may require businesses to adapt their operations.

Humans resist change for a variety of reasons, both emotional and practical. Some of the main reasons include:

Fear of the unknown: Change often means stepping into unfamiliar territory, which can be daunting and unsettling. People tend to feel more comfortable with what they already know and are used to.

Loss of control: Change can also make people feel like they are losing control of their lives. They may feel like they have less say in what happens next, and this can be scary.

Comfort in routine: Humans are creatures of habit and often find comfort in the predictability and routine of their lives. Change disrupts that routine and can be unsettling.

Fear of failure: People may resist change because they are afraid of failing or making mistakes. They may feel that sticking with what they know is safer than taking a risk with something new.

Lack of understanding: If people don't fully understand why a change is necessary or what it will entail, they may resist it out of confusion or scepticism.

Past experiences: Negative experiences with change in the past can make people wary of it in the future. If someone has been hurt or disappointed by a change in the past, they may be less likely to embrace it in the present.

In their work on resistance to change theory, **John P. Kotter** and **Leonard A. Schlesinger** concluded that there are four common situations in which people's resistance to change germinates and grows:

Self-interest: When people believe they may lose something of value as a result of a proposed change, they are likely to resist. People prioritize their own self-interests (all stakeholders have an agenda) which are not necessarily in the best interests of the organization. They may eventually influence support for their position and can develop into group resistance.

Misunderstanding and lack of trust: A lack of understanding about the potential consequences of a change can also be a factor of resistance. If there is a trust deficit between leadership (instigating) versus the workforce expected to implement, this also breeds resistance.

Different evaluations: This situation arises when people assess the impacts of transformation differently to their managers or others who initiate the change. Ambiguous potential outcomes require a little more work in advance, and a data backed vision of the future to create certainty.

Low tolerance for change: Some people fear change because of their own low confidence in their ability to develop the competencies required in the new way of doing things. This is particularly true of agile projects that require rapid change – the bigger and faster the change, lower the confidence for some.

Personality also affects individual attitudes towards change which is a theme that also runs through Peter Drucker's theories on management. Essentially personality types which require more information to reach certainty, are likely to be slower to commit to change.

Overcoming Resistance To Change

So, we understand what change is and the psychology as to why people resist... Let's look at some strategies and tactics to overcome this resistance.

So, a quick reminder of the difference between a strategy and a tactic... Strategies encompass high-level plans and approaches that provide direction and guidance for achieving long-term goals, while tactics involve specific actions and decisions aimed at implementing the strategy and achieving short-term objectives. Strategies focus on the overall vision, competitive advantage, and allocation of resources, while tactics deal with the practical execution of the strategy, adapting to real-time feedback and circumstances.

Simply put a strategy will provide the overarching framework, while tactics drive the day-to-day actions necessary to make the strategy a reality.

6 Strategies To Overcome Resistance

When it comes to overcoming resistance to change, there are six key areas that organizations should focus on.

Communication and education: Resistance often stems from fear of the unknown or a lack of understanding about why change is necessary. To address this, effective communication and education should start even before the change is implemented. By providing clear explanations and rationale for the change, individuals and teams can better grasp its purpose and make informed judgments.

Participation: People are more likely to accept change when they feel involved and have a say in the process. When change is imposed without consultation, resistance tends to increase, especially if job security is perceived as being at risk. It's crucial to engage stakeholders and those affected by the change in its design, fostering collaboration and empowering individuals to contribute their insights and ideas. Studies have shown that participation leads to positive outcomes such as readiness for change, acceptance, and increased trust.

Support: Transformation often disrupts established routines, pushing people out of their comfort zones. This can result in exhaustion, particularly if the organization experiences frequent changes. Even if individuals appear to accept the change, they may be simply resigned

"

It's easy to come up with new ideas; the hard part is letting go of what worked for you two years ago but will soon be out of date

Roger von Oech

to it. Providing support is essential to help them develop new skills and prevent change burnout. Managers need to demonstrate emotional intelligence and connect with their employees, offering coaching and guidance throughout the change process.

Agreement: Resistance arises when people perceive negative consequences for themselves. To address this, organizations can consider offering incentives such as extra pay, improved benefits, or structured career plans. Negotiation plays a crucial role in reaching agreements, although it's important to note that this approach can be costly and does not guarantee full engagement with the change.

Co-opting: People often form emotional connections to established processes and procedures. Co-opting involves involving those who may be resistant to change in key roles during the implementation phase. By giving them ownership and responsibility, it becomes easier to gain their support. However, it's important to be cautious since putting resistant individuals in influential positions may spread resistance further among others.

Coercion: In some cases, coercion becomes necessary when people feel unable to acquire new skills or perceive change as a temporary trend. Coercion involves using disciplinary measures to enforce compliance with the required behaviours and actions. While coercion can expedite change, it doesn't eliminate resistance and may lead to negative consequences in the long run if underlying resistance persists.

It's worth noting that coercion should be a last resort, as it doesn't address the root causes of resistance and can create a hostile environment. Ultimately, organizations should strive for strategies that promote understanding, engagement, and support to successfully navigate resistance and achieve successful transformation.

7 Tactics To Overcome Resistance

Structure the team to maximize its potential: Once you've communicated the change, assess the strengths and weaknesses of each team member. In individual sessions, discuss how they can contribute to the change effort based on their skills and abilities. Assign them roles and responsibilities that utilize their strengths while providing opportunities for personal and team development. This collaborative approach will engage team members and make them active participants in the change process.

Set challenging, achievable, and engaging targets: Clearly define goals and break down the change project into smaller milestones. Celebrate achievements along the way. Ensure that the goals are progressive and aligned with the organization's values and beliefs. It's important to not only focus on team milestones but also acknowledge and track individual progress. Link personal development to the overall goals of the team to motivate and engage employees.

Resolve conflicts quickly and effectively: Address any conflicts or breakdowns in communication promptly. Encourage open and honest dialogue, fostering an environment of trust and respect. Building a strong team spirit is crucial during times of change, so consider team meetings and bonding sessions. These activities help team members understand and appreciate each other, enabling transparent communication and collaborative problem-solving.

Show passion: Communicate with enthusiasm and demonstrate your belief in the future vision. Lead by example, embodying the behaviours and attitudes required by the change. When others witness leaders actively embracing the change, they are more likely to follow suit and become change advocates themselves. By being the change you want to see, you inspire others to adopt the new values and behaviours.

Be persuasive: Engage employees by being an energized and persuasive leader. Focus on the opportunities that come with the change and use persuasion rather than relying solely on authority. Share stories and experiences that highlight positive change and relate them to the organizational motives and goals. Cultivate your storytelling skills to effectively convey the culture, brand, and future vision to employees.

Empower innovation and creativity: Create an environment that encourages feedback and flexibility. Foster a culture of innovation and creativity where people can contribute their ideas and find solutions to challenges that arise during the change process. Remove the fear of taking risks by framing failure as a learning experience and a necessary step toward success. Encourage accountability and collaboration across teams to foster a cross-pollination of innovative ideas and expand everyone's capacity for creative thinking.

Remain positive and supportive: Recognize that change can be unsettling for people, both personally and professionally. As a leader, provide positive support and inspire free thought, honest communication, and creativity. Encourage personal and team development, as employees navigate through the change. Employees expect leaders to manage change, and by creating a culture where change is embraced by all, you foster an environment where everyone becomes a catalyst for positive transformation.

We have seen time and time again organizations ignore the psychology of change and simply tolerate the resistance. They try to bulldoze the change through with their fingers crossed hoping to minimise the casualties. It is all so needless, a little planning with strategies and tactics to mitigate can make all the difference. Remember, effective leadership and a supportive culture are vital for managing resistance to change and achieving successful outcomes.

Friction at the Interfaces

We first heard this term 'friction at the interfaces' working with a large European law enforcement agency going through agile culture change.

Friction at the interfaces refers to the challenges and obstacles that arise when different components or systems interact with each other. In the context of digital transformation, friction at the interfaces can occur when various technologies, processes, departments, or stakeholders within an organization need to work together or when the organization interacts with external partners or customers.

Here's what you can do about technology or process frictions;

1. **Interoperability:** Ensure that different systems and technologies can seamlessly communicate and share data with each other. This may involve integrating legacy systems with new digital solutions.

2. **Data Integration:** Establish mechanisms to consolidate and synchronize data from various sources to provide a unified and accurate view of information across the organization.

3. **Process Alignment:** Identify and address discrepancies or gaps in workflows and processes that may hinder smooth collaboration between different departments or functions.

But in this section we would really like to focus on the people friction... how to improve the inter-department collaboration, stakeholder communication, and how to break down the silos.

As traditional work environments undergo a shift towards remote and hybrid structures, companies are facing the challenge of breaking down team silos and fostering effective collaboration.

Silos occur when teams operate in isolated bubbles, reluctant to interact and share information with other departments. If not addressed, the silo mentality can have detrimental effects on organizations, hindering their overall success.

The Impact of Silo in Organizations

From early adulthood, we are conditioned to adopt a silo mentality, focusing on a specific area of expertise for success. While this approach may seem prudent, it has led to collaboration, productivity, and organizational obstacles in businesses worldwide.

According to a 2016 McKinsey survey, executives identified silo mentality as the top hindrance to building a functional digital culture. As organizations venture into fast-paced global markets, the need for flexibility and efficiency becomes even more crucial. Centralized structures offer focused decision-making, but they may struggle to meet modern business demands.

Recent research on the effects of remote work on collaboration among information workers reveals that the shift to remote work has intensified siloed behavior and reduced synchronous communication. This highlights the importance for organizations to prioritize efforts in preventing and breaking down team silos.

What Are Team Silos?

To effectively address silos in the workplace, we must first understand the problem of silo mentality and its impact on the business environment.

According to the Cambridge dictionary, silos are parts of a company or organization that do not communicate or work well with other parts. The Merriam-Webster dictionary highlights the negative effects of silos, hindering communication and cooperation.

What Causes Silo Mentality?

The term "silo mentality" is derived from physical silos used to store grains on farms. Similarly, team silos occur when information or knowledge flow is restricted to specific teams in a company. This leads to low work morale, ineffectiveness, and power struggles, resulting in losses in resources, opportunities, and revenue.

The intangible nature of organizational silos makes them challenging to detect until poor performance becomes evident, and this is complex as it involves both communication and collaboration issues.

Apart from the lack of information sharing, teams trapped in siloed thinking also tend to neglect the requirements of the new cross-functional work environment. As organizations grow, teams often adopt more focused roles. However, they frequently fail to adapt their processes to meet the demands of enhanced collaboration, especially evident in recent years. The shift to remote and hybrid work environments has posed significant obstacles to successful collaboration for many teams.

Here are the common factors contributing to the silo mentality at work:

Leadership Discord

Leadership discord is a significant factor contributing to organizational silos. When team leaders disagree on a plan or strategy, it creates power struggles that hinder communication and collaboration.

The problem often originates at the top of the organizational hierarchy and trickles down to teams and individuals. As a consequence, productivity is adversely affected, serving as a clear indicator of larger structural issues.

Poor Information-Sharing

Siloed behavior often arises due to a lack of incentives for information-sharing. Teams operate in closed environments without encouragement to share information with other departments.

When departments lack clarity about each other's responsibilities and priorities, it can result in duplicated efforts, mistrust, and various other challenges. Additionally, organizations with multiple communication channels utilized by teams may face issues of miscommunication.

A lack of emphasis on larger organizational priorities can have a negative impact on collaboration, fostering a silo mentality among teams. When there isn't a clear, overarching vision to guide them, teams may become fixated on narrower, department-specific goals.

Communication Obstacles

Team silos often emerge in organizations due to a lack of functional and flexible communication channels. Poor communication tools can be a significant factor. Relying solely on email for team communication may hinder the development of a healthier and more productive digital culture.

Lack of Feedback Opportunities

Siloed behavior is also influenced by the absence of a feedback-driven culture within organizations. When there is a lack of emphasis on prioritizing and encouraging feedback, it can lead to a breakdown in trust and openness between different departments. As a result, collaboration becomes hindered, and teams tend to operate in closed-off silos.

Narrow Expertise

Organizations that prioritize narrow expertise over a broader, cross-functional knowledge and organizational structure often encounter challenges related to isolated team silos. Focusing too much on specific areas can limit the larger perspective required for effective cross-functional collaboration.

Common symptoms of team silos among departments include:

- **Delays:** Inadequate inter-departmental communication and collaboration lead to missed deadlines and unmet goals.

- **Mistrust and rivalry between teams:** Siloed thinking hinders trust-building, open communication, and knowledge sharing across teams.

- **Unwillingness to accept accountability:** Teams in a siloed culture may take pride in their uniqueness but often fail to share responsibility for mistakes.

- **Task duplication:** Lack of regular communication and cooperation causes duplication of tasks, resulting in unnecessary delays and increased costs.

According to a 2019 report, collaboration is a top priority for 94% of office workers, urging companies to focus on improved collaboration strategies. To effectively break down team silos and promote collaboration, organizations should adopt a proactive approach. This approach should include clear leadership examples, the use of appropriate tools, and additional training.

To help organizations foster collaboration and overcome team silos, we have compiled a list of eight actionable strategies.

Breaking down silos in the workplace may sound like an oversimplistic cliché, but it's a vital approach for fostering collaboration and better organizational performance.

Silos occur when teams become overly focused on their own departmental goals, often leading to clashes with other teams and hindering information-sharing.

The problem often starts with leaders and managers who hyper-focus on their specific objectives, losing sight of the bigger picture. This mentality can trickle down to team members, fostering a culture of isolated silos.

To prevent this scenario in your organization, consider implementing steps to build a more connected and collaborative culture.

Develop Cross-Team Transparency

Managers and leaders play a crucial role in breaking away from the damaging silo mentality. By fostering a vision-centered culture, they can put the organization's vision statement into practice. This involves viewing each individual as an essential unit contributing to the greater, unified goal.

Organizations can achieve greater success by setting practical and achievable goals instead of presenting a generic vision. Clear directions and action plans are essential to ensure that all teams prioritize a common goal.

For some organizations, this could involve creating company-wide customer experience councils. These councils would facilitate inclusive discussions on developing better ways to support the overarching vision and effectively communicate it to customers.

Others may benefit from establishing more unified communication channels to foster a sense of community and emphasize shared values and goals.

Create More Opportunities for Cross-Departmental Communication and Interaction

Effective collaboration is essential for success, but in silo-based organizations, it's often a challenge to achieve. A key indicator of a silo mindset is the lack of information-sharing among teams.

This situation may arise due to organizational limitations, such as the failure to prioritize transparency. Many companies lack sufficient incentives to keep all teams updated on processes, projects, and goals. Moreover, the absence of a centralized communication channel exacerbates miscommunication and misalignment among teams.

- **Hold regular cross-department management meetings:** Ensuring that all departments are updated on each other's responsibilities and priorities.

- **Promote cooperation between related departments:** For example, encouraging collaboration between marketing and sales teams, two interdependent departments whose success relies on consistent information exchange.

- **Develop streamlined communication:** Adopting a single communication tool across all teams can greatly improve collaboration.

To rebuild a cross-functional culture, companies must re-evaluate their team communication practices from the ground up. Start by organizing regular check-in meetings across different divisions to encourage interaction. Implement cross-team training sessions and team-building events to improve communication, trust, and empathy, fostering interaction and sharing among all departments.

Encouraging one-on-one work buddy meetings with members from different teams can also effectively inspire better cross-team communication during the process of breaking down silos and improving teamwork.

For building trust and empathy among teams, creating general public channels can be beneficial. These channels provide all employees with opportunities to seek advice or share opinions on various topics beyond work scope, promoting understanding and openness throughout the organization.

Encourage Better Communication

To achieve this, focus on building an open and supportive culture where teams feel comfortable sharing and seeking feedback, as well as asking questions. Improving communication and cross-team collaboration will naturally follow.

When devising an action plan to enhance communication, consider these three crucial steps:

Cultivate a sense of community and support: Facilitate informal weekly check-ins between teams to gauge their well-being. Offer support to new hires to help them integrate seamlessly into the organization. Encourage an atmosphere where everyone feels safe expressing their thoughts and feelings. Leaders can lead by example, sharing their challenges, mistakes, and lessons learned.

Encourage a Constructive Feedback Culture

Constructive feedback is a valuable tool for individual and team growth. Implementing regular feedback sessions across cross-teams allows for reflection on projects, identifying areas for improvement, and optimizing future endeavors. As people become more comfortable with sharing their thoughts, individual projects also benefit from increased feedback opportunities.

When aiming to break down team silos and foster a culture of feedback, it is essential to create a safe and constructive environment. Avoid assigning guilt and blame, and instead, focus on constructive insights. By cultivating a healthy culture that embraces regular feedback, organizations can promote growth, enhance productivity, and shift from a silo mentality to a collaborative and interconnected culture.

Btw we have a great workshop on Feedback Culture.

Promote Curiosity and Openness through Better Questions

Inquiry plays a crucial role in transitioning from siloed work to collaborative cross-team efforts. Research conducted by Francesca Gino from Harvard Business School supports this idea. In her HBR article, Gino emphasizes that curiosity positively influences successful collaboration across departments. To break free from disconnected environments, organizations must embrace the art of asking meaningful questions that propel conversations forward.

By encouraging teams to inquire, learn, and explore, companies can unleash the power of collaboration and innovation, driving better outcomes and continuous improvement.

Enhancing Cross-Functional Collaboration: Creating Pathways for Success

In the quest to break down team silos, companies often discover that the issue doesn't lie in teams' reluctance to collaborate but in the lack of avenues for meaningful collaboration.

By creating more opportunities for cross-boundary work, companies can unlock a wealth of benefits, including increased productivity, improved customer retention, and greater success in achieving company goals.

Research published in Harvard Business Review in 2015 suggests that organizations supporting inter-department collaboration witness enhanced customer loyalty and experience higher revenue.

Encouraging organization-wide input on general projects helps individuals understand the value of joint effort, fostering a sense of connection and contribution.
Another effective approach involves creating cross-functional teams for general projects, such as business runs or industry events. Appointing inter-departmental teams for such initiatives encourages cross-silo dialogue and collaboration.

Improve Virtual Collaboration and Communication With Team Chat Applications

Enhancing Virtual Collaboration and Communication with Team Chat Applications For companies striving to break down team silos and foster better employee engagement in remote and hybrid work environments, maintaining seamless and streamlined communication is of paramount importance.

An effective solution to maximize productivity and collaboration across teams is the utilization of team chat apps. Research reveals that efficient digital collaboration tools can boost workplace satisfaction by 17%, yet only 9% of organizations currently employ such infrastructure.

Inspire Employees To Look Beyond the Organization - Encouraging a Broader Perspective

As organizations strive to break down company silos, it is crucial to inspire teams to shift their focus beyond immediate tasks and embrace a wider perspective both within and outside the firm.

Motivating employees to expand their horizons and visions offers several benefits, such as exposure to the bigger picture and the discovery of new ideas. It also aids in breaking away from the silo mentality.

In addition to fostering cross-team collaboration on shared projects, leaders can encourage teams to explore ideas and knowledge beyond the organization's boundaries. This may involve seeking inspiration from other industries, discovering innovative solutions, and exploring interdisciplinary techniques.

REFLECTION SECTION

Here are 20 great questions to ask for the people part of the Transformation Insight Framework™:

1. What are the key skills and expertise required for each role within the organization?
2. How do we ensure that employees receive adequate training and development opportunities to maintain their skills and expertise?
3. What is the current organizational culture, and is it aligned with our values and goals?
4. How can we improve the organizational culture to foster collaboration, innovation, and teamwork?
5. What are the existing communication channels within the organization, and how effective are they in ensuring clear and consistent communication?

---

6. How can we improve communication channels to ensure that everyone in the organization understands their roles, responsibilities, and objectives?

7. What are the current employee engagement levels, and how can we improve them?

8. How can we create a work environment that fosters a sense of ownership and accountability among employees?

9. What are the current employee motivation levels, and how can we improve them?

10. How can we recognize and reward high performance to encourage employee motivation and engagement?

11. What opportunities do employees have to be involved in decision-making processes within the organization?

12. What is the diversity and inclusion policy within the organization, and how is it being implemented?

13. What initiatives can be put in place to promote diversity and inclusion in the workplace?

14. How can we ensure that all employees feel valued, respected, and included within the organization?

15. What are the current employee retention rates, and how can we improve them?

16. What are the current employee satisfaction levels, and how can we improve them?

17. How can we ensure that employees have a healthy work-life balance?

18. What are the existing health and safety policies within the organization, and how effective are they?

19. How can we create a work environment that prioritizes employee well-being and mental health?

20. What are the long-term career growth opportunities available to employees within the organization?

REMEMBER: You can visit www.Everyday-Transformation.com for the **Transformation Insight Assessment™** which includes more questions to guide you.

Leading Change the Agile Way

Building on the topic of Agile, let's look at it from a leadership perspective...
and btw this topic is one of our most delivered workshops in the last 3
years as organizations recognise the need to install a new leadership
and management operating system.

What's the Difference Between Management and Leadership?

Management and leadership are two distinct but complementary
roles within an organization. While they share similarities, there are
fundamental differences between the two:

Management: Management involves planning, organizing, and
controlling resources to achieve specific objectives and targets. Managers
are responsible for day-to-day operations, implementing processes
and procedures, allocating resources, and ensuring efficiency and
effectiveness. They focus on executing tasks, monitoring performance,
and making decisions to achieve predefined goals. Management is
more task-oriented, focused on operational efficiency, and maintaining
stability within the organization.

We are huge fans of Gary Hamel, a renowned management thinker, who
has made significant contributions to the field of management and has
shared his insights on management change over the last 100 years. One
of his key theories is the need for a fundamental shift in management
practices to adapt to the changing business landscape. He argues that
traditional hierarchical and bureaucratic management models are no
longer effective in today's dynamic and complex world.

According to Hamel, management practices have largely remained
stagnant over the past century, with a focus on command-and-control
structures, top-down decision-making, and rigid hierarchies. However,
he believes that organizations must evolve and embrace more flexible,
innovative, and participative management approaches.

Hamel advocates for the democratization of management, where
decision-making is distributed throughout the organization and employees
are empowered to take ownership and initiative. He emphasizes the
importance of creating a culture of trust, collaboration, and continuous
learning, where individuals at all levels can contribute their ideas and
expertise.

Additionally, Hamel highlights the need for organizations to foster a culture of innovation and adaptability. He encourages leaders to challenge the status quo, promote experimentation, and embrace change as a constant. He argues that organizations must be agile, able to respond quickly to market shifts, and continuously reinvent themselves to stay competitive.

Hamel's theory on management change in the last 100 years centers around the necessity of breaking away from traditional management practices and embracing more innovative, participatory, and adaptable approaches to thrive in an ever-evolving business environment.

Management 3.0: Management 3.0 is an approach to modern management developed by Jurgen Appelo that emphasizes the importance of employee engagement, collaboration, and continuous improvement. It is based on the belief that traditional command-and-control management methods are no longer effective in today's complex and rapidly changing business environment.

Management 3.0 promotes a shift towards more agile and adaptive management practices that empower and motivate employees, foster creativity and innovation, and create a culture of learning and growth. It encompasses a wide range of principles, practices, and tools that aim to improve leadership, team dynamics, decision-making, and organizational culture.

The goal of Management 3.0 is to create a more dynamic, resilient, and employee-centric approach to management that enables organizations to thrive in the digital age.

The 5 Principles of Management 5.0

Energize People: Management 3.0 recognizes that motivated and engaged employees are crucial for organizational success. It emphasizes creating an energizing work environment where individuals feel motivated, inspired, and have a sense of purpose. This principle involves understanding and fulfilling the intrinsic needs of employees, promoting autonomy, mastery, and purpose in their work.

Empower Teams: Management 3.0 promotes self-organization and distributed decision-making within teams. It advocates for empowering teams to make decisions, take ownership of their work, and collaborate effectively. This principle encourages a shift from traditional hierarchical control to a more decentralized and autonomous team structure, where team members are trusted to make decisions that impact their work.

Align Constraints: Instead of imposing rigid rules and processes, Management 3.0 focuses on aligning constraints to foster creativity and innovation. It acknowledges that too much freedom can lead to chaos, while too many constraints can stifle creativity. This principle involves defining clear boundaries and guidelines that enable teams to experiment, learn, and find creative solutions within those constraints.

Develop Competence: Management 3.0 emphasizes the importance of continuous learning and personal growth. It encourages managers to support the development of their team members' skills and competencies. This principle involves providing opportunities for learning, mentorship, and feedback, enabling individuals to enhance their capabilities and contribute more effectively to the team and organization.

Grow Structure: This principle recognizes that organizational structures should be adaptable and flexible to meet the changing needs of the business. Management 3.0 encourages a dynamic approach to organizational design, where structures can evolve and adjust based on the context and requirements. It promotes creating an environment that fosters collaboration, knowledge sharing, and cross-functional communication.

These five principles of Management 3.0 are fully aligned with agile thinking as they aim to empower and engage teams, promote autonomy and innovation, and foster a culture of continuous learning and improvement within organizations.

So What Are The Differences Between Management 1.0 And Management 3.0 We Hear You Ask?

MANAGEMENT 1.0		MANAGEMENT 3.0
Power happens when you are in charge	vs	**Power is greatest when in a unified team**
Focussed on specific roles and responsibilities	vs	**Flexible about changing roles and responsibilities**
Allocates resources and time only when necessary	vs	**Empowers team to make decisions about resources and time**
Keeps information locked down	vs	**Is open and transparent with information**
Focuses on symptoms when troubleshooting	vs	**Focusses on root causes**
Autocratic and rarely invites team input	vs	**Democratic and frequently invites contribution**

Now Let's Look At Leadership

Leadership: Leadership on the other hand is about setting a vision, inspiring and motivating others, and guiding them towards achieving a shared goal. It involves influencing and guiding people, promoting innovation, and fostering a positive culture. Leaders focus on the big picture, long-term strategies, and inspiring others to achieve their full potential. They provide direction, empower their teams, and promote change and growth. Leadership is more focused on people and driving organizational change and innovation.

Leaders today have had to adapt and create a culture where experimentation and learning are encouraged. They understand the importance of allowing employees to make mistakes without fear of blame. Collaboration among all team members has become essential, as everyone is striving for the organization's survival and sustainable growth. With a clear purpose, strategy, and priorities, leaders empower teams to think and act autonomously while ensuring a great customer experience.

All of these aspects align with the concept of Agile Leadership, which is a management style characterized by staying calm under pressure, effectively responding to unique situations, embracing innovation, inspiring others, and keeping teams focused on the right track. By putting people first, prioritizing customer needs, and embracing change as an opportunity to add value, organizations and leaders can not only survive but also thrive amidst crises and periods of change. It's all about finding the right balance and leading with confidence and adaptability.

Agile Leaders embody a new paradigm of leadership that is not only powerful but also profoundly humane, democratic, and inclusive. They empower their teams by communicating the "why" behind the organization's goals and trusting them to figure out the best path to success.

These leaders foster an environment of autonomy, allowing teams to self-organize, unleash their creativity, and take ownership of their work. They understand that true greatness emerges when individuals are given the freedom to create and innovate. Agile Leaders redefine what it means to lead, inspiring and enabling their teams to reach new heights of achievement and fulfilment.

An agile leader is a change leader... a catalyst for transformation in an organization, someone who ignites and guides the process of change. Picture this: they're the kind of person who wears many hats, from being a visionary with a clear direction to being a great communicator who can rally the troops.

They possess a mix of confidence and humility, inspiring others to embrace new ideas and approaches. They're adaptable and open-minded, willing to challenge the status quo and encourage innovation. Change leaders are also empathetic listeners who understand the concerns and fears that come with change, and they take the time to address them.

They lead by example, showing enthusiasm, resilience, and a positive attitude throughout the change journey. In short, a change leader is someone who lights the path forward and brings others along on the exciting adventure of transformation.

The Benefits of Agile Leadership

1. Empowered leaders and organization: Agile Leadership empowers leaders to trust their teams and delegate decision-making, creating a more empowered organization overall.

2. Increased responsiveness at all levels: Agile Leadership fosters a culture of adaptability and quick decision-making, enabling teams to respond rapidly to changing circumstances and customer needs.

3. More motivated and involved employees: By promoting autonomy, Agile Leadership encourages employees to take ownership of their work, resulting in higher levels of motivation and engagement.

4. Better communication and collaboration: Agile Leadership emphasizes open and transparent communication, fostering better collaboration within and between teams.

5. Cultivate individual relationships and appreciation: Agile Leadership focuses on valuing individual contributions and fostering meaningful relationships among team members, creating a culture of appreciation and respect.

6. Continuous learning: Agile Leadership encourages a growth mindset and a culture of continuous learning, where employees are empowered to experiment, learn from mistakes, and constantly improve.

7. Increased confidence: Agile Leadership builds confidence in oneself and others by providing support and creating a safe environment for taking risks and trying new approaches.

8. Employees with greater autonomy: Agile Leadership promotes autonomy and decision-making at the team level, allowing employees to take ownership of their work and contribute their unique skills and expertise.

Examples of Agile Leadership

When we look at companies like Amazon and Facebook, we can see some great examples of Agile Leadership in action. Take Jeff Bezos, the founder of Amazon, for instance. He's known for promoting fast decision-making and learning from mistakes. He encourages his teams to make high-quality decisions quickly and supports them even if he may not initially agree. This kind of trust and empowerment embodies the Agile mindset.

For example, he decided to release an Amazon Studios production even though he had doubts. Amazon Studios isn't afraid to fail quickly by cancelling new programs. He withdrew "The Last Tycoon" two weeks after releasing a season of episodes. This approach embodies Agile thinking.

Facebook, on the other hand, thrives on a culture of continuous improvement and open communication. Sheryl Sandberg, the Chief Operating Officer, emphasizes the acceptance of organizational failure and the importance of all contributors' opinions. At Facebook, they believe in creating a network-based organization where everyone's ideas are valued, and decisions are made collectively.

Both Amazon and Facebook exemplify Agile Leadership by fostering an environment that encourages experimentation, learning, and collaboration. They understand that empowering teams and embracing failure as a learning opportunity leads to sustainable growth and resilience. Additionally, leaders like Jeff Bezos and Sheryl Sandberg emphasize empathy, flexibility, and recognizing the personal lives of employees, which helps create strong relationships and a supportive work culture.

These examples demonstrate how Agile Leadership can positively impact organizations, enabling them to adapt and thrive in a rapidly changing world.

REFLECTION SECTION

We encourage you to answer the following questions spontaneously, without overthinking. Pay attention to your responses and assess whether they reflect behaviors aligned with Agile Leadership. If not, consider what initial actions you could take to embrace Agile Leadership.

1. What drives your passion for leadership?
2. What keeps you motivated to continue leading your team?
3. Why do you place importance on being an effective leader?
4. What inspires your dedication to projects within your organization?

Creativity is thinking up new things. Innovation is doing new things.

Theodore Levitt

5. How does your role impact both your own life and the lives of others?

6. What qualities or attributes make you an appealing leader to others? i.e. Why would people choose to follow?

7. What actions exemplify your leadership style?

8. Reflect on moments of personal pride in your leadership journey (identify at least 10).

9. Choose a person who serves as an inspiration and whom you admire. What aspects of their character do you appreciate the most? Which specific behaviours and actions do you find admirable?

10. Identify the connections and similarities between the actions you take pride in and the qualities you admire in the person you've chosen (name 6).

REMEMBER: You can visit www.Everyday-Transformation.com for the **Transformation Insight Assessment™** which includes more questions to guide you.

Everybody Can Innovate

Innovation culture is a hot topic among companies and entrepreneurs. It's all about fostering creativity and driving innovation within the organization. But how exactly do you build a culture of innovation the right way?

Before we delve into this in any detail, please note that under the Process section we will talk more about how to actually implement innovation initiatives into your organization and more importantly organise them through an Innovation Management System.

We have already discussed many of the culture attributes in this section of the book in relation to digital change, but what does it mean in relation to innovation? Well, it's about recognizing how the values and behaviours within an organization shape its approach to innovation. It encompasses the practices and processes that support and promote innovation as a key driver of progress and growth.

Why is cultivating an innovation culture so important? It should be obvious by now, it helps companies survive and thrive. By encouraging fresh ideas and breaking away from traditional norms, businesses can adapt to evolving market needs, leading to better products and services.

Another crucial aspect is empowering employees to think and work innovatively. Companies that prioritize innovation not only recognize the value of their workforce but also inspire them to contribute their unique insights. Research shows that happy employees are more productive, leading to improved work habits and a greater commitment to company success.

Your culture drives the development of impactful strategies and innovative solutions. By embracing innovation as an attitude rather than just a task, and promoting permission to challenge the status quo, organizations can improve their profitability, drive necessary changes, and enhance overall business performance.

As mentioned previously, diversity can play a crucial part of innovation by bringing together people with different backgrounds and expertise, companies can generate fresh perspectives, unlock new ideas, and avoid biases that may hinder growth.

It Starts With You!

Building a "culture of innovation" can actually start with just one person. It's pretty amazing how a single individual can make a big difference and be the inspiring catalyst. But imagine if you could supercharge your people by giving them the freedom to decide how work should be organized and how tasks should be carried out. Encouraging them to value commitment, taking creative risks, tapping into collective intelligence, and promoting effective communication.

Imagine if someone takes the initiative and shows that every idea is not only needed but also welcomed. That person becomes a catalyst for creating a safe space where colleagues feel comfortable coming forward and sharing their ideas. These conversations are guided by communication strategies that have a clear purpose and remove any barriers by exchanging ideas early on. The key is to focus discussions on what can be done rather than dwelling on what cannot be done.

By embracing the concept of "it takes only one" and adopting an improved communication strategy, the culture starts to cultivate innovation ambassadors. These are the individuals who champion innovation and spread the mindset throughout the organization. They inspire others by their example and encourage a culture of continuous improvement and creative thinking.

1. Focus on Continuous Improvement

When we think about innovation, it's often about coming up with new ideas, methods, or devices. It's about introducing something fresh and exciting. But sometimes, the pressure to create something new can be intimidating, leading to a lack of confidence and even a creative block. That's where the concept of continuous improvement comes in.

Continuous improvement is all about building upon existing processes and ideas without interruptions. It's about constantly generating and evolving ideas to make things better. And when an IT organization embraces this mindset, the results can be transformative.

Imagine a culture where continuous improvement is at the core. In this environment, there's a comfort level in openly discussing what doesn't work. It's a space where everyone contributes to problem-solving and takes ownership of finding solutions. And it's a place where creative thinkers collaborate with strategists, bringing their unique perspectives to the table.

The outcome of this culture is an environment where we constantly strive to see what we can do better, hence the "C what we can do better" mindset. Ideas flow freely, improvements are implemented, and breakthroughs can happen spontaneously. It's a dynamic and ever-evolving process that drives progress and keeps the team engaged.

More about this in the 'Process' Section.

2. Create a Value Statement

A value statement plays a crucial role in shaping an organization's culture and guiding its actions. It serves as a set of core principles that steer decision-making and establish standards for the organization to achieve its goals. When these values are clearly defined, they create a cohesive culture where inclusiveness is fostered, and all ideas are welcomed.

The value statement works hand in hand with the mission statement, which outlines the organization's purpose, objectives, and the approach it takes to accomplish those objectives. It also complements the vision statement, which paints a picture of the desired future state and explains why the organization provides its specific service.

When these three elements the mission, vision, and value statements are aligned, they provide a comprehensive framework that guides the development of a culture of innovation. They set the tone for how the organization operates, interacts, and embraces new ideas. By incorporating innovation as a core value, organizations can create an environment that encourages creativity, risk-taking, collaboration, and continuous improvement.

3. Incorporate the Core Competencies of Innovative Organizations

Innovative organizations understand the importance of attracting top talent with high-demand skills. While some professional development courses may cover these skills to some extent, organizations can reinforce the value of "innovation" as a cultural standard by offering programs that specifically focus on these core competencies. For example we run courses on design thinking, innovation, problem solving, creativity and decision making. We also run extended programs that start with a workshop but then go through an innovation process supported by coaching and mentoring, and culminating in teams presenting new ideas to the business having built the business case and visualised their concept.

Other topics that support innovation competencies include.

- **Resiliency:** Innovation requires individuals who can bounce back from setbacks
- **Agility:** Adapt to change and embrace a growth mindset.
- **Customer-centricity:** Innovation using feedback and evaluations from customers, driven by understanding their needs and preferences.
- **Inclusivity:** Creating an inclusive environment is vital for fostering diverse perspectives and driving innovation.
- **Collaboration and effective communication:** Innovation thrives when there is open and effective communication among team members.
- **Informed decision-making:** Innovation requires making informed decisions based on data and insights.
- **Results-driven:** By emphasizing the value of tangible results, organizations can motivate employees to take ownership of their work and strive for innovative solutions.

By offering programs that specifically target these core competencies, organizations demonstrate their commitment to valuing and nurturing innovation as a cultural standard. These initiatives not only attract top talent but also empower existing employees to embrace the right mindset.

4. Emphasize a Sense of Purpose in the Culture

The desire for authentic purpose in their work is a fundamental need shared by employees at all levels within the organization. However, recent data from a Gallup poll conducted between July and September 2020 reveals a concerning trend. The poll indicated that 51 percent of workers reported being "not engaged" at work, expressing a lack of psychological attachment to their work and company.

By leveraging the values outlined in the organization's value statement and combining them with the "what we can do better" approach, teams have the potential to fulfil employees' need for purpose and facilitate their professional growth.

5. Change the Method of Discussing Ideas

Intentional communication strategies play a vital role in fostering innovation. It is common for discussions to revolve around why an idea might not work or the past failures associated with it. Sometimes, conversations even deviate into listing inhibiting factors, which can hinder progress and creativity. However, by shifting the focus to the "what we can do better" approach, inhibiting factors can be debunked and disregarded when necessary.

Changing the way new ideas are discussed is key. Instead of starting from a place of "we can't do that," teams can adopt a mindset of "how might we do that?" This shift in perspective allows for exploration and encourages the consideration of potential ideas and their benefits.

In the traditional conversational pathway, discussions often focus on the obstacles and limitations, leading to a stagnant and risk-averse mentality. On the other hand, in a culture of innovation, conversations are guided by a mindset that embraces continuous improvement and encourages creative thinking. This pathway facilitates a positive and open exchange of ideas, enabling teams to explore new possibilities and drive innovation forward.

If you have always done it that way, it is probably wrong

Charles Kettering

What Can You Do To Be the One?

So if it is true that the ripple of culture change starts with a single pebble… why not be that pebble?

Be someone's wing person: Take the initiative to encourage others to share their ideas for improving existing services or processes. Create a safe and supportive environment where individuals feel comfortable expressing their thoughts and suggestions.

Share ideas and listen: Actively participate in sharing your own ideas both within and outside the organization. Engage in meaningful conversations and listen attentively to the suggestions and insights of others. Embrace the power of collaboration and diverse perspectives.

Consider the impact on reputation: When discussing potential innovations, emphasize how they can positively influence the organization's reputation. By highlighting the connection between innovation and organizational success, you can inspire others to contribute and support innovative initiatives.

Utilize intentional communication frameworks: Introduce and share communication frameworks that promote open and constructive discussions. These frameworks help guide conversations, ensure all perspectives are heard, and provide a structured approach to address inhibitors or challenges. Additionally, hold separate follow-up discussions to allow ideas to develop and gain input from all team members.

Encourage creative thinking: Empower your team to think creatively without reservations. Create forums or platforms where ideas can be shared freely, knowing that decisions will not be made immediately. This encourages a sense of psychological safety and encourages innovative thinking to flourish.

Successful organizations with strong cultures of innovation share one common factor: they embrace the notion that anyone who is interested can contribute to finding solutions. Collaboration between strategists, creative thinkers, and effective communicators is key to unlocking potential.

REFLECTION SECTION

Here are ten questions to ponder, take your time and brainstorm…
better still do it with your team!

1. How clearly do you define your goals and align your team's
    efforts?
2. How do you encourage out-of-the-box thinking and value
    unconventional ideas?
3. How actively do you seek and value your employees' opinions
    and input?
4. How often do you conduct innovation workshops to develop
    mindset and involve everyone?
5. What fun idea challenges could you create to encourage idea
    sharing and participation?
6. How do you recognize and reward innovative behaviour to
    motivate your team.
7. How does your team provide constructive feedback to each
    other, to refine ideas and promote learning?
8. What do you do to foster an entrepreneurial mindset among
    your employees?
9. What can you do to minimize bureaucracy and support rapid
    experimentation?
10. What can you do to encourage collaboration and break down
    silos within the organization?

REMEMBER: You can visit www.Everyday-Transformation.com
for the **Transformation Insight Assessment™** which includes
more questions to guide you.

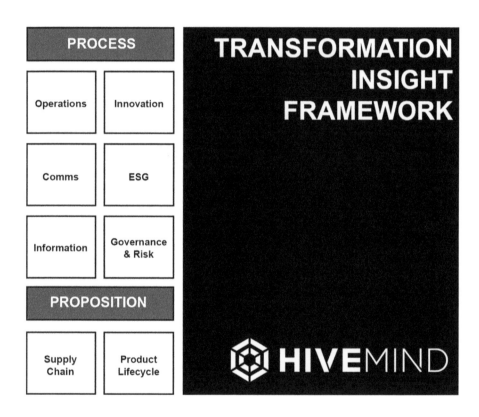

PROCESS ALIGNMENT

How Effective Processes Drive Business Success

Processes are the backbone of any successful organization. They provide structure and control, and help ensure that tasks are completed efficiently and effectively. However, not all processes are created equal. In order to truly drive business success, processes must be designed with specific goals and objectives in mind, and continually evaluated and refined to ensure that they are meeting these objectives.

In relation to the quote above, if you can't describe your activity as a process, then it is almost impossible to teach, replicate and measure. In this section of the book we are going to both talk about process as a topic, as well as introduce you to several processes in their own right for navigating digital transformation, identifying process improvement opportunities, process planning and even a framework for effective communication.

The beauty of a good process is that it manages expectations and creates certainty. The simple act of applying a framework, or methodology or structured approach to doing literally anything, has many benefits, not least though is that it helps you visualise an outcome.

Another key benefit of effective processes is that they help to reduce errors and mistakes. By providing clear guidance on how work should be done, processes help to ensure that tasks are completed accurately and consistently, reducing the likelihood of errors that can lead to costly rework or customer complaints. In addition, processes can also help to identify potential issues before they become problems, allowing businesses to take proactive steps to address them and minimize their impact.

Effective processes can also help to streamline workflows and reduce costs. By eliminating unnecessary steps or tasks, businesses can focus on the most important tasks and complete them more quickly and effectively.

"

If you can't describe what you are doing as a process, you don't know what you're doing

W. Edwards Deming

This can help to reduce overheads and increase productivity, allowing businesses to invest more resources into growth and development.

By providing a consistent level of quality and service, businesses can build a strong reputation for reliability and professionalism, which can help to attract and retain satisfied customers in a competitive marketplace.

However, in order to truly drive business success, processes must be continually evaluated and refined. This requires ongoing analysis and feedback from employees and stakeholders, as well as a commitment to continuous improvement and innovation. Businesses must be willing to create a culture where everyone can challenge the status quo, and constantly look for ways to improve their processes and systems.

One way to achieve this is through the use of process mapping and process improvement methodologies such as Lean Six Sigma. By mapping out the various steps and components of a process, businesses can identify areas for improvement and make data-driven decisions about how to optimize their processes.

Process Improvement is the Catalyst for Digital Transformation

Organizations struggle with digital transformation because it is such a big topic, broader than just process improvement. It requires scrutinizing all areas of the enterprise and asking 'Is there a better way of doing this?', and being prepared to fundamentally change how the organization operates.

As previously discussed, whilst digital transformation may seem like it's just about technology, the transformation that matters most is at a strategic level. **Everyday Transformation™** requires embracing new ways of working that leverage advancements in disciplines like artificial intelligence, process automation and data management. But also reporting structures, communication flow and customer engagement.

Taking the First Steps

So how can you avoid the pitfalls and minimise mistakes? One way is by prioritising process improvement as the main catalyst for change. Digital transformation expects the automation of potentially thousands of processes (depending on company size, number of customer propositions and complexity of your deliverables), so it makes perfect sense to use a process-based approach for strategic change and decision-making. So many process automation tools have emerged in recent years that build and adapt processes quickly to eliminate superfluous steps, inefficiencies and deliver improvements to operational performance.

This is one of the areas that we love the most when working with clients. Guiding teams from all parts of the organization, bottom to top, on how to identify improvement opportunities, ideate, research and prototype. The satisfaction people experience when they discover new and improved ways to deliver is palpable. New revenues, cost savings, efficiency gains and better customer (internal or external) are just some of the potential upsides.

Catalyst for Change

According to the 2018 AIIM study, 67% of organizations report having less than half of their processes automated. If this is true today, there should be plenty of opportunity. Better still we can start by prioritising the more important processes that drive performance and potentially offer the most return on investment.

According to the AIIM research, the prime targets for early productivity gains could be internal departments like Finance, Operations and Human Resources. But strategically, externally focussed departments like sales (34%), customer correspondence (32%), on-boarding (23%), new account opening (23%), and case management (26%) etc. may provide the more competitive benefits.

Process Transformation vs. Business Process Improvement

Process transformation and business process improvement (BPI) are two related but distinct concepts in the realm of process management.

BPI is the act of analysing and modifying an existing process to make it more efficient, effective, and adaptable. The goal of BPI is to optimize the process within the existing framework to improve outcomes such as cost, quality, or customer satisfaction. BPI can involve small, incremental changes or larger, more transformative improvements, but it generally operates within the boundaries of the existing process.

Business process improvement can be seen as a part of the business transformation. It has a limited focus on identifying areas to implement changes, such as

- Standardization of existing process

- Changing business process model

- Improving key performance indicators like cost reduction for example

Process transformation, on the other hand, is a more radical and comprehensive approach to process management. It involves reimagining and redesigning an existing process from the ground up, often with the goal of achieving a fundamental shift in the way the organization operates. Process transformation can involve changes to the technology, people, and culture of an organization, and it often requires a significant investment of time, resources, and leadership commitment.

- Produce better business outcomes

- Create new processes

- Accelerate business growth

- Deliver increased value to customers

- Improve digital experience.

Transformation statistics indicate that process transformation can boost business growth by

- Improving operational efficiency by 40%,

- Providing agility in the market by 36%,

- Increasing revenue by 56%,

- Reducing additional cost by up to 20%.

In essence, while BPI seeks to improve the performance of a current process, process transformation seeks to create a new process that better aligns with the organization's goals and objectives. Process transformation is often seen as a more disruptive and ambitious approach, while BPI is seen as a more pragmatic and incremental one.

Where Are the Key Benefits to Process Improvement?

Pretty much every process change initiative is going to require an investment of both time and money, however, the ROI can be rapid, with most efforts repaid at the revenue and transaction cost level. When we examine closely, we can identify key areas that sum up the main benefits that result from pursuing a digital process approach... Starting with humans.

Improved Employee Experience

Over time, work structures change, largely influenced by the introduction of the new products and services you deliver, and the tools and technology you use to deliver them. On top of this you might spread your wings into new markets or adopt new working practices (think remote working during the pandemic for example). The first consideration for any process should be to the humans involved in its execution.

Here are some considerations that impact the employee experience specifically.

- **Access from everywhere** - Do you use a corporate VPN? Do you make it easy for people to access the systems and do their part?

- **Adequate support** - Do you have responsive remote support services so people are not left frustrated when their own efficiency is impacted?

- **Agile working practices** - This could include smart working hours, new collaboration tools to keep a team united (especially when working remote).

- **Digital Academy** - As previously discussed, a key to retaining top talent is your commitment to upskilling. An online academy and forum for sharing knowledge for all employees no matter where they are working is a good strategy.

A reminder... systems, structures and processes create behaviours and impact culture!

Processes are a fundamental component of how organizations operate, and they can have a significant impact on employee behaviour and organizational performance.

Well-designed processes can create positive behaviours, such as increased efficiency, better communication, and improved decision-making. For example, a well-designed hiring process can help to attract and select the best candidates for a job, while a well-designed sales process can help to close deals more quickly and effectively.

Conversely, poorly designed or implemented processes can create negative behaviours, such as frustration, resistance, and disengagement. For example, a poorly designed customer service process can result in long wait times, frustrated customers, and disengaged employees. Or if you aspire to develop a more agile culture but budget sign off for small projects take too long, then you can't realistically expect your people to identify as agile.

Processes can also influence the culture of an organization, shaping employee attitudes and behaviours. For example, a process that emphasizes collaboration and teamwork can foster a culture of trust and mutual support, while a process that prioritizes individual achievement and competition can create a more cut-throat culture.

It is essential to design and implement processes that support positive behaviours and the organizational culture you desire. By creating processes that are well-designed, efficient, and effective, organizations can improve employee engagement, customer satisfaction, and overall performance.

Improved Customer Experience

Another area we work on with our clients is in the mapping of the customer journey. This means tracking the entire consumer experience from the first contact with the brand as a prospect, through to purchase, onboarding, and ongoing support. Of course, this will differ significantly from one sector to another, but there are consistent steps:

Identification of individual touchpoints – When and why do you as an organization come into direct contact with prospective or existing customers? Whether that is simply a marketing message, to digital customer services, or a physical interaction. Journey mapping is about empathising with the customer, identifying critical issues and desired output for each individual touchpoint.

Multichannel and omnichannel dimensions – Multichannel and omnichannel are two terms used in the context of marketing and customer experience. Both terms refer to the different channels through which a business interacts with its customers, but they have different dimensions and implications.

Multichannel refers to a business's use of multiple channels (such as email, phone, social media, and in-person interactions) to communicate with its customers. In a multichannel strategy, each channel is managed independently, and the customer experience may differ depending on which channel the customer uses to interact with the business. For example, a customer may receive different information or offers on the business's website compared to what they receive through social media or email.

Omnichannel, on the other hand, refers to a seamless, integrated customer experience across all channels. In an omnichannel strategy, the business integrates all its channels to provide a consistent and cohesive customer experience, regardless of which channel the customer uses to interact with the business. This means that the customer can move between channels without any disruption to their experience, and the business has a unified view of the customer across all channels. For example, a customer might start a purchase on the business's website, receive a confirmation email, and then receive personalized follow-up messages through social media or phone.

While multichannel and omnichannel both involve the use of multiple channels to communicate with customers, the key difference is that omnichannel aims to provide a seamless and integrated experience across all channels, while multichannel does not necessarily prioritize integration and consistency.

Information transparency – helping customers significantly reduce frustrations when they need help or more information through the use of chatbots, effective FAQs, tutorials or easy access to a human being.

Digitization and digitalization have introduced many changes in the way we interact with customers. Whilst savings might have been made or processes became more efficient... they don't necessarily best serve the customer.

The Other Benefits can be Summarised in the Following:

Increased efficiency: By streamlining a process and eliminating unnecessary steps or tasks, process improvement can make it faster and more efficient. This can result in cost savings, faster turnaround times, and increased productivity.

Improved quality: Process improvement can help identify and eliminate errors and defects in a process, leading to higher quality outputs and increased customer satisfaction.

Greater consistency: By standardizing a process and ensuring that everyone follows the same steps, process improvement can help achieve greater consistency in the outputs, reducing variation and increasing predictability.

Increased agility: A well-designed process can be more flexible and adaptable, allowing the organization to respond quickly to changing circumstances and customer needs.

Better communication and collaboration: Process improvement can help break down silos and promote cross-functional collaboration, leading to better communication and more efficient problem-solving.

Reduced risk: By identifying and addressing potential risks in a process, process improvement can help reduce the likelihood of errors, accidents, or other negative outcomes.

Best Practices

Organizations from across all industries or professions are finding success using process improvement as the primary catalyst for change. The Everyday Transformation™ approach to process improvement/ transformation gives consideration to these best practices.

1. **Development must be led by process owners**

   The most knowledgeable people in your business, best placed to describe the current state and desired future state are your existing process owners. They will understand the nuances as to why certain things are done in certain ways and address the gaps in the performance. Don't get us wrong, technologists are essential for success, as is strong support at the executive level, but experience tells us empowered process owners ultimately design better solutions, are invested in the outcome, and embrace change more enthusiastically.

2. **Engage ALL Stakeholders**

   In addition to the process owners, in order to reduce future resistance and tap into the 'why' of the process, you should consult all stakeholders. This means your customers, suppliers, distributors, and all others who are part of the function of the process. After all, they have a direct influence on the process performance and a vested interest in the changes and improvements made to the workflow.

3. Where possible seek solutions that allow for agility

We have made the case for business agility earlier in this book. But due to the rapid nature of change (market, workforce, technology), you need to design an approach that allows you to adapt quickly to change and new opportunities. Clunky and overly complicated solutions often slow things down, causing inertia and a loss of focus.

4. Look for low-code BPA solutions

We will take a look at business process automation tools shortly, but there are a number of new options rising to meet the challenge of process transformation. Solutions that enable organizations to seamlessly deploy digital processes without any coding and very little support from technology departments. According to recent research from Forrester, 67% of the organizations they surveyed plan to expand the use of low-code process tools. Our best advice is to seek solutions that are flexible, agile enough to replicate across other processes that may be related or similar, and have the ability to scale.

5. Don't rush the requirements gathering process

Let's face it, there are so many different possible approaches to transformation, as well as technologies to support it. So how do you identify the best methodology for the task? One area we always encourage clients to focus on, is creating a comprehensive brief from the outset. i.e. take the time to fully explore and understand your requirements. Does your solution need to be on site or can you use cloud? Are you prioritising simplicity or ease of use, or are you focusing on expanding features and capacity? What about mobile solutions or other emerging technology?

6. Share best practice

Prioritizing a process-focused approach allows organizations to make faster gains by capitalising on the new learning and experience obtained in every process improvement effort and applying to other key processes. Thus creating a central resource for all process owners across the organization, sharing best practice and insight, and with buy in from leadership.

How can **Everyday Transformation™** in the Form of Process Automation Be Introduced?

Introducing new process automation technology to your company can be very intimidating at first with the sheer variety of options on the market. It's easy to get carried away and want to implement changes all at once, but it is important not to try and eat the elephant all in one go. In other words, it's a mistake to try and take on everything at once, because it will be impossible to accomplish given the reality of the resources at your disposal. A more realistic approach is to eat the elephant one bite at a time, working to a realistic delivery timetable and taking a systematic approach.

The next step is to identify what you need to do the job. Broadly speaking there are four types of automation technology, Workflow, RPA, DPA, and BPM, and there are overlaps between them all in functionality. So let's take a brief look at what each of them do;

Workflows – In the context of process automation, workflows refer to the automated sequence of steps or tasks (often within a single system) that are designed to achieve a specific outcome or goal. They help organizations to streamline processes and improve efficiency. Most applications today come with workflows included, although there are many 3rd-party applications that specialise, specifically on workflows.

For example, workflows within your enterprise resource planning system (ERP) can take a purchase order input and automatically process the order, generate an invoice, and update stock levels. But the important thing to remember is that the workflow does not facilitate the overall end-to-end process, which will likely begin and end well outside the scope of the workflow.

RPA – RPA stands for Robotic Process Automation and is a type of process automation that uses software robots to automate repetitive and rule-based tasks. It can be used to automate a wide range of tasks, such as customer onboarding, accounts payable, data extraction, and report generation, among others. By automating these tasks, organizations can increase efficiency, reduce errors, and save time and money.

RPA tools are designed to be user-friendly and do not require programming skills to use. They can be easily configured to automate specific tasks and can be integrated with existing systems and software. Another main advantage is that it is quite easy to quickly ramp up your bot-workforce. Although a downside to this is that RPA bots have no connection to your process, therefore any upstream changes to your processes or applications (even a simple software update) can render your bots useless. It is almost easier to think of RPA as RTA... Robotic Task Automation, because there is no process governance behind RPA.

DPA – Digital Process Automation is a comprehensive approach to automating business processes that goes beyond Workflows or RPA. DPA uses digital technologies such as artificial intelligence (AI), machine learning (ML), natural language processing (NLP), and robotic process automation (RPA) to automate complex business processes that involve multiple steps and interactions. By its very nature, DPA must be a 3rd-party application that connects to all the existing systems and internally manage the process, tasks, and data.

DPA enables organizations to automate end-to-end processes that involve both humans and machines, such as customer service, supply chain management, and order fulfilment, among others. DPA focuses on optimizing processes to improve business outcomes such as cost savings, efficiency, and customer satisfaction.

In the purchase-order example above, DPA would begin with the start of the process, perhaps the identification of the need for a specific part number, and would navigate the process through approvals, order creation, and receiving; perhaps interfacing with the ERP, CRM, and financial systems along the way.

BPM – Business Process Management includes DPA; and adds a layer of process modelling, management, and governance over the automation. Unlike the other technologies mentioned here, BPM is more than the technology, it is a discipline for process management and continuous improvement that utilises technology as a method to achieve process excellence.

BPM typically involves several key steps, including:

- **Process identification:** identifying the processes within an organization that need improvement.

- **Process analysis:** analysing the current processes to identify inefficiencies and opportunities for improvement.

- **Process redesign:** redesigning the processes to remove inefficiencies and improve effectiveness.

- **Process implementation:** implementing the new processes and monitoring their performance.

- **Process monitoring:** continuously monitoring the processes to ensure they continue to perform effectively and efficiently.

Without BPM, your processes and your automation are two separate entities; one managed by the business and one managed by IT. BPM unites these two, so that your processes and your automation are always in sync. Of course, you can use a BPM application only for DPA, but you cannot use a DPA application for BPM.

Process management is an essential practice to have in any organization – without it, a company will be too slow to manage all the tasks they need to complete. A robust process governance system allows for efficiency among people, processes, and platforms across all industries to ensure maximum productivity gains and competitive advantage across all operations, while also delivering an improved customer experience.

It is also important to remember that the four types of automation technologies listed above, can complement each other. Knowing when to use each approach is vital for maximising return on investment and keeping companies running efficiently.

Mapping the Process

Whenever we work with clients on transformation projects, it starts with a discovery phase, during which we begin by mapping the current state of the company's strategic processes with the ultimate objective to eventually automate and simplify them.

Simply mapping the processes can allow organizations to discover the blind spots they were ignorant of and make small adjustments that can potentially have a large impact. Process mapping involves creating a visual representation of a business process using diagrams and symbols to illustrate the steps, inputs, outputs, and decisions involved in the process. The purpose of process mapping is to document the current process, identify inefficiencies and opportunities for improvement, and develop a plan for optimizing the process. Process mapping is typically a manual process that involves interviewing process stakeholders and analysing data to create the process map.

Process mining, on the other hand, involves using specialized software tools to analyze and visualize the digital traces of the process that are

DISCOVERY PHASE

 HIVEMIND

STAGE ONE

DEFINE THE SCOPE

Identify the specific areas of the organization that need to be transformed and the expected outcomes.

CURRENT STATE ANALYSIS

Evaluate current digital capabilities, technology infrastructure, processes, and systems. Identify gaps.

STAKEHOLDER ANALYSIS

Identify all stakeholders who will be affected, including customers, employees, partners, and suppliers.

STAGE TWO

DEVELOP VISION AND STRATEGY

Based on the assessment and analysis, develop a vision and strategy. Include specific goals, objectives & roadmap.

BENCHMARK ANALYSIS

Identify metrics for comparison, select partners (industry, size, geography and digital capabilities).

IDENTIFY KEY DRIVERS

Customer expectations, competitive pressures, regulatory requirements, and technology advancements.

STAGE THREE

DEFINE GOVERNANCE MODEL

Outline stakeholder roles, including decision-making processes, communication channels, and performance metrics.

IDENTIFY RESOURCES REQUIRED

Identify the resources required for success, including budget, personnel, technology infrastructure, and training.

RISK MANAGEMENT PLAN

Identify all potential risks and develop a risk management plan to mitigate those risks.

captured in event logs or data from IT systems. The purpose of process mining is to identify the actual process flow, uncover process bottlenecks and inefficiencies, and make data-driven recommendations for process improvement. Process mining is typically an automated process that uses data analytics and machine learning algorithms to analyze the event logs and generate process models.

Here is a real-world example of a process mapping case study:

A major telecommunications company (who shall remain nameless) was experiencing issues with its customer service process, resulting in high call volumes, long wait times, and low customer satisfaction. The company decided to use process mapping to identify inefficiencies and streamline the process.

The process mapping team started by interviewing customer service representatives and analysing call data to identify the steps involved in the process. They then created a process map that illustrated each step in the process, including the inputs, outputs, and decision points.

The process map revealed several inefficiencies, including redundant steps, unclear decision points, and inconsistent communication channels. The team used this information to develop a redesigned process that eliminated unnecessary steps, clarified decision points, and streamlined communication channels.

The redesigned process included a new triage system that allowed calls to be routed to the appropriate representative based on the customer's needs, reducing wait times and increasing the likelihood of resolving issues on the first call. The new process also included standardized scripts and communication channels, ensuring consistent and clear communication with customers.

The company implemented the new process and monitored its performance using customer satisfaction surveys and call data analysis. The results were significant, with call volumes decreasing by 25%, wait times decreasing by 50%, and customer satisfaction increasing by 20%. The process mapping approach allowed the telecommunications company to identify inefficiencies and develop a streamlined, customer-centric process that improved customer satisfaction and reduced costs.

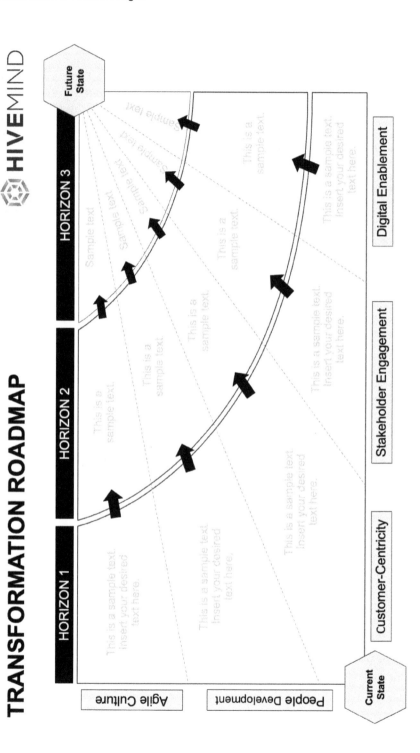

What Is a Digital Transformation Roadmap?

According to Gartner, 91% of organizations are engaged in some form of digital initiative. However, when a business works on digital projects, it does not necessarily mean that they are digitally transforming. Realizing the difference between digital optimization and transformation is key in determining your company's digital transformation roadmap.

So, what exactly is a digital transformation roadmap? In simple terms, it is a strategic plan that sets a clear goal or desired outcome and outlines the major steps or milestones necessary to achieve it. The roadmap encompasses all the essential details to ensure a successful digital transformation, including the existing and new technology, the people involved in facilitating the transformation, and the relevant processes.

Beyond being a guiding document, the digital transformation roadmap serves as a communication tool, articulating the strategic thinking behind both the goal and the plan to accomplish it.

Having a well-defined digital transformation roadmap offers several advantages. It prepares your organization to handle urgent needs for rapid transformation, as exemplified during events like the 2020 pandemic. Additionally, it enables your company to keep pace with digital trends and adapt to new digital tools and changes. Moreover, the roadmap provides critical information for updating software, digital tools, and other technological aspects, ensuring your organization remains technologically relevant.

To create a digital transformation roadmap, you must first understand where digital transformation fits within your organization. Assess its significance, the impact of not keeping up with digital trends, and identify departments that require continuous digital updates. This is especially crucial in today's age, where almost every business operates digitally.

A comprehensive digital transformation roadmap includes the following elements:

1. An inventory of current technology, software, and digital tools used in each department, along with their lifecycle and usage.

2. Identification of current challenges your organization faces with existing tools, addressing them in order of urgency and priority.

3. Opportunities to implement new technologies and digital tools, aligning them with current digital trends.

4. Forward-thinking considerations, such as the investment required in new technologies and the potential for rapid replacements. Map out timelines and lifecycles of the intended tools.

5. Clear objectives for the use of new tools, including assigning responsibilities for troubleshooting, updates, and overall management.

6. Key milestones on the roadmap leading up to the implementation of new digital tools.

These aspects provide an overview of your digital journey. It's essential to remember that a digital transformation roadmap is a dynamic tool that evolves as you progress through your digital transformation journey. As you reach one point (point B) in the roadmap, it's time to start planning for the next (point C), and so on.

To ensure that major objectives are met, utilize the roadmap as a communication tool within your organization. Share the details with all stakeholders involved in the digital transformation, enabling them to understand their roles, create timelines, and manage the overall project effectively.

Sharing the roadmap with the leadership team ensures their support and guidance throughout the process. Successful implementation relies on transparent communication among stakeholders and the inclusion of relevant details to ensure the plan is clear and transparent. With a well-structured digital transformation roadmap, your organization can confidently navigate the digital terrain and thrive in the digital era.

DOWNLOAD: You can visit www.Everyday-Transformation.com to get the **Transformation Roadmap** template to guide you thought your 3 horizons.

Creating the Conditions for Innovation

As mentioned previously it requires cultivating a culture that fosters creativity, risk-taking, and open communication.

Strong leadership support is crucial in driving innovation and setting the tone for the entire organization. Clear goals and objectives align innovation efforts with the company's overall strategy, providing a sense of purpose and direction. Diversity and inclusivity in teams bring together different perspectives and skills, fuelling creativity and fostering broader insights.

Allocating sufficient resources, time, and budget for innovation projects allows for experimentation and iterative development. A learning culture encourages continuous growth and the acquisition of new knowledge and skills. Collaboration across departments and the formation of cross-functional teams can spark collaborative thinking and foster innovative solutions.

Recognizing and rewarding innovative efforts motivates employees to think outside the box and take calculated risks. Embracing failure as an opportunity for learning encourages a healthy attitude towards experimentation. Providing easy access to relevant data and information empowers employees to make informed decisions and identify potential opportunities for innovation.

By combining these elements, organizations can create an environment where innovation thrives, leading to sustainable growth and a competitive edge in the market.

Convergent Thinking Vs Divergent Thinking

Convergent thinking and divergent thinking are two cognitive processes that play essential roles in problem-solving and creativity.

Convergent thinking refers to the ability to narrow down and focus on finding a single, correct solution or answer to a specific problem or question. It involves logical reasoning, deduction, and using existing knowledge to arrive at the most appropriate solution. Convergent thinking is often used in situations where there is a well-defined problem with a clear goal and limited potential solutions. It is commonly associated with standardized tests and academic assessments that require selecting the right answer from a set of choices.

On the other hand, divergent thinking is a thought process that involves exploring multiple possible solutions or ideas in an open-ended and creative manner. It encourages free-flowing and unconstrained thinking, generating a wide range of possibilities, associations, and perspectives. Divergent thinking is a key component of creativity, as it allows individuals to think outside the box, consider unconventional approaches, and come up with innovative solutions to complex problems. It is often used in brainstorming sessions, creative exercises, and ideation processes, where the goal is to generate as many ideas as possible without judgment.

Both convergent and divergent thinking have their place in the innovation process...

*The purpose
of Innovation
Management is
not to promote
innovation, but to
manage innovation
as a process*

Pearl Zhu

...But Let's Not Confuse Creativity With Innovation

Creativity and innovation are related concepts, but they are distinct from each other. Creativity refers to the ability to generate new and novel ideas, solutions, or concepts. It involves thinking outside the box, making connections between seemingly unrelated things, and coming up with original and imaginative concepts. Creativity is about the generation of ideas, regardless of their practicality or implementation.

On the other hand, innovation is the process of turning creative ideas into practical and valuable solutions that bring about positive change. It involves taking the creative ideas and applying them in a real-world context to create something new, useful, and impactful. Innovation requires not only creativity but also execution and implementation to bring the ideas to life and create value for customers, organizations, or society as a whole.

Innovation Management

Innovation management is the systematic and strategic approach that organizations adopt to foster creativity, generate new ideas, and successfully implement innovative solutions in the form of new products, services, or business models. It involves guiding the entire innovation process, starting from idea generation to the practical implementation of these ideas in the market. This strategic discipline involves the decisions, activities, and practices aimed at formulating and executing an innovation strategy.

To bring in new business models and introduce new products and services to the market, organizations need to focus on various aspects of innovation management. This includes developing a deep understanding of customer needs, market trends, and technological advancements. Additionally, firms must encourage a culture of innovation within their teams, enabling employees to think creatively and contribute novel ideas.

As described by Gartner, innovation management constitutes a crucial business discipline that seeks to foster a sustainable culture of innovation within an organization. In many instances, these initiatives employ disruptive methods of change to drive transformative shifts in the business landscape.

Due to the drivers of change we have already discussed in this book, organizations face a compelling need to innovate rapidly and effectively.

HIVEMIND

INNOVATION MATRIX

	SOLUTIONS	
	Existing	New
CUSTOMER (INTERNAL/EXTERNAL) — New	**RADICAL INNOVATION** Technology breakthrough that transforms the environment (12-18 months)	**DISRUPTIVE INNOVATION** New business model that disrupts the market (18+ months)
CUSTOMER (INTERNAL/EXTERNAL) — Existing	**INCREMENTAL INNOVATION** Create a better version of the past by going digital (0-6 months)	**SUSTAINING INNOVATION** Better performing solutions to sustain the market position (0-12 months)

This innovation is the driving force behind business growth and a key differentiator in remaining competitive. By managing innovation effectively, organizations can generate new business models and create products, services, and technologies that cater to the evolving market demands. Furthermore, adept innovation management can enhance customer satisfaction and elevate employee engagement levels.

In the realm of innovation management, various methods can be classified into four primary categories: incremental, sustainable, radical, and disruptive.

Incremental innovation plays a pivotal role in enabling businesses to continuously adapt and flourish. By making constant improvements to existing products, services, processes, or methods, organizations can stay competitive in today's rapidly evolving landscape.

Sustainable innovation, on the other hand, revolves around significant technological advancements that propel a product or service far ahead of its competitors within an established category. This level of innovation can create a substantial competitive advantage.

Radical innovation are transformative ideas capable of fundamentally reshaping market dynamics upon implementation. These game-changing concepts revolutionize industries and often lead to entirely new ways of conducting business.

Lastly, **Disruptive innovation** is an invention that destroys or supplants an existing business model. Unlike architectural or incremental innovation, radical innovation blows up the existing system or process and replaces it with something entirely new.

Achieving success in innovation management requires fostering an innovation-driven culture within the company and recognizing the value of employees' contributions. By doing so, employees are motivated to generate high-quality ideas, leading to a virtuous cycle of innovation.

Modern organizations are harnessing the power of collaborative technology, such as social networking platforms, to facilitate feedback gathering. This approach ensures a continuous influx of ideas from both internal and external stakeholders, enriching the innovation process.

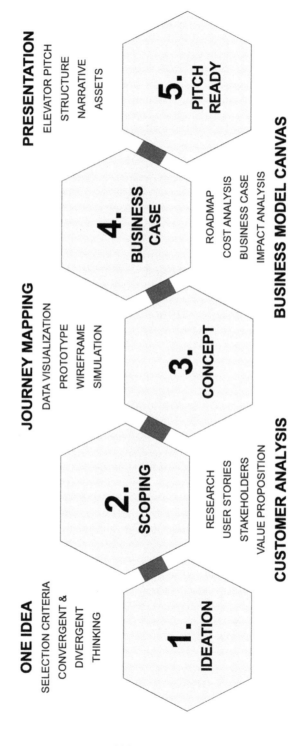

INNOVATION MANAGEMENT SYSTEM

HIVEMIND

ONE IDEA
SELECTION CRITERIA
CONVERGENT & DIVERGENT THINKING

1. IDEATION

CUSTOMER ANALYSIS
RESEARCH
USER STORIES
STAKEHOLDERS
VALUE PROPOSITION

2. SCOPING

JOURNEY MAPPING
DATA VISUALIZATION
PROTOTYPE
WIREFRAME
SIMULATION

3. CONCEPT

BUSINESS MODEL CANVAS
ROADMAP
COST ANALYSIS
BUSINESS CASE
IMPACT ANALYSIS

4. BUSINESS CASE

PRESENTATION
ELEVATOR PITCH
STRUCTURE
NARRATIVE
ASSETS

5. PITCH READY

Establishing Innovation Management as an Integral Part of the Business

Many companies adopt a structured and iterative approach, beginning with the crucial step of ideation, where a diverse range of ideas are generated. Incentives and constructive feedback mechanisms further encourage a consistent flow of innovative concepts.

Subsequently, the process moves on to identifying the most promising ideas that align with the company's objectives and have the potential for successful implementation. The selected ideas are then transformed into prototype products or services, providing tangible representations of their feasibility and value.

The final stage involves full-scale implementation, where the chosen innovations are integrated into the company's operations. It is imperative to carefully evaluate the outcomes against the intended business goals to assess the effectiveness of the implemented ideas.

By following this disciplined and cyclical approach to innovation management, organizations can enhance their ability to drive meaningful change and achieve sustainable growth.

Involving the C-suite and senior leadership in discussions about innovation management is vital to ensure that the generated ideas align with the overall business goals and strategic direction of the organization. Also by involving them you can secure the necessary support, resources, and alignment needed to drive successful initiatives.

As innovation becomes a core component of business success, organizations are recognizing the need for dedicated managers or teams. These professionals possess specific skills and expertise to lead and facilitate the innovation management process effectively. Their roles encompass driving innovation culture, overseeing ideation, evaluating ideas, coaching, and guiding the implementation of innovative projects.

Innovation managers play a crucial role in promoting a collaborative and forward-thinking environment within the organization. They facilitate communication between various departments and stakeholders, ensuring that innovative ideas are explored, refined, and aligned with the company's strategic objectives.

Furthermore, these managers keep a keen eye on market trends, emerging technologies, and customer needs to identify opportunities for innovation and competitive advantage. By focusing on continuous improvement and fostering a culture of experimentation, innovation managers can help organizations stay ahead in today's dynamic business landscape.

Case Study – Let us give you a real example from one of our clients .

One programme we have had the pleasure to support over the last two years (still ongoing) is for a top consulting firm in the Middle East. Working with approx. 25 senior leaders at a time we have taken each cohort through a two-month process which starts with education, showing them the potential application of emerging technology, AI and automation tools and specific products like PowerBi or Alteryx for example.

Then they are guided through an ideation process which helps them to identify both internal and external opportunities to innovate. What to look for? Who to consult? Etc. Working in small teams, we then get them to challenge each other's assumptions and push the boundaries. But this is just the catalyst... From here we get them to land on one initiative to see through the process. We add a technologist to their team and begin the journey of building the business case with regular coaching check ins. A typical process will examine current state, benchmark best practice, perform a gap analysis, set the transformation strategy and build (and present) the business case. Often, we encourage building the prototype or at least some form of concept visualisation to help others understand the vision for the idea.

Out of this one programme delivered over 5 cohorts to 125+ senior leaders in 5 countries, we have seen internal process improvements, new client propositions, better knowledge management and analytics etc. Saving money through new efficiencies and making money from new revenue streams. The outcome certainly justifies the investment, but ultimately we create a new lens for participants to see their world ongoing... so innovation is normalised day to day.

Creating a New Standard for Innovation

The International Organization for Standardization (ISO) has taken a ground-breaking step by developing and publishing the world's first international standard for innovation management systems. This standard involves collaboration with around 50 participating countries, making it a global effort to promote systematic and purposeful innovation.

ISO 56002:2019, the Innovation Management System - Guidance, was published in July 2019 and comprises seven fundamental elements within its framework: context, leadership, planning, support, operations, evaluation, and improvement. This guidance document creates a shared language and credible reference framework for organizations worldwide. It outlines essential innovation management principles that provide managers with a clear understanding of the concept of innovation and the key components required to effectively manage innovation activities.

The system offers organizations a comprehensive and guiding framework to enhance their innovation capabilities. Irrespective of the type of company or organization, this standard serves as a valuable checklist based on a systems approach. It helps organizations identify and implement the most relevant practices to align with their unique innovation aspirations and existing capabilities.

One of the key advantages of this framework is its adaptability and generality. It does not prescribe specific tools or methods but instead provides a flexible structure that organizations can customize to suit their particular needs and context. This enables companies to foster innovation in a manner that aligns seamlessly with their strategic objectives and corporate culture.

It empowers them to systematically pursue and achieve their innovation goals, driving creativity and improvement repeatedly. As a result, organizations gain a competitive edge in today's rapidly evolving market landscape, propelling them towards sustained growth and success.

Adopting this standard empowers companies and organizations to adopt a systemic and systematic approach to address their innovation challenges, significantly enhancing their chances of success. The framework is designed to be compatible with and integrated into other management systems present within the organization, such as quality and environmental management systems. This integration ensures a cohesive and holistic approach to overall organizational management.

Furthermore, ISO 56002:2019 serves as a foundation for consultants and professionals offering innovation management services. It provides them with a structured and authoritative basis for guiding their clients in developing and implementing effective innovation strategies and practices.

"

With the right attitude, self-imposed limitations vanish

Alexander the Great

The Right Approach to Innovation Removing Self-Imposed Limitations

Over the previous chapters in this book, we have discussed many of the key attributes which ultimately result in the right cultural mindset for innovation. Topics like continuous learning, fostering collaboration and diversity, redefining success and failure, empowering people to take initiative are just a few areas to re-visit.

Whilst, not strictly a process, we thought it worth adding a couple more ideas around creating the right environment for innovation and wanted to start with the subject of self-imposed limitations. Self-imposed limitations can be pervasive and detrimental to both individuals and the organization as a whole. These limitations manifest as a result of ingrained beliefs, corporate culture, social conditioning and the pressure to conform to norms and expectations. They can hinder creativity, stifle innovation, and prevent employees from reaching their peak performance. Overcoming self-imposed limitations in a corporate context is essential to foster a culture of growth, resilience, and sustainable success.

We are reminded of the story we heard many years ago about the young girl watching her mother prepare the Sunday roast dinner. As the story goes, the Mother is about to put a Turkey in the oven and chops a bit from each end, before placing in a baking tray and then in the oven. As the little girl watches with curiosity and awe she does the one thing that all children do... constantly ask why!

"Why do you chop the end off, Mummy?" she asks.

"Because that is how we have always prepared the bird" her mum replies... "That's how your grandmother did it".

Not satisfied with the response, the little girl decides to enquire further with her grandmother. "Why do we chop the ends of the Turkey before putting it in the oven, Nanny?" Her grandmother initially looks confused, then realises what she is talking about.

"I used to do that years ago" she replies... "When my oven was too small". The lesson being that in life and in business, we form habits, or ways of working which if we just adopted the curiosity of a child and asked 'why?', we may discover that the routine no longer serves us.

One process we followed with a recent client demonstrated this very principle. One particular team was under enormous pressure to compile a monthly report which absorbed multiple man hours and involved several people to complete. Upon closer inspection we discovered that this report had become obsolete nearly two years prior, and no one had told them. Literally no one was reading it.

Breaking the chains of self-imposed limitations results in a workforce that is resilient, adaptable, and primed for success in an ever-changing corporate landscape. As leaders, it is our responsibility to foster an environment that empowers individuals to rise above limitations and unleash their true potential, benefitting both the individuals and the organization as a whole.

Thinking outside of the box is a phrase that encapsulates the ability to approach problems, challenges, and opportunities in a creative and innovative way. It means breaking away from conventional and traditional methods and daring to explore new and unconventional solutions. When individuals think outside of the box, they open themselves up to a world of possibilities and pave the way for ground-breaking ideas and transformative outcomes.

A dear friend to both Warrens' Barnaby Wynter shares a story of a design agency looking to outsource some of the creative work. One small boutique agency called 'Out of the Box Thinking' arrived to be interviewed. Barnaby's first question was, define the box? Several awkward minutes later they asserted there is no box.

Needless to say the interview didn't go well for them as Barnaby explained that out of the box thinking still requires a box as a reference point or context from which to depart. The "box" represents the established norms, rules, and limitations that govern traditional thinking or the status quo. It provides a framework for understanding the conventional ways of approaching problems and challenges. When we talk about thinking "outside the box," we are encouraging individuals to explore beyond these established boundaries and consider alternative perspectives and solutions.

Here are a few reasons why out of the box thinking still requires a box:

Breaking Away from the Familiar: The "box" serves as a familiar starting point for individuals to recognize what is considered standard or common. By understanding the conventional approaches within this box, individuals can then seek to break away from it and explore new territories.

Providing Context: The box provides context and a baseline understanding of the existing situation or problem. This context is essential for individuals to identify areas where innovative solutions are needed or where current approaches may be limiting.

Challenging Assumptions: To think outside the box, one must be aware of the assumptions that lie within it. By recognizing and challenging these assumptions, individuals can begin to question the validity of established norms and consider alternative viewpoints.

Setting Constraints: While thinking outside the box encourages creativity and exploration, setting certain constraints can be helpful. Constraints can focus thinking and creativity, preventing it from becoming too scattered or impractical.

Making Connections: Thinking outside the box often involves making connections between seemingly unrelated concepts or ideas. The box acts as a repository of knowledge and experience that individuals can draw from to create novel combinations.

Testing Feasibility: The box can also serve as a reality check. While thinking outside the box involves pushing boundaries, ideas must still be feasible and realistic to implement. The box helps individuals evaluate whether their innovative ideas can be practically applied.

Overcoming Resistance to Change: The box can represent the resistance to change or the status quo. By acknowledging these barriers, individuals can address them strategically when proposing novel solutions or innovative approaches.

By understanding the limitations of the box and challenging its boundaries, individuals can open themselves up to a world of possibilities and drive transformative change.

Design Thinking

Design Thinking is crucial for organizations driving through change or transformation in a business.

Design Thinking is a buzzword that you may well have come across. But is it an ideology, a methodology or a philosophy? Whilst you could say it's all three, it's actually a problem-solving approach, which allows teams to systematically identify their customers' issues and generate new opportunities to resolve them.

DESIGN THINKING PROCESS

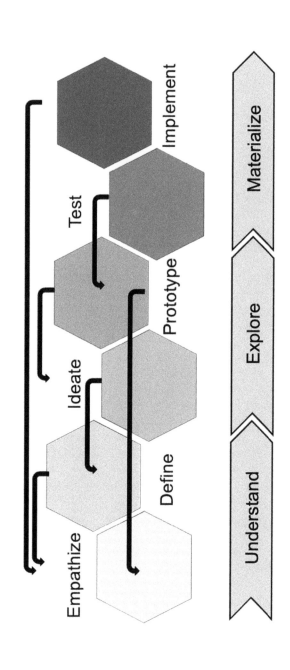

174

Think about it. Everything from a product to an experience can be designed to improve its quality for the end-user and reduce waste – to become more sustainable for both the business and the planet. And as customers become ever more savvy and aware that they can get similar, or even identical, products and services elsewhere, understanding their specific needs and designing user-centric solutions becomes ever more vital to business growth and sustainability.

So, Design Thinking is about solving problems in a user-centric way. It originated as the preserve of the UX team, but embedded across an organization, Design Thinking can help a business produce solutions to seemingly unsolvable issues. It draws on a whole team's imagination, intuition, logic, reasoning, and customer knowledge, promoting creativity and fostering a culture of innovation within the organization.

Design Thinking Origins

Design Thinking came into being as a way of taking the problem-solving methods designers use and applying them to areas designers don't usually get involved with – like organizational design or business or marketing issues. These areas, though not commonly involving the design team, can be resolved by 'thinking like a designer'. It's true; you don't have to be a designer to think like one, and whilst design skills need to be learned and practiced, Design Thinking draws on critical thinking and problem-solving skills which a professional team should already have in abundance. With a little guidance, everyone in an organization can adopt design techniques like observing, interviewing, storyboarding and persona building.

This approach helps a business to focus on its customers in all aspects of the business – offering huge value. It involves really getting to know your customers, so that every area of the business operates from a position of empathy with their wants and needs. By fully understanding its customers' 'pain points' a business can be redesigned around effectively meeting those needs at every point of interaction.

How does the Design Thinking process work?

Although the Design Thinking process can be broadly divided into six phases, the first thing to recognise is that it's not a linear process. A Design Thinking business culture will move backwards and forward, and around the phases – constantly evolving as more is learned about customer needs, and as those needs themselves evolve.

Phase 1 – Empathy

Developing true empathy with your customer involves getting to know and engaging with real people, to understand their needs and relationship with you – from an emotional perspective as well as a practical one. How you do this will depend on the nature of the business and the resources available, but it should ideally include a mix of quantitative data collection and analysis (which the business is hopefully already doing) and reviewing your regular customer feedback, alongside additional qualitative research like focus groups and interviews.

Phase 2 – Definition

Define the problem. Gathering all the insights collected in Phase 1 will allow the business to discover where customers may be coming up against barriers. Are there patterns in behaviour and interactions? Analysing the customer insights will reveal the big problems that the business needs to resolve. Always express that problem from a customer point of view – what is it that THEY want and need?

Phase 3 – Ideas

Once the problem is defined, the team can get to work coming up with ideas for solutions. This is the really creative part, and your Design Thinking workshops can use any number of techniques from brainstorming to storyboarding, role play to mind mapping. Whichever techniques your team uses, you may find it useful to engage someone from outside the business to facilitate this phase – as an objective external perspective often helps to unlock ideas and push beyond the obvious boundaries. Keep an open mind, and don't discard ideas too soon. Once the team has exhausted the creative possibilities, then it is time to whittle down the ideas into those to be taken through to Phase 4.

Top Success Tips for Idea Generation

Encourage the team to look forwards rather than backwards. "This is the way we've always done it" is one of the most dangerous phrases in the English language – it kills creativity stone dead!

Go somewhere that inspires thinking, learning and ideas.

Accept uncertainty. More answers will reveal themselves as the process unfolds (we will be talking about asking better questions shortly).

As ideas arise, allow them out of people's heads, whether through discussion, mind-mapping or whatever technique is being used. Treat every idea as a tangible thing and don't block its path, as you never know where it will lead.

Phase 4 – Prototype

In this phase, ideas are put to the test by becoming scaled down versions of a final product or service. Prototyping is crucial in order to stress-test those new products – highlighting any problems or flaws, as well as feasibility and viability.

Phase 5 – Test

This is where the process often becomes non-linear. As the business tests new products or services, it's common for the results to demand new prototyping, or even a return to Phase 3 to look at new ideas; or to Phase 2, to redefine the problem.

Phase 6 – Implement

During the implementation phase, it's time to consider a longer-term roadmap for your solution. With a clearer understanding of the solution's functionality, target audience, implementation process, and operation, you can now delve into more intricate questions, such as the implications of growth.

Design Thinking, Lean and Agile

We are often asked about how Design Thinking, Lean and Agile work together.

Now you know what Design Thinking is, and how it works, let's remind ourselves about 'Lean' and 'Agile', and look at how the three practices work together.

Lean focusses on streamlining processes as much as possible, to minimise waste and achieve maximum value. It relies on collaboration between several business functions – chiefly design, marketing and management, and involves gathering feedback as you go, so everyone is constantly learning and adapting. Lean focuses less on long-term deliverables and more on making quick decisions in order to enable rapid delivery. So the whole team needs to be engaged and involved.

AGILE works in incremental cycles, and is flexible and adaptive. In order to get new products and services up and running, it prioritizes individuals and interactions over processes and tools, and collaboration and quick response over documentation and a long-term plan.

Whilst Design Thinking, Agile and Lean are often seen by business leaders as three separate approaches – one of the most common questions I get being "which should I use in my business?".

The answer for organizations is that you should be seeing them as interactive processes which can be merged to achieve optimal results for your business. Applying Design Thinking in an environment which is both lean and agile helps to create a customer-centric development process for new products or services. As an effective leader, ensuring that the teams in your business are combining and applying principles from each methodology helps to promote a truly collaborative culture in which everyone is working to a common vision.

In practice, Design Thinking is your solution-based approach to resolving your customers' problems – keeping them at the epicentre of the process. Lean principles drive how you test your ideas and gather feedback to see what works, and Agile ties everything into short 'sprint' cycles, enabling the process to be fully adaptable as circumstances change. In combination, the three methodologies cut out unnecessary processes and bureaucracy and, with the right level of cross-team collaboration, deliver optimum value to the customer and to the business.

The Quality of the Brief Dictates the Quality of the Output

One of the phrases you will often hear us say when talking to leaders who don't get the results they are looking for when giving their team a brief to work to… is that it is entirely their fault. The quality of the brief dictates the quality of the output.

The quality of the brief provided to any team or individual working on a project significantly influences the quality of the final output or deliverable. A well-crafted, clear, and detailed brief lays the foundation for success by providing essential information, expectations, and guidelines to the team. On the other hand, a vague or inadequate brief can lead to misunderstandings, misalignment, and subpar results.

Here's why the quality of the brief is so crucial:

Clarity of Objectives: A good brief clearly outlines the project's objectives, goals, and desired outcomes. It helps the team understand what needs to be achieved, ensuring that everyone is on the same page from the start.

Scope Definition: The brief should define the scope of the project, detailing what is included and, equally important, what is not included. This helps prevent scope creep and ensures the project stays focused.

Target Audience: Understanding the target audience is vital for tailoring the output to meet their needs and preferences. A comprehensive brief includes information about the audience, their characteristics, and their expectations.

Guidelines and Constraints: A well-prepared brief provides guidelines and constraints within which the team should work. This might include budget limits, brand guidelines, or specific technical requirements.

Timelines and Deadlines: Clear timelines and deadlines are essential for managing project timelines and ensuring timely delivery. The brief should specify important milestones and the final delivery date.

Communication and Collaboration: An effective brief facilitates communication and collaboration within the team. It acts as a reference document that team members can revisit throughout the project, reducing the risk of miscommunication.

Quality Standards: The brief should outline the expected quality standards and benchmarks that the output should meet. This helps the team maintain a consistent level of quality throughout the project.

Risk Management: A thorough brief also addresses potential risks and challenges that the team might encounter during the project. This allows the team to be proactive in addressing potential issues before they escalate.

Flexibility and Adaptability: While a brief provides clear guidelines, it should also allow for some flexibility and adaptability. This enables the team to respond to unforeseen circumstances or make necessary adjustments without compromising the project's overall vision.

A good brief acts as a roadmap, guiding the team towards achieving the desired outcome. Investing time and effort in crafting a well-thought-out

*To ask the
right question
is already half
the solution of a
problem*

C.G. Jung

brief ensures that the team is aligned, empowered, and fully equipped to deliver high-quality results that meet or exceed expectations. As the saying goes, "a well-begun is half done," and a well-crafted brief sets the stage for a successful project from the outset.

Ask Smarter Questions

The Power of Great Questions

A significant portion of an executive's workday is dedicated to seeking information by requesting updates from team leaders or engaging in probing conversations during negotiations. Surprisingly, unlike professionals such as litigators, journalists, and doctors who are trained in the art of questioning, many executives overlook questioning as a skill that can be developed. They rarely contemplate how their own responses to questions can impact the productivity and effectiveness of conversations.

It's a missed opportunity not to recognize the powerful impact of questioning in unlocking value within organizations. Questioning not only spurs learning and fosters the exchange of ideas but also fuels innovation and drives performance improvement. Additionally, it plays a significant role in building rapport and trust among team members, while also mitigating business risks by revealing unforeseen pitfalls and hazards.

While some individuals possess a natural talent for questioning due to their inquisitiveness, emotional intelligence, and ability to read people, many of us fall short in asking enough questions or framing them optimally.

The good news is that by actively engaging in questioning, we can enhance our emotional intelligence, leading to a cycle of continuous improvement in our questioning abilities. Here we draw on insights from behavioral science research to explore the impact of question framing and response choices on conversation outcomes. By providing guidance on selecting the right type, tone, sequence, and framing of questions, as well as determining the appropriate amount of information to share, we can maximize the benefits of our interactions, not only for ourselves but also for our organizations.

"If We Don't Ask, We Don't Get"

In his timeless classic "How to Win Friends and Influence People" published in 1936, Dale Carnegie advised readers to be good listeners and to ask questions that others would enjoy answering.

Surprisingly, even after more than 80 years, most people still overlook this sage advice. A foundational insight from all our work is that people don't ask enough questions. How many times have you heard the common complaint after an interview, a sales presentation, or a work meeting along the lines of... "I wish they had asked me more questions" or "I can't believe they didn't ask me anything."

Numerous reasons contribute to this hesitance. Some individuals might be preoccupied with impressing others with their own thoughts and ideas, neglecting to inquire further. Others might show apathy towards asking questions, fearing boredom from the answers they receive.

Overconfidence in one's knowledge can lead to the belief that they already possess all the answers. There may also be worries about asking the wrong questions and being perceived as rude or incompetent. However, the biggest obstacle, in our view, is that many people fail to realize the immense benefits of skilful questioning. If they did, they would likely use question marks more and full stops less in their conversations.

Research dating back to the 1970s suggests that people engage in conversations with two primary goals: information exchange (learning) and impression management (liking). Recent studies reveal that asking questions is effective in achieving both objectives.

In research conducted by Harvard, extensive analysis of natural conversations among participants in various settings, such as online chats and in-person speed dates were examined. Some participants were instructed to ask multiple questions (at least nine in 15 minutes), while others were encouraged to ask very few (no more than four in 15 minutes).

In the online chats, those randomly assigned to ask numerous questions were better liked by their conversation partners and gained deeper insights into their partners' interests. For instance, high question askers were more adept at accurately guessing their partners' preferences for activities like reading, cooking, and exercising.

Similarly, among speed daters, individuals who asked more questions were more likely to secure a second date. Astonishingly, asking just one additional question on each date resulted in persuading one extra person (out of 20 dates) to go on a second outing.

Asking numerous questions is a catalyst for learning and enhances interpersonal connections.

The potency of questions as tools becomes particularly evident in situations where question asking goes against social norms. Take, for instance, job interviews where prevailing norms dictate that candidates should primarily answer questions.

However, research by Dan Cable of the London Business School and Virginia Kay of the University of North Carolina reveals that many candidates tend to excessively self-promote during interviews, often neglecting to ask their own questions. However, candidates who take the initiative to inquire about the interviewer, the organization, and the work create a more engaging atmosphere and leave a favorable impression.

Moreover, such questioning helps candidates gain insights into whether the job would offer satisfying work. An insightful question like, "What am I not asking you that I should?" not only showcases competence but also builds rapport and unlocks crucial information about the position.

Interestingly, many individuals fail to grasp the significance of asking numerous questions in fostering learning and stronger interpersonal bonds. These are two of the main ingredients required for innovation... learning gives us the 'context of the box', and the improved relationship enhances collaboration.

The New Socratic Method

To become a better questioner, the first step is simply to ask more questions. However, the quality of a conversation is influenced not only by the sheer number of questions but also by factors such as the type, tone, sequence, and framing of those questions.

Based on our research, we have identified several approaches that can enhance the power and effectiveness of queries. The best approach depends on the goals of the conversationalists whether the discussion is cooperative, aimed at building a relationship or accomplishing a task together, or competitive, with the parties seeking to uncover sensitive information or serve their own interests, or a combination of both.

Consider the Following Questioning Tactics

Favor follow-up questions.

Not all questions carry the same weight. The same Harvard research identified four types of questions: introductory questions ("How are you?"), mirror questions ("I'm fine. How are you?"), full-switch questions (ones that change the topic entirely), and follow-up questions (ones that elicit more information). While each type is prevalent in natural conversation, follow-up questions possess a special power. They signal to your conversation partner that you are actively listening, genuinely interested, and eager to delve deeper into the topic.

As a result, people engaging with a person who asks plenty of follow-up questions tend to feel respected and heard. An unexpected advantage of follow-up questions is that they flow effortlessly and naturally.

Know when to keep questions open-ended.

Avoid putting someone in a yes-or-no corner by utilizing open-ended questions strategically. These types of questions are particularly valuable in gathering information and uncovering novel insights. They act as wellsprings of innovation, often leading to unexpected answers that no one had considered before.

Survey design research has extensively demonstrated the dangers of narrowing respondents' options with closed questions, which can introduce bias and manipulation. For instance, in a study asking parents about the most important thing for children to prepare them in life, about 60% chose "to think for themselves" from a list of predefined options. However, when the same question was posed in an open-ended format, merely about 5% of parents spontaneously provided an answer along those lines.

Of course, open-ended questions may not always be the ideal choice. In tense negotiations or dealings with individuals who are guarded, open-ended questions might leave too much room for evasion or deception by omission. In such scenarios, closed questions can be more effective, especially when framed appropriately. Closed questions zoom in on the detail, seeking specificity and allow for accuracy.

A Characteristic of Great Leaders.

Effective leadership involves the art of asking the right questions, but there are situations where direct inquiries may not yield the desired information, regardless of how tactfully they are posed. In such sensitive circumstances, a survey tactic can be a valuable tool for discovery instead.

While this tactic might prove useful at the organizational level such as when managers need to assess sensitive information like salary expectations we must exercise caution in its application. If individuals perceive that they are being tricked or manipulated into revealing something, it can erode trust, leading them to be less willing to share information in the future and potentially damaging workplace relationships.

Another tip is to get the sequence right when asking questions. The most effective order of your questions depends on the context of the conversation. In tense encounters, starting with tough questions, even if it initially feels socially awkward, can encourage your conversational partner to be more open and less defensive for later, less intrusive questions.

Strike the right tone when asking questions.

A casual and approachable manner tends to elicit more openness from people compared to a formal and official tone. Again from the Harvard studies, participants were presented with a series of sensitive questions through an online survey. For some participants, the website's user interface had a fun and playful appearance, while for others, it had a formal look. The results showed that participants were approximately twice as likely to disclose sensitive information on the casual-looking site than on the more formal ones.

Furthermore, providing an escape hatch or offering an "out" during a conversation can also encourage greater openness. When people are assured that they can change their answers at any point, they tend to be more candid, even though they rarely take advantage of this option. This is akin to the productivity seen in brainstorming sessions within teams or groups. In a setting where ideas can be freely expressed on a whiteboard and judgment is withheld, participants are more inclined to respond honestly and share thoughts they might otherwise keep to themselves.

However, it's essential to recognize that there will be situations where a more structured approach is necessary. Nevertheless, in general, maintaining an overly formal tone is likely to inhibit people's willingness to share information.

Be mindful of group dynamics.

Conversations can take on a whole new dimension when they occur one-on-one versus in a group setting. The presence of others not only affects people's willingness to answer questions but also influences how group members follow one another's lead. In a series of other studies, participants were presented with sensitive questions, including ones about finances and sex. Some participants were informed that most others in the study had been forthcoming with stigmatizing answers, while others were told that others had been reticent.

Those who believed that others had been open were 27% more likely to reveal sensitive information compared to those who believed others had been reserved. In a group or meeting, the dynamics can shift significantly, and just a few closed-off individuals can diminish the probing power of questions. Conversely, when one person starts opening up, it often prompts the rest of the group to do the same.

Moreover, group dynamics can influence how question askers are perceived. Research reveals that participants in a conversation enjoy being asked questions and tend to hold those asking questions in higher regard than those providing answers. However, when third-party observers watch the same conversation unfold, they usually favor the person who answers questions. This is understandable, as question askers tend to reveal little about themselves or their thoughts during the conversation. To listeners, they may come across as defensive, evasive, or unremarkable, while those who answer questions seem more engaging, open, present, or memorable.

The Art of Answering

Engaging in a conversation is akin to a well-choreographed dance, requiring partners to move in harmony a mutual push-and-pull that unfolds over time. Just as the manner in which we pose questions can foster trust and information sharing, our responses to those questions hold equal significance.

Answering questions entails a delicate balance between privacy and transparency, where we must make thoughtful choices. Should we respond to the question at hand? If so, to what extent should we be forthcoming? What about those questions that, if answered truthfully, might expose less flattering facts or put us in a strategically disadvantaged position? Both ends of the spectrum complete opacity and full transparency offer their own advantages and drawbacks.

Keeping certain information private can offer the freedom to experiment and learn without judgment. In negotiations, withholding sensitive information, such as the weakness of your alternatives, can help secure more favorable outcomes. On the other hand, transparency is vital for forging meaningful connections. Even in negotiation scenarios, transparency can lead to mutually beneficial deals. By openly sharing information, participants can identify elements that hold little importance to one party but are crucial to the other forming the foundation of a win-win outcome.

However, maintaining secrets comes with its costs. Research from the University of Virginia suggests that concealing secrets during social interactions can lead to intrusive recurring thoughts about those secrets. Additionally, studies conducted by Columbia indicate that keeping secrets, even outside of social interactions, can have cognitive consequences. It interferes with our ability to concentrate, impacts memory retention, and even affects long-term health and well-being.

Striking the Balance: Transparency in Organizational Context

In the realm of organizations, there is a prevailing tendency to lean towards privacy, often overlooking the potential benefits of transparency. It's not uncommon to realize the missed opportunities for true bonding with colleagues only after they have moved on to new ventures. Similarly, better deals and breakthroughs in negotiations frequently emerge after the formalities have ended, and the atmosphere becomes more open for candid conversation.

To make the most of answering questions while minimizing risks, it's crucial to proactively decide what information to share and what to keep private before engaging in any conversation.

Certainly, there are instances where keeping information confidential serves both you and your organization better.

*Too often we forget
that genius, too,
depends upon the
data within its reach,
that even Archimedes
could not have devised
Edison's inventions*

Ernest Dimnet

As Albert Einstein famously proclaimed, "Question everything." The essence of personal creativity and organizational innovation lies in the willingness to seek out novel information. Thoughtful questions and answers facilitate smoother and more effective interactions, cultivate trust and rapport, and guide groups toward discovery these findings are well-documented in our research.

However, beyond mere performance, we believe questions and answers possess a profound power. At the core of all questions lies fascination, curiosity, and the capacity for delight. We engage in this exchange with the belief that the magic of conversation will yield a complete picture greater than the sum of its parts. In both our lives and work, sustained personal engagement and motivation necessitate a mindful acknowledgment of the transformative joy that arises from asking and answering questions.

Data-Driven Decision Making

As human beings, our decisions are often influenced by emotions and intuition, leading us to make split-second choices without fully considering the potential outcomes or consequences. Our emotional and empathetic nature plays a significant role in these instances, and while we can't entirely eliminate this aspect of decision-making, it's crucial to approach business decisions differently.

In the realm of business, taking into account all external factors before making decisive actions becomes paramount. This is where data-driven decision-making (DDDM) comes into play, ensuring that organizations base their business goals and objectives on cold, hard evidence.

In the following section, we will delve into what data-driven decision-making entails, explore its benefits for you and your business, and examine case studies that illustrate how it has driven success for brands worldwide.

Data-Driven Decision Making (DDDM) refers to the practice of making strategic business decisions based on concrete facts, metrics, and insights that align with a company's goals, strategies, and initiatives. This process involves collecting and analyzing data through market research to draw valuable insights that can benefit the organization.

At its essence, DDDM emphasizes the importance of relying on real and verified data rather than making decisions based on assumptions. There

Data is like garbage. You'd better know what you are going to do with it before you collect it

Mark Twain

are various methods of data gathering, each suited for different research objectives and contexts. Some common methods include:

- **Surveys:** Surveys involve asking a series of structured questions to collect data from a group of respondents. They can be conducted through online surveys, phone interviews, or face-to-face interactions.

- **Interviews:** Interviews are in-depth conversations with individuals or small groups to gather qualitative data. They can be structured (with predefined questions) or unstructured, allowing for more open-ended discussions.

- **Observations:** Observational methods involve directly observing and recording behavior, events, or phenomena in their natural settings. This can be done through field observations, participant observations, or video recordings.

- **Experiments:** Experiments are controlled studies designed to investigate cause-and-effect relationships by manipulating variables and observing their effects on outcomes.

- **Focus Groups:** Focus groups bring together a small group of participants to discuss a specific topic or product, providing qualitative insights and group dynamics.

- **Case Studies:** Case studies involve in-depth analysis of a single individual, group, organization, or event to gain a comprehensive understanding of a particular subject.

- **Content Analysis:** Content analysis is used to examine and categorize written, visual, or audio content to extract meaningful insights.

- **Social Media Listening:** This method involves analyzing data from social media platforms to understand public opinions, sentiments, and trends related to a specific topic or brand.

- **Secondary Data Analysis:** Secondary data refers to existing data collected by others, such as government agencies, research organizations, or databases. Analyzing secondary data can save time and resources.

- **Online Analytics:** Web analytics tools track and analyze online user behavior, providing valuable data on website traffic, user engagement, and conversion rates.

- **Mixed Methods:** Combining quantitative and qualitative data collection techniques, this approach provides a comprehensive understanding of the research topic.

Selecting the most appropriate data gathering method depends on research objectives, resources, target audience, and the nature of the data needed to address the research questions effectively.

Making decisions without a solid data foundation can lead to detrimental consequences for both external and internal strategies. On the other hand, by embracing data-driven approaches, businesses can effectively shape their marketing strategies. Consumer insights play a significant role in driving ad design, messaging, channel selection, and more. In fact, it's reported that 49% of marketing professionals leverage data-driven strategies to enhance customer outreach efforts.

Data-Driven Decision Making has a profound and positive impact on every aspect of your business, fostering improvement and growth. Here are some key areas where DDDM proves its value:

Improves customer retention: By utilizing customer surveys, you can identify crucial key performance indicators (KPIs) such as satisfaction levels, Net Promoter Score, likelihood of switching, and areas of dissatisfaction. This enables you to ensure that your customers are genuinely content with your organization, leading to higher retention rates.

Reduces customer attrition: Non-customer surveys offer valuable insights into what drives prospects to use your products or services. Understanding factors such as sources of awareness, brand perception, and current competitor usage can help you enhance your offerings and attract more customers.

Enhances employee satisfaction: Partnering with an employee survey company allows you to gain insights into areas where your team seeks improvements. These valuable insights can then drive cultural changes within your organization, directly impacting employee engagement and retention.

Informs Innovation: By understanding what's important to the people you serve both internally and externally, we can let data focus our attention on the areas that matter, driving innovation to improve experience and operational efficiencies.

Essential Steps in the Data-Driven Decision-Making Process

To ensure high-quality data for making informed decisions, it is crucial to follow these key steps:

- **Define your objectives:** Clearly outline your goals and what specific insights you need to achieve them.

- **Agree metrics for analysis:** Clearly specify the measurement metrics

- **Craft questions and decide collection method:** Design well-structured questions that align with your objectives and gather relevant data.

- **Collect data:** Implement the data collection strategy using various data collection methods.

- **Analyze the results:** Thoroughly examine the collected data, draw meaningful insights, and identify patterns or trends.

- **Take action based on the data:** Use the analyzed data to inform your decision-making process and take appropriate actions to achieve your objectives.

Key Factors When Making Data-Driven Decisions

When employing data-driven decision-making, two key factors play a critical role in ensuring its effectiveness:

Data Accuracy and Relevance

The foundation of sound data-driven decision-making lies in the accuracy and relevance of the data used. It is essential to verify that the data collected is not only precise but also directly applicable to the goals and objectives of your organization.

Relying on inaccurate data can lead to misguided decisions, negatively impacting business outcomes. Similarly, analyzing data that is not relevant to your specific goals can lead to inefficiencies and wasted resources. Collaborating with a reputable third-party online survey company can help ensure the data's accuracy and quality through rigorous data cleaning and verification processes.

Fostering a Data-Driven Culture

Having access to accurate and relevant data is not enough; it must be accompanied by a thriving "data culture" within the organization. Cultivating an environment that encourages employees to think critically about the data and its implications is crucial. A data-driven culture fosters curiosity, empowering individuals to explore and analyze the data, extract insights, and make informed decisions. By encouraging employees to be proactive in seeking data-driven solutions, organizations can unlock the full potential of data-driven decision-making and drive success.

By considering these key factors, organizations can leverage the power of data-driven decision-making to steer their strategies, enhance performance, and achieve their business objectives effectively.

Where Is Your Data and Analytics Strategy Today?

Data Analytics has emerged as a prominent buzzword in the 21st century, gaining significant traction over the past decade. Giants such as Amazon, Alibaba, Coca-Cola, Facebook, Google, IBM, Microsoft, and SAP were among the pioneers to embrace data analytics by incorporating into all aspects of their operations, from strategic planning to daily activities, these companies have reaped substantial benefits.

Today, numerous companies, regardless of their size, are harnessing the power of data analytics and displaying a keen eagerness to explore ways to further enhance their adoption journey. The recognition of data analytics as a crucial driver for informed decision-making has spurred a growing interest among businesses to unlock its full potential.

In this section, we'll explore Gartner's Analytics Maturity Model, which comprises four distinct phases, with a twist on it to incorporate a fifth phase. But before that, let us assess where you are today? Read the five Gartner levels below and consider your organization.

Level One – Basic

- Data is merely used, not exploited
- Data and Analytics is managed in silos
- People disagree over whose data is correct
- Analysis is ad hoc

- Spreadsheet and information firefighting
- Transactional

Level Two – Opportunistic

- IT attempts to formalize information availability requirements
- Progress is hampered by culture and inconsistent incentives
- Organizational barriers and a lack of leadership
- Strategy is over 100 pages; not business relevant
- Data quality and insight efforts, but still in silos

Level Three – Systematic

- Different content types are still treated differently
- Strategy and vision formed (5 Pages)
- Agile emerges
- Exogenous data sources are readily integrated
- Business executives become data and analytics champions

Level Four – Differentiating

- Executives champion and communicate best practice
- Business-led/driven, with Chief Data Officer (CDO)
- Data and Analytics is an indispensable fuel for performance and innovation, and linked across programs
- Program management mentality for ongoing synergy
- Linked to outcome, and data used for ROI

Level Five – Transformational

- Data and analytics is central to business strategy
- Data value influences investments

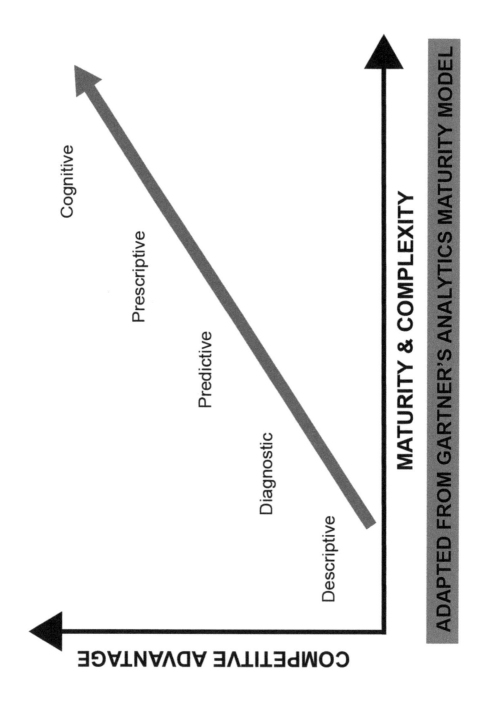

- Strategy and execution aligned and continually improved\ Outside-in perspective

- CDO sits on the board

Five Types of Analytics

- **Descriptive Analytics** – What happened?

- **Diagnostic Analytics** – Why did it happen?

- **Predictive Analytics** – What will happen?

- **Prescriptive Analytics** – How can we make it happen?

- **Cognitive Analytics** – AI and machine learning, Neurological and behavioural analysis

These phases represent different levels of maturity in an organization's analytics adoption journey.

Descriptive Analytics

Descriptive Analytics focuses on looking backward to analyze past events (hindsight), while Diagnostic Analytics gathers insights from historical data to aid decision-making. On the other hand, Predictive Analytics and Prescriptive Analytics shift the focus to predicting the future (foresight), with decision-making becoming increasingly automated as you progress from Descriptive to Prescriptive Analytics.

The value derived from analytics significantly increases as organizations develop into the more advanced phases. Let's delve into each of these four phases in detail.

Descriptive Analytics is the initial phase that focuses on answering the question "What happened" in the past by analyzing historical data. It deals with queries related to quantities, occurrences, timing, and locations based on past data. For instance:

- "How many iPhones were sold by Apple Stores in Dubai last month?"

- "How many users downloaded the recently launched social media app from the play store yesterday?"

- "During the last week of the SALE, how many customers visited the store?"

- "Which regions have less than 20% coverage in the COVID-19 vaccination program?"

Example: In the retail industry, Descriptive Analytics plays a crucial role in uncovering valuable insights such as the best-selling brands/ products, most searched items, and regions with high product demand. By analyzing this data, retailers can make informed decisions on various aspects, such as optimizing inventory levels for popular products, ensuring stores with higher demand receive frequent restocking of fast-moving items, and effectively managing resources like manpower, logistics partners, and infrastructure to handle increased customer traffic during SALE periods. These actions are primarily guided by human interpretation of the data obtained through Descriptive Analytics.

Diagnostic Analytics

Diagnostic Analytics represents the next stage in the analytics adoption journey and addresses the question "Why did it happen?" This phase involves delving deeper into data understanding through statistical techniques like statistical summary, correlation analysis, bi-variate and multi-variate analysis to uncover patterns and trends not captured in the Descriptive Analytics phase. The primary focus of Diagnostic Analysis is to reveal hidden insights from the data.

During this phase, you can find answers to questions such as:

- "Does gender have an impact on the sale of the newly launched iPhone 12?"

- "Are there significant differences in plant operations costs between two locations?"

- "Is there a positive relationship between age and sales revenue from protein bars?"

- "Which factors contribute to the increase in COVID-19 fatalities in the state, such as age, comorbidity, number of vaccination doses administered, gender, and lifestyle?"

Additionally, various hypothesis tests like t-tests, ANOVA, and Chi-square tests can be conducted to validate or disprove assumptions and hypotheses. This statistical analysis aids in gaining a deeper understanding of the underlying reasons behind observed trends and patterns in the data.

Example: The hospital makes a claim that the average waiting time for patients is less than or equal to 30.15 minutes. To verify this claim, data can be collected and analyzed using hypothesis tests. By conducting this analysis, the hospital can assess the factors that influence patient waiting time and implement measures to enhance operational efficiency accordingly.

Predictive Analytics

Predictive Analytics represents an advanced phase of analytics that leverages data mining and various advanced techniques, such as machine learning and artificial intelligence, to create models capable of making predictions based on historical data. This phase seeks to answer the question "What will happen in the future." By identifying hidden patterns in the data and establishing relationships between the outcome variable (in supervised machine learning scenarios) and predictor variables, mathematical/statistical models are built to predict the outcome for new data.

This phase encompasses stages like data preparation, data cleaning, feature engineering, model building, and model evaluation. Predictive Analytics enables the automation of decision-making processes through these predictive models, equipping businesses with valuable insights to make informed and timely decisions.

In this phase, you can find answers to questions such as:

- "How many iPhones smartphones are projected to be sold in the next month?"

- "Will John likely purchase a new car in the upcoming quarter, and should I add him to the list of prospective customers for next month?"

- "What is the probability of hospitalization for a 62-year-old male weighing 69 kg with a fatty liver, residing in Texas, North America, if he contracts the COVID-19 virus?"

- "Do middle-aged men (35–50 years) in London, UK prefer dark-grey suits?"

Predictive Analytics empowers businesses with the ability to make data-driven decisions and anticipate future outcomes, leading to better planning and improved outcomes.

Example: Consider building a predictive model that forecasts whether a customer is likely to purchase the annual subscription pre-paid plan from a telecom service provider. By analyzing various factors such as usage patterns, recharge frequency, recharge amounts, data consumption, and customer profiles, telecom companies can identify potential customers with a significant propensity to buy the offer. Subsequently, they can launch targeted promotional campaigns to maximize return on investment (ROI) from their marketing efforts, effectively reaching out to those customers most likely to avail the annual subscription plan.

Prescriptive Analytics

Prescriptive Analytics represents the next level of advancement in analytics, addressing the question "How can I achieve it? What should be done?" This advanced phase empowers decision-makers to select the optimal analytics solution to solve business problems by evaluating various mathematical models and comparing their performance on available data for a specific industry, ultimately choosing the most optimal approach.

During this phase, you can find answers to questions like:

- "How many ground staff members will be required to handle the volume of passengers on 25-Dec in Mumbai?"

- "What are the top 3 combo offers that will boost staple sales in the upcoming month?"

- "In which Cafe-Coffee Day outlets across India should I open mini book stores for effective cross-selling?"

Prescriptive Analytics equips businesses with actionable insights, enabling them to make well-informed decisions and take the most effective course of action to achieve their objectives.

Example: When searching for a video on a specific topic like "How to play Chess" on YouTube, the platform's search engine employs an algorithm to sort through numerous videos and provide you with the most relevant and useful results. This algorithm takes into account factors such as relevance, engagement, and video quality to determine the ranking of the search results.

Moreover, YouTube's search engine refines the relevance of recommended videos based on your search and watch history. As a result, your search results may differ from those of another user who performs the same search query, as the algorithm tailors the suggestions to each individual's preferences and viewing behavior.

Cognitive Analytics

Cognitive Analytics is an advanced technology that encompasses various analytical techniques to analyze vast data sets and bring structure to unstructured data.

In simple terms, a cognitive analytics system examines its knowledge base to find sensible solutions for the given questions.

Cognitive analytics can be seen as analytics imbued with human-like intelligence. It involves understanding the context and meaning of sentences or recognizing objects in images based on substantial amounts of information. It often leverages artificial intelligence algorithms and machine learning, allowing cognitive applications to continuously improve over time. By revealing patterns and connections that basic analytics cannot, cognitive analytics offers deeper insights.

Organizations can utilize cognitive analytics to monitor customer behaviour patterns and identify emerging trends. This enables them to predict future outcomes and plan objectives to enhance performance.

Certain aspects of cognitive analytics also overlap with predictive analytics, wherein business intelligence data is used to make predictions.

Example: The medical industry is embracing cognitive analytics to efficiently match patients with the most suitable treatments. Notable examples of cognitive analytics in use today include Microsoft's Cortana, Apple's Siri, and IBM's Watson.

Organizations are harnessing cognitive analytics to access and analyze unstructured data from various sources, such as images, emails, text documents, and social media posts.

While still in its early stages, cognitive analytics shows promise in providing real-time solutions for vast and diverse data, potentially revolutionizing traditional analytics practices.

Data Sources

Data forms the bedrock of any project; however, not all data sources deliver the same level of trustworthiness and usefulness. Assessing the quality and reliability of data sources before integrating, transforming, and analyzing them is crucial. To achieve this, consider following this 4 step process to effectively evaluate your data sources and ensure they align with your requirements and expectations.

STEP ONE – Establishing clear data quality goals is the initial step in the process. Define what data quality entails for your specific project and context. Data quality encompasses various dimensions, such as accuracy, completeness, consistency, timeliness, validity, and relevance. Depending on the objectives of your data architecture, you may prioritize certain dimensions over others or set distinct thresholds for acceptable quality levels. For instance, if you are developing a real-time dashboard, you may require data that is frequently updated with minimal errors. Conversely, for historical analysis, you may need comprehensive and consistent data over time.

STEP TWO – The next step involves identifying the data sources intended for use in your project and gathering essential information about them. This information may include the source type (whether internal or external, structured or unstructured, primary or secondary), the data format (such as CSV, JSON, or XML), the data provider (organization, department, vendor, website), the data access method (via API, FTP, or web scraping), and the data license or terms of use (whether it's open, proprietary, or restricted). Additionally, documenting the data lineage, which traces the data's history from generation to collection, processing, and storage, can be valuable.

STEP THREE – The third step involves evaluating your data sources based on the criteria established in the first step. This evaluation process may include data profiling, which examines the data to reveal its structure, content, quality, and metadata. Through data profiling, you can answer questions such as the number of records, fields, and values within the data source, as well as their data types, formats, and ranges. It also allows assessment of the consistency, completeness, and accuracy of the fields and values. Additionally, data profiling helps determine the frequency of updates and how current the data is. Lastly, it aids in understanding the relevance and usefulness of the data for your project.

Comparing different data sources that offer similar or overlapping information and assessing their strengths and weaknesses can also be essential. For instance, you may examine how well they align with your data quality goals and standards, the reliability and credibility of their methods, the compatibility and interoperability of their formats, and the ease and efficiency of accessing and utilizing them.

STEP FOUR – In the final step, you need to select and prioritize your data sources based on the evaluation results. You can rank the data sources according to their quality and reliability scores and decide which ones to use, exclude, or combine for your project. It's essential to consider the trade-offs and costs associated with using different data sources, including the time, effort, and resources required to acquire, prepare, and integrate them. Additionally, you may plan data quality improvement actions, such as data cleaning, validation, enrichment, or transformation, to enhance their value and usability.

By following these steps and criteria, you can effectively assess the quality and reliability of your data sources and make informed decisions for your project. Remember that data quality is not a fixed or objective attribute; it is relative and subjective, depending on your context and goals. Thus, it's crucial to continually review and update your data quality assessment as your project evolves and your requirements change.

Market Research

For reliable and accurate data, consider collaborating with an outsourced team (partner) to conduct market research. Follow these essential steps to deliver the best possible results for your decision-making needs.

1. Establish Your Objectives

In every market research study, having well-defined goals and objectives is crucial. When partnering with a market research company, these objectives will be thoroughly discussed during a kickoff meeting. This initial meeting serves as an excellent opportunity for both the team and the client to become familiar with one another. Kick-off meetings encompass a broad range of topics. Regardless of the specifics, certain factors are always addressed in such meetings:

- **Project Objectives:** Clearly outline the goals and objectives of the research project.

- **Key Target Audiences:** Identify the primary audiences that the research will focus on.

- **Timeline Review:** Discuss the project timeline and milestones.

- **Reporting Requirements:** Determine the specific reporting needs and formats.

- **Address Additional Questions:** Provide a platform to address any further inquiries or concerns.

2. Survey Design

With clear project goals in place, the market research team embarks on the task of designing and crafting the survey. Crafting an effective survey involves more than just writing well-structured questions. Here are some recommendations from our online survey agency:

Keep it Concise: For online surveys, it is essential to maintain brevity. Keeping the survey under 20 minutes, and ideally between 10 to 15 minutes, is crucial. Lengthy surveys can lead to respondent disinterest, and attention spans can wane beyond the 20-minute mark.

Vary Question Styles: Incorporating variety into question styles is vital for successful market research. By avoiding uniform formatting, respondents are more likely to stay engaged throughout the survey. Using diverse question types keeps the survey interesting and enhances respondent participation.

3. Collecting Survey Data

Once the survey is finalized, it is transferred from its original document into an online survey platform. The next step is fieldwork, during which responses are collected. The duration of this phase usually spans a couple of weeks, depending on the project's timeline. During this period, participants provide their valuable input and insights.

4. Analysis and Customized Report

The last stages of a comprehensive market research process involve conducting a thorough analysis of the collected data and creating a customized report. Before the analysis, the survey data is carefully cleaned to ensure that only the highest-quality data is used.

Once the data is prepared, the research team proceeds with the analysis, drawing meaningful insights and trends from the information gathered. The resulting market research report covers essential aspects, including a review of the methodology employed, a comprehensive examination of main themes, and additional contextual information. The report also includes in-depth suggestions tailored to the specific needs and objectives of the client. Depending on the available budget, there are options to adjust the scope and level of detail in the final deliverable.

A comprehensive report is of utmost importance for any market research project, particularly in the context of Data-Driven Decision Making (DDDM). Our dedicated research team invests significant effort in reviewing the report with the client, meticulously going through each section to ensure a clear understanding of all the key findings.

Beyond merely presenting the findings, our report goes a step further by providing action-driven recommendations that the client can implement. For instance, when dealing with consumer data, the report identifies sources of awareness, enabling the client to focus on specific marketing channels for targeted outreach. Our goal is to equip clients with valuable insights and actionable steps to make informed decisions and drive their business forward.

Advantages of the Data-Driven Approach

Implementing a data-driven approach in decision-making yields numerous benefits that positively impact all aspects of an organization, spanning from human resources to sales and from marketing to leadership. We identify three key advantages when utilizing data-driven insights for critical business decisions.

Enhanced Confidence in Decision-Making

Embracing data-driven decision-making empowers organizations to make decisions with heightened confidence. Whether it involves entering a new market, launching a new product, or discontinuing an existing one, having verified data at your disposal provides clarity and certainty about the potential impact of each decision. This is why businesses, from start-ups to Fortune 500 companies, invest in market research for their new product development endeavours.

Cost Savings and Increased ROI

Another significant advantage of adopting a data-driven approach is the potential for cost savings and improved return on investment (ROI). By relying on data from the outset, organizations can avoid the trial-and-error method and its associated expenses. Instead of making decisions based on guesswork, data-driven decision-making keeps businesses informed about prevailing trends and consumer preferences.

Operating with up-to-date insights enables companies to streamline their processes and align their strategies with the actual needs of consumers, rather than assumptions about those needs. For instance, leveraging ad concept testing surveys allows businesses to gather valuable feedback on messaging, design, layout, and other critical components of advertising campaigns before launching them. This ensures that the marketing messaging resonates with the intended target audience, leading to more effective and cost-efficient marketing efforts. For further insights on ad concept testing, watch the video from our advertising and marketing research company below.

Embrace Proactive Decision-Making

The final and crucial advantage of data-driven decision-making is its ability to transform you and your organization into proactive decision-makers. Instead of constantly reacting to events and challenges that could have been anticipated, data-driven approaches enable you to identify and address potential issues beforehand.

By carefully considering all relevant information before making decisions, you adopt a proactive stance, ensuring that you take necessary steps to avoid future roadblocks. Being armed with a wealth of data and insights can save you significant time and resources in the long run, as you make informed choices that set your path for success and mitigate potential risks. Embracing data-driven decision-making empowers you to navigate uncertainties with confidence, positioning yourself to thrive in a rapidly changing business landscape.

Foster Team Unity

Data-driven decision-making is a powerful tool for fostering team unity within your organization. When all team members are equipped with the right data and insights, they operate on the same wavelength, working collaboratively towards shared company goals.

By adopting a data-driven approach, you create a learning environment where employees can grow together while implementing the valuable data they have acquired. This shared experience enhances team cohesion and boosts cooperation among team members.

Moreover, internal data-driven decision-making builds a foundation of trust between employees and leadership. When both teams have access to accurate and transparent data, communication improves, leading to better outcomes. This sense of trust contributes significantly to increased employee retention, creating a thriving workplace where everyone feels valued and empowered to contribute to the organization's success.

Forge Personalized Connections With Customers

Data-driven decision-making offers a tremendous advantage by facilitating genuine connections with clients and customers. By continuously analyzing market data, businesses stay ahead of consumer trends, enabling them to truly understand the motivations that drive their audience.

This understanding of consumer preferences goes beyond surface-level benefits. Brands can leverage these insights to create impactful, personalized marketing campaigns that resonate deeply with their target audience. When consumers feel a personal connection to a campaign, they are more likely to invest their time, attention, and loyalty. In fact, leading marketers recognize that personalization plays a crucial role in boosting marketing profitability, with a staggering 90% acknowledging its positive impact.

By using data to inform their marketing strategies, businesses can build authentic relationships with their customers, fostering loyalty and long-term engagement. This level of personalization not only enhances customer satisfaction but also ensures that the brand remains relevant and influential in a competitive market landscape.

Case Study – Lufthansa: As the second-largest airline company in Europe based on passengers carried, the Lufthansa Group operates a vast network of over 500 subsidiary companies. In the past, the company faced challenges with inconsistent data analytics practices across its numerous subsidiaries.

To address this issue and improve overall efficiency, Lufthansa made a strategic decision to implement a unified analytics platform company-wide. This data-driven approach brought about a significant transformation, with efficiency levels soaring by 30% across the entire organization.

With a cohesive data analytics system in place, decision-makers throughout Lufthansa's subsidiaries gained access to comprehensive and reliable insights. The availability of accurate data allowed them to make better-informed decisions, leading to streamlined business objectives and enhanced operational efficiency.

By fostering a data-driven culture, Lufthansa empowered its employees to harness the power of data in their decision-making processes. This cultural shift paved the way for better collaboration, increased productivity, and a deeper understanding of their customers' needs, ultimately driving the company's success in the highly competitive airline industry.

Case Study – Walmart: In the summer of 2004, Hurricane Frances threatened the Florida peninsula, prompting Walmart to take proactive measures to understand and meet their customers' needs during the impending disaster.

Leveraging the power of data-driven decision-making, Walmart analyzed historical data from stores located in regions previously affected by similar environmental disasters. By examining purchasing patterns during those times, the retail giant identified areas where demand had spiked compared to regular periods.

Surprisingly, the data revealed that two seemingly unrelated items, Pop-Tarts and beer, experienced significant increases in demand during storm preparation. Armed with this valuable insight, Walmart strategically increased the supply of these items in stores located in the hurricane's projected path.

The result was twofold: Walmart not only maximized profit by catering to customers' specific needs during the crisis but also played a crucial role in aiding those affected by the hurricane. By relying on verified data rather than making assumptions, Walmart demonstrated the power of data-driven decision-making in enhancing both business outcomes and their contribution to the community in times of need.

Final Thoughts

DDDM, is a powerful process that empowers businesses to make well-informed choices based on gathered insights and figures. Its impact extends across all facets of a company, from nurturing client relationships to enhancing consumer outreach and boosting employee satisfaction. Integrating DDDM into the core of strategic decisions can lead to transformative outcomes.

However, to harness the full potential of DDDM, it is essential to ensure the accuracy and relevance of the data used. Collaborating with a reputable market research company can instil confidence that the insights gathered are trustworthy, fuelling strategic thinking and fostering the generation of innovative ideas.

By embracing data-driven decision-making as a fundamental aspect of their operations, businesses can stay ahead in a rapidly evolving market landscape and drive sustained growth and success.

Communicate Clearly and Often

Change can be unsettling, so it's important to communicate clearly and frequently. This can help to build trust and keep everyone informed of what is happening and why and ensure that they understand the impact of the transformation on their roles and responsibilities.

One example of a great internal communication strategy during a digital transformation is the case of Coca-Cola. Their digital transformation initiative aimed to streamline operations by integrating digital technologies across the organization.

Coca-Cola communicated clearly and consistently with its employees about all initiatives, their purpose, and the expected outcomes. The company used multiple communication channels, including email, video conferencing, social media, and intranet, to reach employees across the organization.

Messaging was backed by the company's CEO, James Quincey, who led by example by embracing digital technologies and encouraging other employees to do the same. The company also created a dedicated digital transformation team, which provided support and guidance to employees throughout the process.

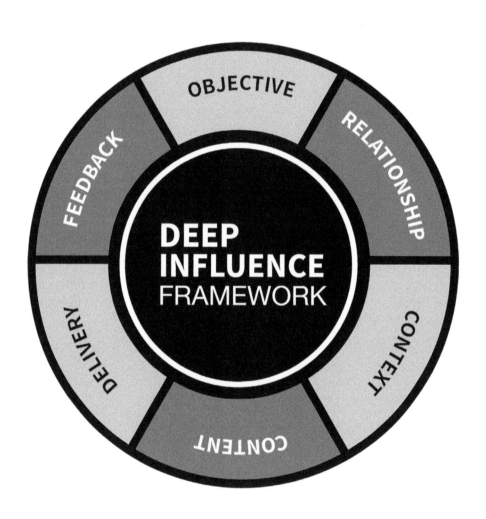

Coca-Cola's internal communication strategy is an excellent example of how effective communication can help drive successful digital transformations. Clear and consistent communication, employee empowerment, and leadership support helped to build trust and confidence with employees.

Deep Influence Framework

The following 'Deep Influence Framework' is a simple structure developed by Warren Cass and regularly taught to our clients. It is designed to encourage consideration for the desired outcome to be achieved from the communication, and the best way to achieve that based on person(s) on the receiving end.

The Deep Influence Framework can be used in any communication scenario to ensure the message lands with a deeper resonance. By simply giving consideration to each of the six steps, we will be able to craft a more impactful message.

STEP ONE – OBJECTIVES

All good communication design starts with clarity of the desired outcome. Spending a little time clearly defining the objective(s).

Questions you may ask yourself:

- What do you want your audience to know or understand?

- What do you want your audience to do after receiving your message?

- How do you want your audience to feel or think after receiving your message?

STEP TWO – RELATIONSHIP

By considering the relationship between the sender and the receiver, communication can be more effective and positive. For example, is there a power dynamic at play? Power dynamics can influence communication and can impact the receiver's willingness to engage in open and honest communication. It's important to be aware of any power imbalances and to strive for open and respectful communication, even in difficult or sensitive situations.

Good communication is not about you! It is always about the person on the receiving end of the message

Warren Cass

They may not know you at all, or are a customer, stakeholder, supplier or colleague. How would this impact tone of voice or professionalism?

Questions you may ask yourself:

- How have you communicated historically, and how might they expect to receive from you now?

- Any previous conflicts or history relevant to how the message might be received?

- What are the trust levels between you?

- How do they feel about you?

- What is the power dynamic?

STEP THREE – CONTEXT

Contextual communication is about being mindful of the person(s) on the receiving end of the message and adapting accordingly to ensure effective communication.

For example, if you are communicating with someone from a different cultural background, you may need to adjust your communication style to account for differences in communication norms and expectations. This might mean using more formal language, avoiding humour or sarcasm, or using different nonverbal cues.

Contextual communication is also important in the workplace. Different departments and teams may have their own jargon, acronyms, and communication styles, so it's important to be aware of these differences when communicating across teams.

Understanding who you are communicating with can help you tailor your message to their interests, needs, feelings, beliefs and communication style. This can include demographic and psychographic information (defined below).

Demographics refers to a particular section or subset of a population, categorized by various criteria such as age, gender, race, education, income, occupation, marital status, location, or any other characteristics that can be used to differentiate people into distinct groups. It is often used in research, marketing, public policy, and other fields to gain insights into patterns of behaviour, preferences, needs, and trends among different groups of people.

Psychographics refers to the study and analysis of people's attitudes, beliefs, values, interests, personalities, and lifestyles. It involves examining psychological characteristics of individuals or groups to understand their behaviour and decision-making processes. Psychographic information can be used to create targeted marketing campaigns, tailor product offerings to specific consumer segments, and understand consumer preferences and behaviour.

So, determine who your audience is, their needs, and their level of knowledge on the topic. This will help you tailor your message to their specific needs and interests. Consider using an empathy map to really understand who they are and how they think.

Questions you may ask yourself:

- What do they think or feel?
- How do they behave?
- What have they experienced before in relation to the topic?
- What are their values?
- What is important to them?
- What do they already know?
- What bias might they have?
- Where do they currently get information in relation to the topic?

STEP FOUR – CONTENT

Designing the content of a message requires careful consideration of the message's purpose, audience, their relation to you, and desired outcomes. Essentially your answer to the first 3 stages.

Consider the language you use as it can impact the relationship between you and the receiver. Using appropriate language can help build trust and respect. This includes avoiding words that could be perceived as offensive, being mindful of tone, and using simple, clear and concise language.

The message should be easy to understand. Avoid using technical jargon or industry-specific terms that the audience may not be familiar with. Use simple language, short sentences, and bullet points to make the message more accessible.

The structure of the message should be compelling and engaging. Start with a strong opening that captures the audience's attention, provide supporting evidence or examples, and end with a clear call to action. Consider using visuals and multimedia. This can help to enhance the message and make it more engaging. This includes images, videos, charts, and graphs that support the message and make it more memorable.

Questions you may ask yourself:

- What format will you create the message in?

- What does your audience prefer?

- Is this short form or long form? Overview or detailed?

- Have you contextualised in this format?

- Have you considered language, visuals, colours, design and font size?

STEP FIVE – DELIVERY

Decide on the delivery format that will best convey your message, such as face to face, virtual meeting, phone call, email, a presentation, a social media post, or a video. It's important to choose the appropriate medium for the message and the audience.

Questions you may ask yourself:

- How frequently should they receive communication?

- What are the methods of delivery?

- What are the appropriate timings?

- How does your audience prefer to receive communication?

- How can you amplify?

STEP SIX – FEEDBACK

Lastly, before you send your message, take a moment to understand how you intend to evaluate its effectiveness and adjust your approach if necessary. Identify the metrics you will use to measure the success of your message. This might include website traffic, click-through rates, engagement rates, or sales figures, behavioural change, agreement/ sign off etc.

Use the metrics you identified to determine if your message achieved its objectives and make changes as needed to improve future messages. Evaluate and adjust.

Questions you may ask yourself:

- How do you know your message was received?

- How do you know your message was understood?

- How do you know if your audience took action?

- How did it make your audience feel?

- What did we learn?

Of course, not all communication requires significant planning, for more trivial exchanges of information this might just be a quick structured thought process before going into a meeting. But in a digital transformation change process, some of the more significant communications to colleagues, stakeholders and customers can have serious consequences if not thought through.

Bad communication impacts trust and confidence, both required for change. It can even have a significant impact on a company's share price. Inaccurate, misleading, or inadequate communication from a company's management team or spokesperson can cause confusion, uncertainty, and mistrust among investors and analysts.

On the other hand, clear and effective communication can help to build investor confidence and trust, which can have a positive impact on a company's share price.

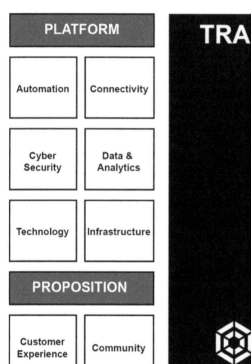

PLATFORM ALIGNMENT

Let us ask you a question... What do some of the most famous tech giants all have in common? Of course, besides their incredible success, market share and valuations...

The answer is that they all also operate on a platform-based business model which when well executed significantly increases customer value whilst also introducing new integrated products and services. This has led to significant market power and higher margins.

Today, more and more companies are choosing to adopt a platform-based approach, from the most valuable start-ups that are disrupting traditional markets, to established organizations that have shifted their business model from a traditional linear to a platform-based approach in order to keep up with the competition. All placing innovation and ownership of the customer relationship at the forefront of their strategy.

Platform based businesses like Airbnb, Amazon, and Uber are household names and have caused huge disruption in their respective industries. As the platform strategy becomes more ingrained, more and more traditional companies are exploring ways to stay competitive.

It is worth noting that platforms don't belong to tech giants alone. Other companies that enjoy strong relationships with their customers, and possess a keen willingness to collaborate can also benefit from the platform approach.

According to Accenture, digital platforms are the "most profound and global macroeconomic change since the industrial revolution." 50 percent of organizations recently surveyed by them defined platforms as central to their business strategy, with 40% citing platforms as a critical enabler.

At least 40% of all businesses will die in the next 10 years… if they don't figure out how to change their entire company to accommodate new technologies

John Chambers

So What Exactly Is a Platform?

What we mean by a platform business is a business model (not a technology infrastructure) that facilitates exchanges between two or more interdependent groups, usually consumers and service providers or producers. They typically create value by enabling interactions with each other more efficiently and effectively than they would be able to do on their own.

Platforms create large, scalable networks of users and resources that can be accessed on demand, creating communities, markets and facilitating transactions.

The concept of a platform business is not actually new. Think about traditional marketplaces, massive shopping malls or even exhibition centres housing B2B and B2C events. These are just traditional single location (bricks and mortar) approaches to enable interactions between buyers and sellers and facilitate value exchanges. Today platforms are supported by global and scalable digital technology infrastructures which enable participation and collaboration.

Case Study – LEGO: This time the LEGO Group embarked on a digital transformation journey in 2019 to elevate its supply chain management and enhance customer experience. The initiative involved integrating cutting-edge digital tools and technologies like IoT sensors, robotics, and data analytics into their manufacturing processes for improved efficiency and streamlined supply chain operations.

Additionally, the company focused on creating a new e-commerce platform that offers customers a more personalized and engaging shopping experience. By leveraging these digital advancements, The LEGO Group aimed to achieve higher levels of operational excellence and deliver enhanced value to its customers.

Different Platform Types

There are several platform business models, each with their own unique characteristics and approach to creating value. Here are 11 different types of platform businesses, organized by the type of value that's exchanged in the platform's core purpose.

Services Platform: Service platforms provide a mechanism for connecting customers with service providers. Examples include TaskRabbit, fiverr, and 99Designs.

Product Platform: Product platforms facilitate transactions between buyers and sellers of physical or digital goods. Examples include Amazon, Ebay, Gumtree or Etsy.

Payment Platform: Payment platforms facilitate financial exchanges (including P2P, B2B and B2C) Examples Venmo, Apple Pay, GoCardless and Paypal.

Investment Platform: Investment platforms exchange money for a potential financial return, be it equity or a loan or good will. Examples include Crowdfunder, Kickstarter and GoFundMe.

Social Platforms: Social platforms facilitate user interactions by sharing content, messaging, or forming groups. Examples include Facebook, LinkedIn, and Twitter.

Mobilization Platforms: Mobilization platforms enable people to work together to accomplish something beyond the capabilities of any individual participant. In a business context this could be advancing a project or co-designing. Examples include Trello, Monday, Google Jamboards or Miro.

Learning Platform: Learning platforms facilitate learning by bringing participants together to share insights. They tend to foster deep, trust-based relationships and have both a business and consumer application. Examples include Medium, Quora, Udemy and Teachable.

Communication platform: direct social communication (e.g., messaging) Examples include Messenger, WhatsApp and Telegram.

Development platforms:

- Closed development platform: software built across access to data (usually via an API)

- Controlled development platform: software built in a controlled, integrated development environment

- Open development platform: open-source and free software

Content Platform: Content platforms provide a framework for distributing content, such as music, videos, or articles. Examples include YouTube, Spotify, and Medium.

Social Gaming Platform: Social gaming platforms promote interactions, collaboration and competition involving multiple users. Examples include Twitch, Xbox Live and Discord.

Case Study – Estonian Government: Estonia is a small Baltic nation that has become a global leader in digital government. In the 1990s, Estonia embarked on a digital transformation journey that included the development of a secure, national digital identity system that allows citizens to access a range of government services online.

The digital identity system, called ID-card, is a smart card that contains a microchip with the citizen's personal information and a digital signature that is used to verify their identity. The ID-card allows citizens to access a range of services online, including voting, tax filing, healthcare, and banking.

Additionally, Estonia has developed a range of digital services that are available to citizens and businesses, including e-Residency, which allows non-Estonians to access Estonian digital services and establish a business in Estonia remotely. The country also uses blockchain technology to secure and verify data, such as land registry and health records.

Estonia's digital government has significantly improved the efficiency and accessibility of government services while reducing bureaucracy and corruption. The digital government has also helped to create a thriving start-up ecosystem in the country, with many start-ups leveraging Estonia's digital infrastructure to develop new products and services.

An excellent case study of how a small nation can leverage advanced technologies to improve the accessibility, efficiency, and transparency of government services, and create a thriving innovation ecosystem.

What a Platform Is Not

Many make the mistake of conflating a platform with a mobile app or a website, but a platform isn't just a piece of software. It is important to reiterate that a platform is a business model, not just technology. It creates value by bringing together consumers and producers, buyers and sellers, creators, and customers.

Probably the most common misuse of the term "platform" is when it's used to describe an integrated suite of software solutions. This is indeed very common among SaaS companies, who love to claim they provide a complete platform. However, in this example, the term "platform" really is just being used for marketing, and these SaaS companies are still linear businesses.

We refer to these traditional, non-platform companies as linear businesses, because their operations are best described by the typical linear supply chain. SaaS companies build and sell products, not networks, so don't have the financial models that make platform businesses successful.

Generally speaking, linear companies exchange value in the form of products or services, sold downstream in their supply chain. They own their inventory (unlike platform businesses) and it shows on their balance sheets, whether it's a phone manufacturer like Apple or a subscription content provider like Disney, which either creates or directly licenses all of its content. It also includes resellers like Carrefour, Jarir or WHSmiths.

This also includes technology companies like Netflix, which pays for or licenses all its content. Even though it is a technology company, Netflix is still a linear business. Remember: Platform design isn't just about creating the underlying technology. It's about understanding and creating the whole business and how it will create value for, and build a network.

Simply put, what a company owns matters less than the resources it can connect to its audience. Meaning the supply chain is no longer the central aggregator of business value.

You Can Still Benefit From Platform Thinking

The platform trend is worth paying very close attention to even if your company isn't a platform business. There may be opportunities for you to introduce a new proposition built on a value-adding platform or to pivot to a platform model. But even if there isn't an opportunity to do this, you can still take inspiration and improve performance by applying 'platform thinking'.

'Platform thinking' is about focusing on increasing agility while providing more value to customers. In fact, organizations can use this mindset to restructure their technology foundations or recalibrate their business operating model. How could you better network your internal talent? Or introduce better ways to collaborate and create new efficiencies or knowledge sharing?

Unfortunately, the majority of initiatives towards platform transformation fail to achieve their full potential. This is largely because many organizations don't take a strategic approach and/or limit themselves when it comes to build, integration, or partnership by not considering the big picture.

For us it is clear... Whether your organization is motivated by fear of being left behind (stick) or driven by new opportunities or possibilities for your customers (carrot), the platform approach is here to stay and is worthy of your serious consideration.

Platforms Work for Most Businesses, and the Time to Move is Now

The right time for companies to start executing a platform strategy is now, especially since more agile competitors, or new players uninhibited by legacy approaches are likely already doing so.

To maintain competitive advantage requires more business intelligence, awareness of emerging game changers and data-driven insights to steer strategy. That's one of the big drivers motivating many to accelerate the migration towards the platform play, with the focus on delivering more value.

Organizations that experience high levels of bureaucracy will struggle more than most due to their lack of nimbility ... think governments for example. But when you address the philosophical, people and process Ps... Platform thinking is easier to apply.

"

Empirically speaking, there is no such thing as history, destiny and even future for that matter, what there really is, is the 'now'. And this very "now" – this very moment, is the only thing which you have in your hands... in fact, it is the only time that actually exists – the 'now'.

Abhijit Naskar

So What Does This Mean for Technology Departments?

IT departments are already very familiar with new ways of working. Agile techniques, practices and ceremonies are now the norm along with self-managed teams, multi-disciplinary teams, DevOps approaches, and much more. They are all transforming how IT generates value and engages with its internal customers and their business challenges. However, these don't necessarily add up to begin a platform organization. Forming an integrated technology model creates value but can be extremely hard to do.

A wide range of approaches are currently in place for IT departments. At one end of the scale are operating models where traditional IT and customer distinctions have been completely removed. At the other end of the spectrum these distinctions are well and truly locked in place. Most companies sit somewhere in between but are looking for new and better ways to increase IT's value delivery and role they play in innovation.

The right approach focuses teams on tech products and platforms related to business goals, helping them prioritize technology work. Dramatically different outcomes can be achieved from a deliberate strategy of thinking, organising, operating and behaving as a platform organization.

An increasing number of companies are choosing to blur the lines between digital programs (cross-functional teams applying new technologies and working practices focussed on user experience, such as agile) and traditional IT services (technical specialists developing and maintaining core systems).

According to research from McKinsey, companies with an integrated or fully digital technology model are 30 percent less likely to face digital-transformation challenges. They are also less likely to face issues when integrating new digital efforts with core architecture. Interestingly, respondents at companies with integrated operations are 60 percent more likely to say their companies' investments in technology create business value.

Migrating to an integrated technology operating model requires significant change. Prioritizing the following three actions will ease the process.

- Organize technology teams around user-facing products and the platforms that enable them
- Create a governance structure to keep the technology initiatives focused on the strategic priorities

- Establish a robust system for prioritizing and delivering technology projects

Here are five great examples of platform thinking from five different industries.

Lloyds Banking Group: In 2019, Lloyds Banking Group launched a digital transformation program aimed at improving customer experience and operational efficiency. The program included the development of a new digital platform that provides customers with a more personalized banking experience and enables them to access a range of services online. The program also involved the implementation of advanced analytics and automation tools to improve the bank's back-office operations.

Starbucks: In 2020, Starbucks implemented a digital transformation program aimed at improving its mobile ordering and payment system. The program included the implementation of a new cloud-based digital platform that enables customers to order and pay for their drinks online and pick them up at a designated store location. The program also

Allianz: In 2019, the global insurance company launched a digital platform called Allianz Business System (ABS), aimed at providing its customers with a more streamlined and efficient insurance experience. The platform was designed to enable customers to access a range of insurance services online, including purchasing insurance policies, managing claims, and accessing customer support.

The ABS platform was built on a cloud-based infrastructure, using modern technologies such as microservices, containerization, and DevOps practices. This enabled Allianz to rapidly develop and deploy new features and services on the platform and quickly respond to changing customer needs.

The ABS platform also utilized advanced analytics and AI technologies to provide customers with personalized insurance recommendations and automate claims processing. The platform's intelligent automation capabilities helped Allianz to reduce the time and cost involved in manual claims processing and improve the accuracy of claims assessments.

Allianz's ABS platform is an excellent example of how building a digital platform can enable organizations to provide their customers with a more seamless and efficient experience, leverage emerging technologies to improve their operations and reduce costs, and quickly adapt to changing market conditions and customer needs.

Dubai Electricity and Water Authority (DEWA): is a utility company in the United Arab Emirates that provides electricity and water services to the Emirate of Dubai. DEWA recognized that digital transformation was necessary to improve customer experience, reduce operational costs, and enhance the sustainability of its services.

DEWA embarked on a digital transformation journey that included investing in advanced technologies such as IoT, AI, and data analytics. One of the key initiatives was the development of the world's largest smart grid, which uses IoT sensors and analytics to monitor and optimize energy consumption in real-time.

DEWA also implemented a customer engagement platform that provides personalized services and allows customers to track their energy usage, view bills, and make payments through a mobile app or website. The platform includes AI-powered chatbots that provide immediate assistance and answers to customer queries.

Siemens AG: is a German multinational conglomerate that specializes in electrification, automation, and digitalization. In the early 2010s, Siemens recognized the need for a digital transformation to stay competitive in the global marketplace.

Siemens embarked on a digital transformation journey that included investing in advanced technologies such as IoT, AI, and data analytics. One of the key initiatives was the development of MindSphere, a cloud based IoT operating system that collects and analyzes data from industrial machines.

MindSphere allows Siemens to offer its customers a range of digital services, such as predictive maintenance and remote monitoring. The platform also provides customers with real-time data and analytics, enabling them to optimize the performance and efficiency of their machines.

Emerging Technology Trends

Whatever we write next will of course make this book immediately dated due to the pace of technology advances. But it would be remiss of us not to discuss some of the current and emerging technology trends which are extremely likely to have a significant impact on the way we work. Do remember to subscribe to our newsletter (visit www.everyday-transformation.com) if you want to be kept abreast of the latest advances on all of the topics discussed in this book, from technology to strategy, culture and beyond.

The Rise of the Cobot

Ooooooh that sounds very Terminator, doesn't it? Or Matrix or any other popular sci-fi which imagines a world where computers rule. Panic not, we are talking about the world of cobots, where humans and machines team up to conquer today's challenges.

So, what exactly is a cobot? Well, think of them as robots designed to work side by side with humans, in perfect harmony. In today's fast-paced world, where technology continues to advance at a rapid pace, the concept of collaboration between humans and machines has gained significant attention. One such innovative development is the rise of cobots, short for collaborative robots. Traditionally associated with the manufacturing industry, until recently, cobots employed some combination of exteroceptive technology that simulate key human senses, most commonly sight/vision, hearing and touch. Consequently, the exteroceptive sensors found in cobots generally include vision, touch, hearing, temperature, range finding, acceleration and other similar sensors.

But with the advances in technologies like AI, cobots have expanded their presence beyond the factory floor and are now making waves in various sectors, including organizational settings. In this chapter, we will explore the concept of cobots and delve into how they can be utilized as personal assistants in organizations, going beyond their conventional role in manufacturing.

In the context of the service sector and organizational environments, a Cobot takes the form of software that operates on PCs, tablets, or smartphones. Rather than physically interacting with tasks like their manufacturing counterparts, these cobots utilize voice interfaces, touch screens, or keyboards to communicate and assist employees in their daily work.

History Lesson... Cobots were invented in 1996 by two Northwestern University professors, J. Edward Colgate and Michael Peshkin; the term cobot was coined by Brent Gillespie, a researcher at the same university: cobot was chosen by the Wall Street Journal as one of the "The words of the future", in 2000

The Functionality of a cobot: Unlike traditional software or virtual assistants, cobots excel at reasoning and delivering personalized responses based on a vast amount of data. They have the ability to process and analyze information swiftly, allowing them to provide well-argued responses tailored to each specific context.

Applications in Organizational Settings: The potential in organizational settings is becoming increasingly evident. By leveraging them as personal assistants, organizations can streamline workflows, improve employee productivity, and enhance decision-making processes.

Personalization and Contextualization: One of the key strengths of cobots as personal assistants is their capability to personalize their responses. They can draw upon vast repositories of data, including the organization's knowledge base, previous interactions, and external sources, to provide tailored recommendations and insights. This personalized approach enables them to adapt to individual users and their unique requirements, ultimately enhancing productivity and efficiency.

Utilizing Close-Ended Questions: To achieve accurate and relevant responses, cobots often employ close-ended questions. These questions serve as a means for them to gather specific information from the user and narrow down the context of the query. By understanding the user's needs more precisely, cobots can offer more targeted assistance.

Efficient Task Management: Cobots can assist employees in managing their tasks and deadlines effectively. They can help prioritize assignments, set reminders, and provide suggestions for optimizing workloads. This proactive support allows employees to stay organized and focused on their responsibilities, leading to increased productivity and reduced stress levels.

Knowledge Repository and Information Retrieval: Organizations accumulate vast amounts of information over time. Cobots can serve as repositories of institutional knowledge, making it easier for employees to access relevant data and insights. Through natural language processing and intelligent search capabilities, they can swiftly retrieve information, saving valuable time that would otherwise be spent on manual searches.

Decision Support and Analytics: Cobots can contribute to decision-making processes by providing data-driven insights and analysis. By analyzing patterns and trends within an organization's data, they can offer valuable recommendations, helping employees make informed choices. This analytical capability can be particularly beneficial in areas such as sales forecasting, resource allocation, and strategic planning.

Enhanced Communication and Collaboration: Cobots act as intermediaries in communication, facilitating efficient collaboration within organizations. They can assist in scheduling meetings, coordinating tasks between team members, and even summarizing discussions. By automating routine communication tasks, cobots free up time for employees to focus on more meaningful and strategic activities.

By all measures, the market for collaborative robots (in the manufacturing context) is expected to experience robust growth over the next several years. A recent report from Interact Analysis predicts the collaborative robot market to be worth $7.5 billion by 2027. This would equate to roughly 29% of the global industrial robot market.

Let's compare this to the evolution of cobots into the office environment. Keeping in mind the likely utilization of AI to drive advances. According to Next Move Strategy Consulting the market for artificial intelligence (AI) will show strong growth in the coming decade. Its value of nearly 100 billion U.S. dollars is expected to grow twentyfold by 2030, up to nearly two trillion U.S. dollars. The AI market covers a vast number of industries.

Let's Talk Artificial Intelligence

Deep learning, a fascinating field of artificial intelligence (AI), has undergone significant developments over recent years. Let's explore the journey of deep learning, its milestones, and the role Google has played in this AI revolution.

Early Foundations: The groundwork for deep learning began in the 1950s with the introduction of neural networks. These networks, inspired by the human brain, consisted of interconnected artificial neurons. However, progress was limited until the 1980s when the backpropagation algorithm enabled neural networks to improve their performance through iterative learning.

Rediscovering Neural Networks: In the 1980s and 1990s, researchers like Geoffrey Hinton, Yann LeCun, and Yoshua Bengio rekindled interest in neural networks. Their work emphasized the potential of these networks to model complex processes. However, computational limitations and data scarcity hindered progress during this time.

Image Recognition Advancements: During the 1990s, Yann LeCun's pioneering work on convolutional neural networks (CNNs) revolutionized image recognition. CNNs were specifically designed to process visual data, enabling breakthroughs in tasks like object detection and facial recognition. These advancements laid the foundation for future developments in computer vision.

Language Processing Breakthroughs: In the late 1980s and early 1990s, researchers began exploring recurrent neural networks (RNNs) capable of modelling sequential data. RNNs paved the way for advancements in natural language processing (NLP), speech recognition, and machine translation. The introduction of LSTM networks in 1997 further improved RNNs' ability to understand and process language.

Deep Learning Renaissance: The 2010s marked a renaissance for deep learning, driven by the availability of large labelled datasets, powerful graphics processing units (GPUs), and advancements in computing infrastructure. Deep learning models, with their ability to learn hierarchical representations, demonstrated remarkable performance in diverse domains. This era witnessed breakthroughs in image recognition, speech recognition, and natural language processing (NLP).

Google's Contribution: Google has been at the forefront of the AI revolution and has made significant contributions to the field of deep learning. It has harnessed the power of deep learning across its various products and services. Google's research teams have developed state-of-the-art deep learning models, pushing the boundaries of what AI can achieve.

Google's deep learning advancements have fuelled innovations in areas such as computer vision, natural language understanding, and machine translation. Google Translate, Google Photos, and Google Assistant are prime examples of how deep learning has been integrated into everyday experiences.

Continuing Advancements: Deep learning is an evolving field with ongoing advancements. Researchers are exploring exciting techniques like generative adversarial networks (GANs) for realistic content generation, reinforcement learning for training autonomous agents, and transfer learning for leveraging pre-trained models. As computational power and data availability continue to grow, the future of deep learning holds promising possibilities.

The history of deep learning is a testament to the perseverance, creativity, and collaborative efforts of researchers and organizations like Google. Through their dedication, deep learning has transformed the way we understand and utilize AI, driving innovation and shaping the future of technology.

"

*AI won't take
your job…
someone using
AI will*

Warren Knight

Generative Artificial Intelligence

In the realm of artificial intelligence, one remarkable innovation stands out: Conversational AI, also known as generative AI. This transformative technology is revolutionizing the way we interact with machines, paving the way for more intuitive and human-like conversations. However, there is a prevailing misconception that AI will replace human jobs. In reality, it is the symbiotic relationship between people and AI that holds the key to job security and professional growth.

Conversational AI has come a long way since its early days, with a goal of bridging the gap between humans and machines, fostering seamless communication and improving user experiences. So your proficiency using AI will be your competitive advantage. Typically, organizations prize resourcefulness over knowledge, i.e., you don't need to know all the answers, you need to know how to find the answers. At the time of writing the job role of 'Prompt Engineer' is appearing on job boards all over the world... BTW with an average salary of $300k!

With developers releasing language model iterations left and right, companies need full-time employees to manage them. Communicating with AI has become a legitimate job. That said, prompt engineering is also at risk of obsolescence. We firmly believe that in a short period of time, the skills of a prompt engineer will be commonplace and a minimum requirement for all job roles. Essentially everyone will need to be able to ask better questions and understand the conversational pathways with AI.

Conversational AI represents a new era of human-machine collaboration, where AI is not a threat to job security but a catalyst for professional growth.

Here are just some of the exciting applications for generative AI right now.

Enhancing Customer Support and Service: One of the most significant applications of Conversational AI is in customer support and service. By utilizing AI-powered chatbots or virtual assistants, organizations can offer 24/7 support, promptly addressing customer queries and concerns. These AI-driven systems can handle repetitive tasks, freeing up human agents to focus on more complex and strategic aspects of customer interactions. Rather than replacing jobs, Conversational AI augments human capabilities, allowing businesses to provide efficient and personalized customer experiences.

Boosting Productivity and Efficiency: Conversational AI acts as a force multiplier, enhancing productivity and efficiency in various industries. With AI-powered virtual assistants, professionals can delegate time-consuming tasks such as scheduling appointments, managing emails, or conducting research. By offloading mundane activities to AI, individuals can redirect their energy towards more high-value activities, fostering creativity, problem-solving, and strategic decision-making. This symbiotic relationship between people and AI amplifies productivity, leading to better outcomes and job satisfaction.

Enabling Personalized Experiences: Conversational AI excels in its ability to deliver personalized experiences. By analyzing vast amounts of data and user interactions, AI systems can understand individual preferences, anticipate needs, and offer tailored recommendations. For instance, personalized marketing campaigns powered by Conversational AI can engage customers with relevant content and recommendations, leading to higher conversion rates and customer satisfaction. By leveraging AI's ability to understand and adapt to human preferences, professionals can deliver exceptional experiences that nurture long-lasting relationships.

Augmenting Creativity and Innovation: Contrary to popular belief, Conversational AI doesn't stifle human creativity; it fuels it. By automating routine tasks and providing quick access to relevant information, AI systems empower individuals to think more strategically and creatively. Freed from the shackles of monotonous tasks, professionals can explore new ideas, experiment with innovative approaches, and push the boundaries of their respective fields. Conversational AI acts as a catalyst, unlocking human potential and fostering a culture of continuous learning and innovation.

Collaboration between Humans and AI: The true power of Conversational AI lies in collaboration between humans and machines. Rather than replacing jobs, AI becomes a trusted partner, supporting professionals in their daily work. Humans bring unique qualities such as empathy, critical thinking, and emotional intelligence to the table, while AI enhances these qualities with data-driven insights, processing power, and scalability. This collaboration enables individuals to achieve new levels of productivity, creativity, and efficiency, leading to professional growth and expanded job roles.

By leveraging the capabilities of Conversational AI, individuals can delegate mundane tasks, focus on higher-value activities, and deliver exceptional personalized experiences. The synergy between humans and AI unlocks new opportunities for creativity, innovation, and productivity.

It is through embracing and harnessing the potential of Conversational AI that individuals can secure their roles in an increasingly automated world.

Case Study – Mercedes Benz: A great example of a brand looking to enhance the customer experience using (a Cobot) AI is Mercedes-Benz who are collaborating with Microsoft (Partner) to introduce ChatGPT, an artificial intelligence software, into its vehicles. The aim is to enhance the existing "Hey, Mercedes" voice command feature, providing drivers with a more natural and seamless voice-command experience. Over the past decade, the auto industry has focused on developing sophisticated voice command systems to improve safety by enabling hands-free interactions with vehicles.

The current "Hey, Mercedes" system allows drivers to adjust in-car settings and find navigation destinations through simple commands. With the integration of ChatGPT, interactions will become more enriching, allowing the system to engage in more natural conversations, remember context, and respond to a broader range of requests, even unrelated to driving, like asking for recipes or travel recommendations.

Moreover, the integration enables the system to interact with other applications, facilitating tasks such as making reservations or purchasing tickets. The ChatGPT software accepts natural voice commands and conducts conversations, enabling drivers to ask complex questions or get details about their destination while keeping their focus on the road.

The voice command data is stored in the Mercedes-Benz Intelligent Cloud for analysis, aiming to enhance the voice assistant further and expand language model rollouts to more markets and languages.

As technology continues to evolve, the role of AI in driving remains uncertain, and the true significance of these features will depend on their practicality and value in the long run.

Before we move on… an important reminder worth repeating. It's not AI that will take people's jobs; it's people using AI that will shape the future of work. Therefore whatever your role, understand how you can utilise this revolutionary resource now and in the future.

REFLECTION SECTION

When considering the potential application of AI, organizations should ask themselves the following questions:

1. What specific business challenges or opportunities can AI help address?
2. Are there any areas of our operations that could benefit from automation, optimization, or enhanced decision-making through AI?
3. What are the potential risks and ethical considerations associated with implementing AI in our organization?
4. Do we have the necessary data infrastructure and quality to support AI initiatives effectively?
5. What AI technologies and tools are available in the market, and how do they align with our business objectives?
6. What are the costs and resource requirements associated with implementing AI, and what is the expected return on investment?
7. How will AI impact our workforce, and what measures should be taken to upskill or reskill employees to work effectively alongside AI systems?
8. How will AI affect our customer experience and interactions with stakeholders?
9. How can AI be integrated with existing systems and processes to ensure a seamless transition?
10. What regulations and compliance standards must be considered when deploying AI in our industry?
11. What are the potential limitations and biases of AI algorithms, and how can we mitigate them to ensure fair and responsible use?
12. How will AI affect our competitive advantage in the market, and what is the level of readiness among our competitors?
13. What are the short-term and long-term goals for AI implementation, and how will progress be measured?
14. Are there any legal or privacy implications related to the data used in AI applications, and how will data security be ensured?
15. How will AI align with our overall business strategy and support our mission and vision?

By addressing these questions, organizations can gain a clearer understanding of the opportunities, challenges, and implications of applying AI in their operations and make well-informed decisions about its adoption.

REMEMBER: You can visit www.Everyday-Transformation.com for the **Transformation Insight Assessment™** which includes more questions to guide you.

PARTNER
Distribution
Development
Support
PROPOSITION
Collaboration

TRANSFORMATION INSIGHT FRAMEWORK

HIVEMIND

PARTNERSHIP ALIGNMENT

Let's just briefly re-cap, change is inevitable, but the dramatic shifts required for a successful digital transformation are among the most challenging to navigate today. We have explored the importance of being philosophically aligned, the impact of aligning your people and culture, the benefits of process improvement or reinvention and how to underpin it all with platform thinking. All of this to create a more experience-led business.

So here is the but... it is rare for organizations to have all the tools, expertise or experience to do so without a little outside help. Delivering digital transformation initiatives requires a broad mixture of skills. Leaders require digital experience and a digital mindset, as well as the political intelligence to navigate organizational dynamics.

On top of this they also should be able to demonstrate emotional intelligence, collaboration, tenacity, resilience, pragmatism, critical thinking, creativity, and learning agility.

Businesses often underestimate the skills and expertise of the people required to deliver successful digital transformation outcomes. For the 70% of transformations that fail, failure (in part) can be attributed to organizations that have tried to build digital capabilities internally without external guidance.

So here is the good news... The complex, evolving work of digital transformation doesn't need to be tackled alone. Partnerships are now amongst the most powerful resources available for companies to navigate from where they are to where they want to be. Whether the partnership is focussed on technology, innovation, co-creation of customer value or knowledge and up-skilling... Organizations can accelerate growth by leveraging insight and ideas from those already wearing the battle scars.

Partnerships are of course nothing new. Both established and emerging industries have historically built value through partnership strategies. Recent research from BPI Network suggests that 44% of businesses

It is the long history of humankind (and animal kind, too) those who learned to collaborate and improvise most effectively have prevailed

Charles Darwin

"seek alliances for new ideas, insights and innovation," and another report in the Harvard Business Review suggests that 94% of technology executives see innovation partnerships as necessary to their strategy.

Working with the right company (or internal team) that specializes in solving a problem which complements your own competencies can be one of the most efficient ways to make progress.

Businesses must ask these critical questions of themselves:

- Is this really our corporate core competency?

- Do we have the time and budget to develop the skills we need?

- Could we accelerate the process with a partner with a track record of delivering measurable results?

- In what areas do we need support, and what transformation services should the right partner offer?

There are five key areas in a digital transformation programme where partners can add significant value:

Transformation Strategy

Strategy partners can help flesh out your transformation process, work with you to uncover opportunities and threats, and map out your value dependency network.

Strategy partners can also identify key applications and services you'll need to implement or develop to unlock new business value. Working with you in the discovery stage with your current state analysis, benchmarking and a deep dive on your market to really understand the future needs of your customer.

They can assist in assessing your organizational culture and whether it needs to evolve to achieve your transformation goals. As well as ensuring the systems processes and structures in place support your ambitions.

This is where we are now spending much of our time with clients helping.

Collaborate with people you can learn from

Pharrell

Learning and Development

Often the skills required for this type of organizational change are either specialist in their nature or address mindset. This of course plays a large part of the work we do at Hivemind, creating tailored learning experiences bespoke to your industry or profession, and centred around your values and culture. Normally L&D initiatives run parallel alongside other change programmes, prioritising those likely to play a part in successful implementation or adoption.

As well as the broad deployment programmes typically addressing topics like agile mindset, collaboration, innovation, leadership and digital skills, we also get involved in workshops (particularly with C-Suite and Senior Leadership) early on in the process to ensure everyone is not only on the same page, but understands what is going to happen and the benefits to the organization.

Innovation Programmes

Connected to our L&D initiatives a growing part of our work is running the innovation programmes previously discussed in this book. Working with leaders, process owners and technologists within the business to ideate using design thinking techniques to create both internal and external customer facing projects that have a tangible impact. Often this results in new revenue streams but almost always in efficiency improvements and savings.

Better still, by participating in these programmes, participants create new instincts for ongoing improvements and have a framework to realise them.

Technology Services

There are many different kinds of technical partnerships from software/ app development, to platform, integration, infrastructure and support. Technology partnerships are a way for businesses to implement and optimize their technical systems with the help of outside expertise. These relationships typically happen between technology vendors who provide the product, and agencies or companies using these in daily operations.

Tech partnerships can provide not just platform integration support but also help companies with smooth implementation processes. They allow for seamless cooperation between different IT systems and partners to avoid hassles during the transition from old technology to new ones to make your business run more smoothly.

Change Management

New digital services and applications only add value when your organization embrace them and exploit the opportunities they provide. A change management partner understands the psychology of change and how humans respond and engage with technology. They recognise how the nature of the work will change and understand that your workforce must be trained, incentivised, organised and motivated to take advantage of the new systems and processes.

Joint Venture Partnership

Occasionally two or more organizations will come together to innovate and disrupt, leveraging their combined resources for R&D or to penetrate new markets. Joint ventures can serve a variety of purposes, for example exploring a new market or territory, actualizing high-investment projects, innovating new products, tax benefits, resource pooling etc. These ventures can be a partnership, a separate legal entity, or a contractual agreement. Additionally, there is no designated governing body for joint venture oversight, although they may of course be subject to various laws and regulations depending on the industry.

Here are just a few examples of companies coming together to create something new:

- Uber + Volvo = Autonomous cars

- Verily + GlaxoSmithKline = Biometric medicines (asthma and diabetes)

- Sony + Ericsson = Mobile phones plus other gadgets

- NBC + Disney = Hulu (valued at over $25 Billion)

- Kellogg's + Wilmar = Kellogg's expansion into the Chinese market

- ExxonMobil + Indian Oil Corporation = Innovative new supply chain methods across India

- Honda + General Motors = Electric cars

- Amazon + Berkshire Hathaway + JPMorgan Chase = New healthcare company for employees

- Nike + Michael Jordan = Air Jordan

While partnerships play a huge role in value creation, they take on even greater importance during times of economic uncertainty. Over the next 10 years we can expect to see organizations invest in more strategic partnerships to efficiently deliver innovative technologies to a broader market and leverage a common platform through which a more powerful round of digital transformation can be unlocked.

Innovative, human-centred solutions to transformation challenges can't be developed without diverse expertise and capabilities. That's why it's important to find transformation partners that use both a technology-enabled and service-based approach to generate a unified solution. Here are some strategies to help you in the process:

Clearly define your objectives: Before seeking partners, have a clear understanding of your digital transformation goals and the specific areas where you need assistance. This clarity will enable you to identify partners who align with your objectives.

Assess your internal capabilities: Evaluate your organization's internal capabilities and identify the gaps that need to be filled through partnerships. This will help you understand the specific expertise and resources you require from potential partners.

Conduct thorough research: Conduct extensive research to identify potential partners who specialize in the areas relevant to your digital transformation. Look for companies with a proven track record of success, domain expertise, and a strong reputation in the industry.

Seek recommendations and references: Ask for recommendations from industry peers, attend relevant conferences and networking events, and reach out to your professional network for suggestions. Gathering insights and references from trusted sources can help you find reliable partners.

Evaluate expertise and experience: Once you have identified potential partners, assess their expertise, experience, and capabilities in the specific areas you require assistance with. Review their previous projects, case studies, and client testimonials to gauge their suitability.

Cultural fit and alignment: Consider the cultural fit and alignment between your organization and potential partners. Ensure that their

Alliances and partnerships produce stability when they reflect realities and interests

Stephen Kinzer

values, work ethic, and approach to problem-solving align with yours. A strong cultural fit can significantly enhance collaboration and the overall success of the partnership.

Collaborative approach: Look for partners who adopt a collaborative approach to working. Digital transformation often requires close collaboration, so choose partners who are willing to work together, share knowledge, and actively contribute to your organization's success.

Financial stability and scalability: Assess the financial stability and scalability of potential partners. Digital transformation initiatives may span a significant period, so partnering with financially stable organizations ensures continuity and minimizes the risk of disruptions.

Request proposals and conduct interviews: Once you have shortlisted potential partners, request detailed proposals outlining their approach, methodologies, and deliverables. Conduct interviews or meetings to discuss their proposals in-depth, ask relevant questions, and assess their communication and responsiveness.

Negotiate and establish clear agreements: After selecting the right partner, negotiate terms, and establish clear agreements regarding project scope, timelines, deliverables, responsibilities, and pricing. Clearly define key performance indicators (KPIs) to track progress and ensure accountability.

Remember that finding the right partners takes time and careful consideration. Investing effort in the selection process will help you form strong partnerships that contribute to the success of your digital transformation journey.

Five Examples of Digital Transformation-Inspired Partnerships

AXA: In the early 2010s, AXA faced significant challenges, including a highly competitive marketplace, changing consumer preferences, and increasing regulatory demands. The company's leadership recognized that a digital transformation was necessary to remain competitive and relevant in the market.

AXA embarked on a digital transformation journey that included investing in advanced technologies such as AI, machine learning, and data analytics. One of the key initiatives was the creation of AXA's Open Innovation Lab, which is a startup accelerator that partners with early-stage companies to develop new products and services.

Mercedes-Benz: plans to build its own branded navigation using new in-car geospatial data and navigation capabilities from the Google Maps Platform. The partnership enables Mercedes-Benz to create a driving experience that pairs the trusted, reliable information from Google Maps with its own unique luxury brand and feel.

Accenture and Sumitomo Chemical: have formed a collaborative venture named SUMIKA DX ACCENT. The joint venture aims to harness the potential of artificial intelligence (AI), data analytics, and other cutting-edge technologies to revolutionize Sumitomo Chemical Group's operations and foster the creation of innovative businesses. The venture is predominantly owned by Sumitomo Chemical (80%) and Accenture (20%).

With Accenture's extensive expertise in various industries and digital transformation, the joint venture will optimize Sumitomo Chemical's supply chain and drive intelligent automation across its operations, employing AI, data analytics, and robotic process automation.

Accenture's role encompasses providing consulting services and implementing a practical training program to cultivate digital technology and intelligent operations skills within the organization. Through this collaboration, both companies aim to achieve greater efficiency and excellence in their business practices.

Capgemini and Audi: have jointly launched their new venture, named XL2, to offer digital technology and consulting services focused on SAP S/4HANA and cloud services, primarily catering to Audi and the entire Volkswagen Group. The company's vision is to progressively expand its project portfolio and build a strong workforce over the next five years.

The collaboration jointly lead, aims to provide comprehensive digital solutions to drive efficiency and innovation within the automotive industry.

Saudi Telecom Company (STC) partnered with Huawei: to launch a transformative program, Corporate Customer Experience Management (CCEx), in 2019, aimed at enhancing digital customer experience. Led by the office of the Group CEO, CCEx establishes a unified method for measuring customer experience throughout the STC Group. At its core, CCEx utilizes Huawei's SmartCare platform, incorporating customer experience management, network performance management, and service quality management. This platform enables a comprehensive 360-degree view of customers and fosters a customer-centric culture at STC. The program's implementation is a significant initiative that seeks to elevate customer experience across the organization.

REFLECTION SECTION

When considering partners in the context of a digital transformation, organizations should ask themselves the following questions:

1. What are the specific skills and expertise that our partners bring to the table in terms of digital transformation?
2. How well do our partners align with our organization's digital transformation goals and vision?
3. Are our partners capable of supporting us throughout the entire digital transformation journey, from planning to implementation and beyond?
4. How will our partners collaborate with our internal teams and stakeholders to ensure seamless integration of digital solutions?
5. What level of flexibility and adaptability do our partners demonstrate in response to changing digital trends and technologies?
6. How do our partners address data privacy, security, and compliance concerns in the context of digital transformation?
7. What is the communication and reporting structure with our partners to ensure transparency and timely updates on project progress?
8. How will our partners assist in building digital capabilities within our organization and ensure knowledge transfer?
9. What are the financial implications and costs associated with partnering in the digital transformation initiative?
10. How do our partners measure success and what key performance indicators (KPIs) will they use to track the impact of the digital transformation efforts?
11. How do our partners plan to support us in scaling and sustaining the digital transformation changes in the long term?

Asking these questions will help organizations assess the suitability and compatibility of potential partners and make informed decisions to ensure a successful digital transformation journey.

REMEMBER: You can visit www.Everyday-Transformation.com for the **Transformation Insight Assessment™** which includes more questions to guide you.

Your value proposition is an answer to the question: 'Why should I buy from you and not your competitor?

Neil Patel

PROPOSITION ALIGNMENT

And so we come to our final P in the **Transformation Insight Framework™**, although your Proposition has been hopefully front of mind through-out the book so far.

By Proposition we mean the products and services you sell and the value you create for your customers. But at a higher level we simply mean your value proposition... The statement that communicates the unique value a company offers to its customers and how it addresses their needs or solves their problems. It defines why customers should choose the company's products or services over competitors.

Every impactful value proposition possesses these five essential characteristics:

Specificity: A powerful value proposition reflects the unique value of your company with precision, avoiding vague statements that lack clarity and substance.

Clarity: The best value propositions provide prospects with a clear understanding of what your company does. If your value proposition is unclear, potential customers may quickly seek alternatives.

Uniqueness: Your value proposition should set your company apart from others, demonstrating that it cannot easily apply to a different industry. Avoid generic statements like "Customers First" that fail to highlight your distinctiveness.

Customer Focus: Shift the focus away from your company and concentrate on your customers. A compelling value proposition goes beyond detailing the longevity of your business or the specifics of your products or services. Instead, it emphasizes the value you bring to your customers' lives and work.

Promises: Your value proposition should make a compelling promise to customers, offering something they won't find elsewhere. Provide insight into the commitment you make to deliver on this promise through your value proposition.

Ask Yourself... Is Yours Still Fit for Purpose?

Digital transformation and value proposition form a perfect partnership, resulting in significant benefits for businesses. When organizations embrace digital transformation, they leverage the power of technology to enhance their value proposition and elevate their offerings to customers.

Through digital transformation, businesses can better understand customer needs and preferences, leading to the development of more personalized and targeted products and services. By incorporating innovative digital technologies, companies can deliver convenience, efficiency, and seamless experiences, aligning with their value proposition.

It also empowers organizations to streamline processes, optimize operations, and improve overall cost efficiency, which contributes to the enhancement of their value proposition. By leveraging data analytics and artificial intelligence, businesses gain valuable insights into market trends, customer behavior, and competitor landscapes, allowing them to fine-tune their value proposition to stay competitive and relevant.

This enables businesses to respond swiftly to changing market demands, customer expectations, and emerging opportunities, ensuring that their value proposition remains compelling and adaptable.

When going through Everyday Transformation™, it is essential to ensure that the changes being made align with and reinforce the organization's value proposition. This alignment helps maintain consistency in messaging and customer experience throughout the transformation process.

Here's a reminder of some key aspects of being proposition aligned during a digital transformation:

Customer-Centric Focus: Prioritize understanding customer needs and preferences to ensure that digital initiatives are designed to enhance the customer experience and deliver on the value promised to customers.

Value Delivery: Evaluate how digital technologies and processes can enable the delivery of the value proposition more effectively and efficiently.

Brand Consistency: Ensure that the brand identity and messaging remain consistent across all digital channels and touchpoints.

Innovation: Embrace digital innovation and technologies that align with the organization's value proposition, rather than adopting technology for the sake of it.

Data-Driven Decision Making: Utilize data and analytics to inform decisions and validate that digital initiatives are aligned with customer expectations and the value proposition.

Cross-Functional Collaboration: Foster collaboration among different departments, such as marketing, sales, customer service, and IT, to ensure that digital initiatives are integrated and collectively reinforce the value proposition.

Employee Alignment: Ensure that employees understand the value proposition and are trained and empowered to deliver on it through digital initiatives.

Continuous Evaluation: Regularly assess the impact of digital transformation efforts on the value proposition and make adjustments as needed to stay aligned with changing market dynamics and customer expectations.

An excellent example of meeting evolving customer expectations is evident in the evolution of automated teller machines (ATMs) in banks. In the 1960s, ATMs had limited functionalities as most transactions required human cashiers. However, in the 21st century, ATMs have transformed to offer almost everything a human cashier can. This transformation is a response to the modern customer's desire for convenience.

Customers no longer want to wait in queues and explain their needs to a cashier. Instead, they prefer the simplicity of pressing a few buttons on an ATM to get their needs fulfilled quickly and efficiently. This shift in approach caters to the demand for immediate solutions, reflecting the changing expectations of today's customers.

Digital technology has the potential to enhance your team's productivity significantly. Take the example of ATMs in banks; advanced ATMs can handle multiple customer requests, efficiently filtering those who don't need human assistance from those who do.

For instance, customers requiring simple transactions like cash deposits or withdrawals can easily use the ATM, freeing up cashiers to attend to customers who need personalized assistance. This improved efficiency not only contributes to customer satisfaction but also allows cashiers to focus on other value-adding tasks.

In a B2B-focused scenario, implementing technology like automation and machine learning can revolutionize manufacturing processes. By increasing production speed without compromising quality, automation and machine learning reduce the likelihood of human errors, consequently improving product quality.

Furthermore, the integration of artificial intelligence (AI) and Internet of Things (IoT) technologies can take productivity to new heights. IoT-enabled devices can provide real-time data to your ERP system through multiple sensors, consolidating essential information like machine performance and maintenance records in one central place. AI goes a step further by offering in-depth insights by cross-referencing real-time data with market and consumer trends.

This level of technological integration empowers your business to meet consumer demand more effectively, ensuring that the right products are delivered in the right quantities when and where they are needed most. Overall, embracing digital technology streamlines processes, optimizes productivity, and facilitates a more agile response to market demands.

Digital transformation often leads to increased cost efficiency. If a business lacks access to the latest digital technology, it may continue running on outdated legacy software and systems. This raises concerns about operational efficiency and the possibility of better alternatives.

Introducing new technology may require initial investments in costs and resources, such as time and labor. However, in the long run, the benefits become evident. Digital transformation can save time for employees, enhance internal productivity, streamline processes, improve output quality, and achieve the goals discussed earlier.

By integrating digital technology, businesses can observe a boost in productivity, effectively meet customer expectations, and ultimately enhance their value proposition. Embracing digital transformation empowers businesses to remain competitive, adapt to changing market demands, and foster continuous improvement and growth.

Challenging the norm can lead to positive outcomes, as demonstrated by Amazon's remarkable journey. Starting as a seller of music, videos, and books, Amazon has now evolved into the world's largest e-commerce company, thanks to its embrace of innovation.

In the realm of e-commerce, apprehensions about selling items online are understandable. Customers may hesitate to purchase items they haven't seen in person. While B2C customers may be more open to online buying, B2B customers often approach it with scepticism due to differences in their buying journey, involving a longer process and more decision-makers, and being process-driven rather than emotionally-driven.

Despite these distinctions, the ideal B2B customer experience should be as convenient as the B2C alternative. Both types of customers seek fast answers to their questions and a straightforward solution-searching process.

For businesses relying on e-commerce, leveraging digital technology can enhance the customer journey and experience. Consider the following approaches:

- Meet customers where they already are by utilizing social selling through targeted native ads and sharing relevant content on social media channels instead of cold calling

- Offer personalized recommendations based on specific customer profiles or individual preferences, using existing knowledge about your customer base.

- Treat returning customers like VIPs, even through simple gestures like addressing them by their first name or providing personalized treats such as unique promotional codes, sales, or content.

- Provide omnichannel customer support, ensuring a consistent and seamless customer service and experience across all channels.

The union of digital transformation and value proposition creates a potent force that propels businesses to new heights, facilitating customer satisfaction, competitive advantage, and long-term success. By embracing digital transformation, organizations can amplify their value proposition and deliver unmatched value to their customers, ultimately positioning themselves as industry leaders in the digital age.

REFLECTION SECTION

1. How will digital transformation enhance our value proposition to customers?

2. Will digital transformation enable us to deliver products or services more efficiently, resulting in cost savings that we can pass on to customers?

3. How will digital transformation improve the customer experience and satisfaction with our products or services?

4. Can digital transformation help us differentiate our offerings from competitors and create a unique selling proposition?

5. Will digital transformation allow us to offer new or additional features, benefits, or services to customers?

6. How will digital transformation address customer pain points and provide solutions that meet their specific needs?

7. Will digital transformation enable us to offer personalized or customized experiences to customers?

8. Can digital transformation help us reach new customer segments or expand into new markets?

9. How will digital transformation enhance our ability to communicate and engage with customers effectively?

10. Will digital transformation improve our ability to collect and analyze customer data, leading to better insights and decision-making?

11. How will digital transformation impact our pricing strategy and overall value proposition in the market?

12. Can digital transformation help us build stronger customer loyalty and retention?

13. How will digital transformation contribute to our brand reputation and perception in the market?

14. Will digital transformation allow us to offer faster and more efficient customer support and service?

15. How will digital transformation impact the overall perceived value of our products or services?

> **REMEMBER:** You can visit www.Everyday-Transformation.com for the **Transformation Insight Assessment™** which includes more questions to guide you.

"

Information with context, transforms into knowledge you can apply!

Warren Cass

CONTEXTUALISING DIGITAL TRANSFORMATION

Digital transformation holds unique significance for different organizational departments. Each department can leverage digital technology to achieve specific objectives and enhance their overall efficiency and effectiveness. Here's how Everyday Transformation™ can be contextualized for different departments:

Marketing Department: Digital transformation enables the marketing department to reach and engage with a broader audience through various online channels. It provides opportunities for targeted advertising, personalized messaging, and real-time data analytics to understand customer behaviour and preferences better. Marketing automation tools can streamline campaign management, lead generation, and customer relationship management, leading to improved customer experiences and increased conversion rates.

Note: We haven't gone into detail in this book about Digital Marketing, but we have some great courses to help should you want to connect the dots.

Key Considerations

- **Digital Customer Journey:** Understand and map the digital customer journey to identify touchpoints and opportunities for engagement across various digital channels, such as social media, websites, email, and mobile apps.

- **Data-Driven Marketing:** Embrace data-driven marketing by leveraging customer data and analytics to gain insights into customer behavior, preferences, and buying patterns. Use this data to personalize marketing messages and improve targeting.

- **Integrated Marketing Technology:** Adopt and integrate marketing technology stack, including customer relationship management (CRM), marketing automation, data analytics, and content management systems, to streamline marketing workflows and enhance efficiency.

- **Content Marketing Strategy:** Develop a comprehensive content marketing strategy that includes creating valuable and relevant content to attract and retain customers. Content can be in the form of blogs, videos, infographics, and other formats that align with customer interests.

- **Social Media Engagement:** Engage customers and prospects on social media platforms through active participation, responding to comments, and sharing valuable content. Leverage social media as a channel for customer support and relationship building.

- **Search Engine Optimization (SEO):** Optimize website content and structure to improve organic search rankings. Implement SEO best practices to drive more qualified traffic to the website.

- **Mobile Marketing:** Optimize marketing strategies for mobile devices, as mobile usage continues to grow. Ensure that websites and marketing campaigns are mobile-friendly and provide a seamless user experience.

- **Marketing Personalization:** Utilize data and technology to deliver personalized marketing messages based on customer preferences, behavior, and demographics. Personalization enhances customer engagement and conversion rates.

- **Customer Segmentation:** Segment the target audience based on demographics, behaviors, and interests to create targeted marketing campaigns that resonate with specific customer segments.

- **Performance Measurement:** Define key performance indicators (KPIs) and use analytics to measure the success of marketing campaigns. Continuously analyze data to optimize marketing efforts and improve ROI.

- **Collaboration with Sales:** Foster strong collaboration between marketing and sales departments to align on lead generation, nurturing, and customer engagement strategies. Ensure a seamless handoff of leads from marketing to sales.

- **Privacy and Compliance:** Adhere to data privacy regulations and best practices to protect customer data and maintain trust with customers.

- **Agile Marketing:** Embrace agile marketing practices to adapt quickly to changing market dynamics and customer needs. Test and iterate marketing strategies to find the most effective approaches.

Sales Department: Digital transformation empowers the sales team with tools for remote selling, lead tracking, and customer relationship management. CRM systems can centralize customer data, facilitating better communication and personalized sales interactions. E-commerce platforms enable online sales, while advanced analytics help identify upselling and cross-selling opportunities. Sales automation streamlines processes, allowing the team to focus on building relationships and closing deals.

Key Considerations

- **Customer-Centric Approach:** Emphasize a customer-centric mindset, understanding their changing needs, preferences, and behaviors in the digital landscape. Use data and analytics to gain insights into customer behavior and tailor sales strategies accordingly.

- **Digital Sales Tools:** Adopt and integrate digital sales tools such as customer relationship management (CRM) software, sales automation platforms, and analytics tools. These tools can streamline sales processes, improve data management, and enhance customer engagement.

- **Sales Team Training:** Provide comprehensive training and upskilling programs to enable the sales team to effectively use digital tools and embrace new sales methodologies. Ensure they are proficient in leveraging technology to engage customers and close deals.

- **Sales Enablement Content:** Develop and curate sales enablement content, including product information, case studies, and multimedia assets that empower sales representatives to deliver compelling presentations and address customer inquiries effectively.

- **Omnichannel Selling:** Implement an omnichannel sales approach that allows customers to interact seamlessly across various digital channels, such as websites, social media, email, and live chat. Ensure consistency in messaging and customer experience across all channels.

- **Data-Driven Sales Strategies:** Utilize data and analytics to inform sales strategies, identify high-value leads, and forecast sales trends. Data-driven insights can help optimize sales processes and prioritize sales efforts effectively.

- **Personalization and Customization:** Leverage digital tools to personalize sales pitches and tailor product recommendations based on individual customer preferences and past interactions.

- **Virtual Selling Capabilities:** Equip the sales team with the necessary technology and skills to conduct virtual meetings and sales presentations, especially in remote or hybrid work environments.

- **Integration with Marketing:** Foster strong collaboration between the sales and marketing teams to align on lead generation, nurturing, and customer engagement strategies. Marketing-generated leads should seamlessly flow into the sales pipeline.

- **Continuous Improvement:** Encourage a culture of continuous learning and improvement within the sales department. Regularly evaluate the effectiveness of digital sales initiatives and identify areas for refinement and optimization.

- **Security and Compliance:** Ensure that all digital sales activities comply with data privacy regulations and cybersecurity best practices. Protect customer data and maintain trust with clients.

- **Performance Metrics and Analytics:** Establish clear sales performance metrics and leverage analytics to track progress, measure success, and identify areas of improvement. Use data to recognize top-performing sales representatives and reward achievements.

Human Resources Department: Digital transformation in HR involves leveraging technology to optimize talent acquisition, onboarding, and employee engagement. Applicant tracking systems facilitate efficient recruitment processes, while digital onboarding tools streamline the integration of new employees. HR analytics and employee feedback platforms aid in workforce planning and talent development, ultimately contributing to a positive work culture.

Key Considerations

- **Talent Assessment and Development:** Assess the existing workforce's digital skills and identify skill gaps that need to be addressed. Develop training and upskilling programs to equip employees with the necessary digital competencies to thrive in the transformed environment.

- **Change Management:** Implement a comprehensive change management strategy to facilitate smooth adoption of digital tools and processes. Communicate the vision, benefits, and impact of digital transformation to employees, and address any concerns or resistance to change.

- **Talent Acquisition:** Attract and hire candidates with relevant digital skills and experiences to support the organization's digital initiatives. Redefine job roles and job descriptions to align with new digital requirements.

- **Employee Engagement:** Foster a culture of innovation and continuous learning. Engage employees by involving them in the digital transformation process and seeking their input on improving processes and operations.

- **Performance Management:** Align performance metrics and evaluation criteria with the objectives of the digital transformation. Set clear performance goals related to digital capabilities and reward employees for embracing digital tools and driving innovation.

- **Data and Analytics:** Leverage HR analytics to gain insights into employee performance, engagement, and learning progress. Use data-driven insights to make informed decisions about talent development and retention.

- **Employee Wellbeing:** Monitor and address employee stress and burnout during the digital transformation. Provide support and resources to help employees manage workloads and adapt to new technologies.

- **Collaboration and Communication:** Encourage cross-functional collaboration and open communication channels between HR and other departments involved in the digital transformation. Ensure that HR is actively involved in planning and implementing digital initiatives.

- **Digital HR Tools:** Adopt and integrate digital HR tools and platforms that streamline HR processes, such as recruitment, onboarding, performance management, and learning management systems.

- **Data Privacy and Security:** Ensure compliance with data privacy regulations when implementing digital HR solutions. Safeguard employee data and protect sensitive information from cybersecurity threats.

- **Diversity and Inclusion:** Prioritize diversity and inclusion efforts during the digital transformation. Ensure that digital initiatives consider the needs of all employees, including those with diverse backgrounds and abilities.

Operations/Supply Chain Department: Digital transformation enhances supply chain efficiency by incorporating IoT devices, sensors, and AI-driven analytics to monitor inventory, logistics, and production processes in real-time. Smart manufacturing technologies can optimize production, minimize downtime, and reduce waste. Automation and data-driven decision-making enable smoother operations and more accurate forecasting.

Key Considerations

- **End-to-End Visibility:** Aim to achieve end-to-end visibility of the supply chain through the integration of data from various sources, including suppliers, manufacturers, logistics providers, and customers. This visibility enables better decision-making and proactive management of supply chain disruptions.

- **Data Integration and Analytics:** Implement advanced data analytics and data integration solutions to process and analyze large volumes of supply chain data in real-time. This helps in identifying patterns, trends, and potential bottlenecks, allowing for data-driven decision-making.

- **Cloud-Based Solutions:** Adopt cloud-based supply chain management solutions to facilitate collaboration, data sharing, and accessibility across different locations and stakeholders in the supply chain.

- **Internet of Things (IoT) and Sensors:** Utilize IoT devices and sensors to monitor and track inventory levels, equipment performance, and transportation conditions. IoT-driven data can optimize inventory management and reduce waste.

- **Demand Forecasting and Planning:** Use predictive analytics and machine learning to improve demand forecasting accuracy. This ensures that inventory levels are optimized, and stockouts or overstock situations are minimized.

- **Supplier Collaboration:** Establish strong digital collaboration channels with suppliers to streamline procurement processes, reduce lead times, and improve supplier performance.

- **Warehouse Automation:** Invest in warehouse automation technologies, such as robotic process automation (RPA) and autonomous mobile robots, to enhance order picking, packing, and shipping efficiency.

- **Last-Mile Delivery Optimization:** Optimize last-mile delivery through route optimization, real-time tracking, and delivery notifications, enhancing customer satisfaction.

- **Supply Chain Resilience:** Develop contingency plans and supply chain risk management strategies to address potential disruptions and build resilience in the supply chain

- **Digital Twin Technology:** Utilize digital twin technology to create a virtual representation of the supply chain network. This allows for scenario modeling and optimization to test different supply chain strategies.

- **Blockchain for Supply Chain Traceability:** Implement blockchain technology to enhance supply chain traceability, ensuring transparency and authenticity of product information.

- **Integration with ERP Systems:** Integrate supply chain management systems with enterprise resource planning (ERP) systems to ensure seamless flow of information and data synchronization between departments.

- **Continuous Improvement:** Embrace a culture of continuous improvement and agility to adapt to changing market demands and technologies. Regularly assess and optimize supply chain processes and technologies.

Customer Service Department: Digital transformation revolutionizes customer service by implementing AI-powered chatbots, virtual assistants, and self-service portals. These tools handle routine queries, freeing up human agents to address complex issues. Omni-channel support ensures seamless customer interactions across various touchpoints, leading to increased customer satisfaction and loyalty.

Key Considerations

- **Omni-channel Customer Support:** Implement an omni-channel customer support system that allows customers to interact seamlessly across various channels, such as phone, email, chat, social media, and self-service portals. Ensure consistent and personalized support regardless of the channel customers choose.

- **Self-Service Capabilities:** Offer self-service options such as knowledge bases, FAQs, and chatbots to empower customers to find answers to their queries independently. This reduces the volume of incoming requests and provides quick resolutions.

- **CRM Integration:** Integrate customer relationship management (CRM) software with customer service systems to have a centralized view of customer interactions and histories. This enables agents to access relevant customer information quickly and provide personalized support.

- **AI and Chatbots:** Utilize artificial intelligence (AI) and chatbot technology to automate routine customer inquiries and support interactions. AI-powered chatbots can handle repetitive tasks, freeing up agents to focus on more complex customer issues.

- **Real-Time Analytics:** Implement real-time analytics to monitor customer service performance and identify areas of improvement. Analyze customer feedback and sentiment to enhance service quality.

- **Customer Feedback Mechanisms:** Gather feedback from customers through surveys, feedback forms, and social media listening. Use this feedback to continuously improve customer service processes and meet customer expectations.

- **24/7 Support:** Offer round-the-clock customer support to cater to customers in different time zones and ensure timely responses to urgent queries.

- **Personalization:** Leverage customer data and AI-driven insights to deliver personalized experiences to customers. Tailor support interactions based on customer preferences, history, and behavior.

- **Proactive Customer Support:** Anticipate customer needs and proactively address potential issues before they escalate. Use data analytics to identify patterns and trends that might indicate customer dissatisfaction.

- **Employee Training and Skill Development:** Provide training and skill development programs to customer service agents to enhance their digital competencies. Equip them with the knowledge and tools to excel in the digital customer service landscape.

- **Collaborative Tools:** Invest in collaborative tools that enable seamless communication and information sharing among customer service agents and other departments. This ensures quick problem-solving and efficient issue resolution.

- **Social Media Engagement:** Engage with customers on social media platforms to address queries, concerns, and complaints promptly. Social media has become a significant channel for customer service interactions.

- **Measure Customer Service Metrics:** Track key customer service metrics, such as response time, resolution time, customer satisfaction score (CSAT), net promoter score (NPS), and first-call resolution (FCR). Use these metrics to gauge performance and make data-driven improvements.

Finance Department: Digital transformation in finance involves automating financial processes, like invoicing, expense management, and budgeting, to enhance accuracy and efficiency. Cloud-based financial systems provide real-time visibility into financial data, supporting data-driven decision-making. AI-driven financial analytics can uncover valuable insights to optimize financial planning and forecasting.

Key Considerations

- **Integrated Financial Systems:** Implement integrated financial management systems that consolidate data from various sources, such as accounting, budgeting, and reporting. This ensures seamless data flow and reduces manual errors.

- **Cloud-Based Solutions:** Consider adopting cloud-based financial software to enhance accessibility, scalability, and data security. Cloud solutions enable remote access and real-time collaboration for finance professionals.

- **Automation of Manual Tasks:** Automate repetitive manual tasks, such as data entry, reconciliation, and invoice processing, using robotic process automation (RPA). This frees up finance staff to focus on more strategic and value-added activities.

- **Data Analytics and Reporting:** Utilize data analytics tools to gain valuable insights into financial performance, trends, and forecasts. Real-time reporting capabilities enable faster decision-making based on accurate data.

- **Compliance and Risk Management:** Ensure that the digital transformation adheres to regulatory compliance requirements and enhances risk management capabilities. Implement robust controls to safeguard financial data and transactions.

- **Mobile Financial Management:** Enable mobile access to financial data and reports for finance professionals on the go. Mobile apps allow timely decision-making and quick responses to financial inquiries.

- **Data Integration and Accuracy:** Focus on data quality and integrity to ensure that financial information is accurate, consistent, and reliable across all systems and reports.

- **Real-Time Financial Visibility:** Provide real-time visibility into financial data to key stakeholders, enabling better financial planning and resource allocation.

- **Cost Optimization:** Evaluate the cost-effectiveness of digital solutions and tools to ensure that the digital transformation delivers tangible financial benefits.

- **Continuous Training and Skill Development:** Invest in training and skill development programs for finance professionals to enhance their digital competencies and adapt to new technologies.

- **Cybersecurity Measures:** Strengthen cybersecurity measures to protect financial data from potential threats and cyberattacks. Ensure data encryption, user authentication, and regular security audits.

- **Vendor Selection:** Thoroughly evaluate and select reputable vendors for financial software and solutions. Consider factors such as functionality, scalability, customer support, and integration capabilities.

- **Collaborative Tools:** Implement collaborative tools that enable seamless communication and data sharing between finance and other departments. This fosters cross-functional collaboration and better financial planning.

- **Scalability and Future-Readiness:** Ensure that the digital solutions chosen for the finance department are scalable and capable of accommodating future growth and changes in business needs.

Research and Development Department: Digital transformation empowers R&D teams with advanced simulation and modelling tools, facilitating faster product development cycles. Collaborative platforms enhance knowledge-sharing and interdisciplinary teamwork. IoT and big data analytics support data-driven research and help identify trends and patterns for innovation opportunities.

Key Considerations

- **Embrace Emerging Technologies:** Stay informed about the latest digital technologies and trends that can enhance R&D processes, such as artificial intelligence (AI), machine learning, big data analytics, Internet of Things (IoT), and cloud computing.

- **Cross-Functional Collaboration:** Foster collaboration between R&D and other departments, such as IT, marketing, and operations. Encourage knowledge-sharing and joint problem-solving to create holistic and innovative solutions.

- **Data-Driven Decision Making:** Utilize data analytics and insights to drive R&D decisions. Data-driven approaches can help identify customer needs, market trends, and potential areas for innovation.

- **Agile Development Methods:** Adopt agile development methodologies to promote flexibility, responsiveness, and rapid prototyping. Agile practices enable quicker iterations and faster response to changing requirements.

- **Intellectual Property Protection:** Ensure proper measures are in place to protect intellectual property rights and maintain confidentiality during the development of new technologies and products.

- **Customer-Centric Approach:** Focus on understanding customer needs and pain points to develop products and solutions that address real-market demands and deliver superior customer experiences.

- **Digital Collaboration Tools:** Implement digital collaboration tools and platforms that facilitate real-time communication and knowledge sharing among R&D teams, even if they are geographically dispersed.

- **Virtual Prototyping and Simulation:** Leverage virtual prototyping and simulation technologies to accelerate product development cycles, reduce costs, and optimize designs before physical prototypes are created.

- **Experimentation and Test Environments:** Establish test environments and sandboxes for R&D teams to experiment with new technologies and conduct proofs of concept before full-scale implementation.

- **Continuous Learning and Skill Development:** Invest in training and development programs to enhance digital competencies within the R&D team. This ensures that team members are equipped with the necessary skills to leverage digital tools effectively.

- **Vendor and Technology Selection:** Carefully evaluate and select vendors and technologies that align with the R&D

department's objectives and can support the organization's long-term innovation strategy.

- **Data Security and Privacy:** Implement robust data security measures to protect sensitive R&D data and adhere to privacy regulations. Data encryption, access controls, and regular security audits are essential.

- **Innovation Metrics and KPIs:** Define clear metrics and Key Performance Indicators (KPIs) to measure the success and impact of R&D initiatives within the digital transformation journey.

- **Alignment with Business Strategy:** Ensure that R&D efforts are aligned with the overall business strategy and support the organization's vision for growth and market leadership.

Technology Department: Digital transformation is at the core of the Technology department's responsibilities. It involves adopting cutting-edge technologies and innovative solutions to modernize the organization's IT infrastructure, systems, and processes. Cloud computing enables scalable and flexible IT resources, while cybersecurity measures protect against potential threats. Embracing DevOps practices fosters collaboration between development and operations teams, resulting in faster software deployment and continuous improvement. The Technology department plays a vital role in implementing and integrating new digital solutions across the organization.

Key Considerations

- **Alignment with Business Strategy:** Ensure that the technology initiatives and investments align with the organization's overall business strategy and objectives. Understand the business needs and requirements to provide technology solutions that add value and drive growth.

- **Scalability and Flexibility:** Select technologies and infrastructure that are scalable and flexible to accommodate future growth and changing business needs. Scalability ensures that the technology can handle increased demand, while flexibility allows for adaptation to emerging trends and opportunities.

- **Data Integration and Interoperability:** Ensure seamless integration and interoperability between different systems and applications. This enables data flow across the organization and supports real-time decision-making.

- **Cybersecurity and Data Privacy:** Implement robust cybersecurity measures to safeguard sensitive data and protect against cyber threats. Ensure compliance with data privacy regulations to maintain customer trust.

- **Cloud Computing Adoption:** Consider adopting cloud computing to enhance agility, reduce infrastructure costs, and enable easier access to scalable resources.

- **Digital Talent and Skill Development:** Invest in training and skill development programs to equip technology staff with the necessary digital competencies and expertise. This ensures that the team can effectively manage and leverage digital tools and technologies.

- **Automation and Artificial Intelligence:** Explore opportunities to automate repetitive tasks and leverage artificial intelligence to enhance decision-making and efficiency within the department and across the organization.

- **User-Centric Design:** Emphasize user-centric design principles when implementing new technology solutions. Focus on creating intuitive and user-friendly interfaces to enhance the overall user experience.

- **Data Analytics and Business Intelligence:** Utilize data analytics and business intelligence tools to derive insights from data and drive data-informed decision-making processes.

- **Legacy System Modernization:** Assess and modernize existing legacy systems to ensure they are compatible with digital initiatives and can support future technological advancements.

- **Continuous Innovation and Experimentation:** Foster a culture of continuous innovation and encourage experimentation with emerging technologies to identify new opportunities and stay ahead of the competition.

- **IT Governance and Project Management:** Establish robust IT governance frameworks and project management methodologies to ensure that technology initiatives are effectively planned, executed, and monitored.

- **Vendor and Partner Selection:** Select technology vendors and partners that align with the organization's digital transformation goals and can provide reliable support and solutions.

- **Disaster Recovery and Business Continuity:** Develop comprehensive disaster recovery and business continuity plans to mitigate the impact of potential technology failures or disruptions.

Risk Department: Digital transformation empowers the Risk department to enhance risk management strategies and practices. Advanced analytics and AI-driven algorithms can analyze large datasets to identify potential risks and trends, enabling proactive risk mitigation. Real-time monitoring of operational and market data aids in early detection of emerging risks. Automation streamlines compliance processes, ensuring adherence to regulatory requirements. The Risk department can leverage digital tools to build robust risk models and scenario simulations for better decision-making.

Key Considerations

- **Risk Assessment and Mitigation:** Conduct a comprehensive risk assessment to identify potential risks associated with the digital transformation initiatives. Develop strategies and action plans to mitigate these risks and ensure a smooth transition.

- **Data Security and Privacy:** With increased reliance on digital technologies and data-driven processes, data security and privacy become critical. Implement robust cybersecurity measures and comply with data protection regulations to safeguard sensitive information.

- **Compliance and Regulatory Requirements:** Stay up-to-date with relevant laws and regulations that impact digital operations. Ensure that the digital transformation initiatives comply with industry-specific and general regulatory requirements.

- **Vendor Risk Management:** Assess the risks associated with technology vendors and third-party service providers. Evaluate their security practices and data handling capabilities to mitigate potential risks from external partnerships.

- **Business Continuity Planning:** Develop and update business continuity plans to address potential disruptions to digital operations. Plan for contingencies to ensure seamless operations in case of cyber incidents or technology failures

- **Risk Communication and Training:** Foster a risk-aware culture by providing regular training to employees on digital risks and best practices for risk management. Encourage open communication about potential risks and incidents.

- **Data Governance and Integrity:** Establish data governance frameworks to ensure the accuracy, consistency, and integrity of data used in digital processes. Implement data quality controls to minimize errors and discrepancies.

- **Fraud Prevention and Detection:** Leverage data analytics and artificial intelligence to proactively detect and prevent fraud in digital transactions and operations.

- **Technology Risk Assessment:** Assess the risks associated with adopting new digital technologies and platforms. Evaluate the impact of technology upgrades or changes on existing systems and operations.

- **Monitoring and Reporting:** Implement robust risk monitoring and reporting mechanisms to track the effectiveness of risk mitigation strategies and identify emerging risks in real-time.

- **Cross-Functional Collaboration:** Work closely with other departments involved in the digital transformation to understand their risk exposures and collaborate on risk management strategies.

- **Resilience Testing:** Conduct regular resilience testing to evaluate the organization's ability to recover from cyber-attacks or technology failures. Use the insights to improve risk mitigation measures.

- **Continuous Learning and Adaptation:** Stay informed about emerging digital risks and evolving best practices for risk management. Continuously adapt risk management strategies to address changing threats.

- **Risk Appetite and Tolerance:** Define the organization's risk appetite and tolerance levels concerning digital initiatives. Align risk management practices with the organization's strategic objectives.

For the C-suite Executives: a digital transformation is a critical strategic initiative that can significantly impact the organization's success and future growth. Here are key considerations for the C-suite in the context of a digital transformation:

Key Considerations

- **Vision and Strategy:** Define a clear vision and strategic direction for the digital transformation. Align the digital initiatives with the overall business objectives and long-term goals of the organization.

- **Leadership and Culture:** Foster a digital-first culture by leading by example and encouraging a mindset of innovation and adaptability. Ensure that the entire leadership team is committed to the transformation journey.

- **Talent and Skills:** Assess the organization's digital capabilities and identify skill gaps. Invest in talent development and recruit skilled professionals to support the digital transformation efforts.

- **Customer-Centric Approach:** Put the customer at the center of the digital transformation strategy. Understand customer needs and expectations to design digital experiences that deliver value and enhance customer satisfaction.

- **Data-Driven Decision Making:** Embrace data-driven decision making and leverage analytics to gain valuable insights. Use data to make informed strategic choices and improve operational efficiency.

- **Risk Management:** Collaborate with the Risk Department to assess and mitigate potential risks associated with digital initiatives. Balance innovation with risk management to ensure a secure and compliant transformation.

- **Agility and Flexibility:** Embrace agility and flexibility to respond to rapidly changing market dynamics and technological advancements. Be open to adapting strategies based on real-time feedback and insights.

- **Collaboration and Communication:** Facilitate cross-functional collaboration and communication throughout the organization. Break down silos and encourage teams to work together towards common digital goals.

- **Investment and ROI:** Allocate appropriate resources and investments for the digital transformation projects. Continuously monitor and evaluate the return on investment to ensure the initiatives' success.

- **Customer Engagement:** Engage with customers and stakeholders to gather feedback and input on the digital transformation initiatives. Incorporate customer feedback to refine and improve digital experiences.

- **Change Management:** Develop a robust change management strategy to address potential resistance to digital transformation. Communicate the benefits of the transformation and provide support to employees during the transition.

- **Competitive Landscape:** Stay informed about competitors' digital initiatives and industry trends. Benchmark the organization's digital capabilities against industry leaders and identify areas for improvement.

- **Innovation and Experimentation:** Encourage a culture of innovation and experimentation. Be open to piloting new ideas and technologies to identify what works best for the organization.

- **Alignment with Partners:** Collaborate with technology partners, vendors, and other stakeholders to ensure alignment and successful implementation of digital solutions.

- **Sustainability and Scalability:** Consider the long-term sustainability and scalability of digital initiatives. Ensure that the technology infrastructure can support future growth and expansion.

By addressing these key considerations, the C-suite can effectively drive and lead the organization's digital transformation, positioning the company for success in a digitally driven future.

HIVEMIND GROUP: YOUR CATALYST FOR DIGITAL TRANSFORMATION AND PEOPLE DEVELOPMENT

Hopefully having read the book, you have increased your understanding of the process and have a more complete picture of how to approach digital change. We hope to have also convinced you that your success depends on the human factor.

Organizations are now prioritising ways to align with dynamic customer expectations, making digital transformation a central focus in boardroom discussions.

The common mistake is to underestimate the pivotal human aspect while disproportionately emphasizing the technological. The key to getting it right rests in an exceptional, integrated, and adaptable approach to nurturing talent and fostering cultural evolution.

Recognizing the 'why' behind transformation is the catalyst for embracing the 'how' of execution. Whilst no two initiatives are the same, we have presented our Everyday Transformation™ framework and assessment to guide you and ask the pertinent questions.

Our purpose is to shape thinking, instilling excellence by focussing on proficiency and clarity of process. Inspired by human potential and technological advancement, our team is dedicated to sharing wisdom through ongoing education, applied learning projects, and consultancy.

We embrace each individual challenge, proactively immunising businesses against future uncertainties by driving cultural shifts, deploying pioneering technologies, and harnessing disruptive innovations.

Our associates hail from diverse domains, each a subject matter expert in their field, with extensive industry experience spanning a myriad of sectors.

We firmly believe that selecting the right partner to guide your transformation journey is essential.

"Empowering Digital Change through Innovative People First Initiatives"

To discover more about how we can work in partnership with you, we invite you to reach out to us at enquiry@hivemind-group.com or connect through the information provided below.

Websites
www.hivemind-group.com
www.everyday-transformation.com

Connect with Warren Cass
WarrenC@hivemind-group.com
https://www.linkedin.com/in/warrencass
https://twitter.com/warrencass

Connect with Warren Knight
WarrenK@hivemind-group.com
https://www.linkedin.com/in/warren-knight
https://twitter.com/WarrenKnight

Milton Keynes UK
Ingram Content Group UK Ltd.
UKHW022036190923
428911UK00010B/63